Human Resource Issues in International Tourism

D1560349

Human Resource Issues in International Tourism

Edited by Tom Baum

BUTTERWORTH
HEINEMANN

Butterworth-Heinemann Ltd
Linacre House, Jordan Hill, Oxford OX2 8DP

A member of the Reed Elsevier plc group

OXFORD   LONDON   BOSTON
MUNICH   NEW DELHI   SINGAPORE   SYDNEY
TOKYO   TORONTO   WELLINGTON

First published 1993
Reprinted 1994

British Library Cataloguing in Publication Data
Human Resource Issues in International Tourism
   I. Baum, Tom
   338. 4791

ISBN 0 7506 0091 8

Photoset by Deltatype Ltd, Ellesmere Port, Cheshire
Printed and bound in Great Britain by
Redwood Books, Trowbridge, Wiltshire

Contents

Contents

Contributors

Sudhir Andrews is Principal of the Institute of Hotel Management, Catering and Nutrition, New Delhi, India.

Dr Tom Baum is Course Director, International Hotel Management and Deputy Dean of the School of Accounting, Business and Economics at the University of Buckingham, England.

Michael Conlin is Dean of the Faculty of Hotel and Business Administration and Director of the Centre for Tourism Research and Innovation at Bermuda College, Bermuda.

Dr John Fletcher is a Senior Lecturer in the Department of Management Studies for the Tourism and Hotel Industries at the University of Surrey, England.

Dr Yvonne Guerrier is a Senior Lecturer in the Department of Management Studies for the Tourism and Hotel Industries at the University of Surrey, England.

Dr Michael Haywood is with the School of Hotel and Food Administration at the University of Guelph, Canada.

Vincent Heung is a Lecturer in the Department of Tourism and Hotel Management at Hong Kong Polytechnic, Hong Kong.

Els Lowyck is a Researcher with the Department Vrijetijds–, Toekomst– en Beleidsolanning at the Vrije Universiteit, Brussels, Belgium.

V. S. Mahesh is Vice-President (Human Resources) with WIPRO Ltd, India. Previously, he was Vice-President (Human Resources) with the Taj Group of Hotels, the Indian Hotel Company.

Dr Jim Pickworth is with the School of Hotel and Food Administration at the University of Guelph, Canada.

Dr Michael Riley is a Lecturer in the Department of Management Studies for the Tourism and Hotel Industries at the University of Surrey, England.

List of contributors

M. K. Sio is Principal of Kenya Utalii College, Nairobi, Kenya.

Dr Luk van Langenhove is a Lecturer with the Department Vrijetijds–, Toekomst– en Beleidsolanning at the Vrije Universiteit, Brussels, Belgium.

Mary Ena Walsh is Manager of Curricula Development and Research with CERT, the state tourism training agency, Ireland.

Kenneth Wilson is with the Department of Applied Economics, Faculty of Business at the Victoria University of Technology, Australia.

David Worland is with the Department of Applied Economics, Faculty of Business at the Victoria University of Technology, Australia.

Preface

The international travel and tourism industry is continuing to maintain the positive growth curve which will see it attaining the number one spot in terms of its value, relative to other sectors, by the end of the century. This growth has been maintained, albeit at a somewhat reduced rate, despite the impact of economic recession; regional conflicts and terrorism; and environmental concerns during the early 1990s. What is of particular note is the growing dispersal of tourist movements, to an ever increasing number of locations which, until recently, were the preserve of a small minority of travellers.

Within this context, human resource issues, such as staff turnover; recruitment; promotion and succession planning; motivation; rewards and benefits; and education and training have been widely identified as critical concerns for the tourism industries of both developing and developed countries. While, to a certain extent, there are clear variations in the impact that these concerns have in different countries and localities, there are also evident common themes which appear to transcend continents and differing economic conditions.

The purpose of this book is to consider these and related human resource issues in the context of the macro international tourism environment. The focus is on areas such as human resource planning for tourism; the tourism labour market; methodologies for determining manpower and training needs within national tourism industries; and educational and training provision for tourism. This focus provides the book's main distinction from much of the human resource literature in the tourism and hospitality field, which emphasizes issues at the micro or company level within the industry.

The book incorporates two distinct approaches. In Part One, key generic human resource concerns, within international tourism, are addressed and possible broad responses considered by authors with particular specialisms in these areas. Part Two contains ten national or regional case studies, generally by locally-based authors, from Africa, Asia, Australia, the Caribbean, Europe and North America. These case studies address the wider themes of the book in the context of specific national environments. The book concludes, in Part Three, with the case for and presentation of a general conceptual framework, designed to assist in the development and implementation of national human resource policies for tourism.

The book was conceived and written with a broad-based audience in mind. The themes will be of interest to students and others who are studying the development of international tourism and who wish to gain further insights into a specialist and, arguably, neglected aspect of the industry. Much of the information contained in all three parts of the book can be interpreted and applied in the field and, therefore, the book will also be of use to practitioners with professional responsibility for the development and implementation of policies for human resource management within the tourism industry. It will also be of value to readers who are approaching tourism from a human resource management perspective and have an interest in the application of HRM principles within a specific industry sector. Many of the conclusions, which can be drawn from consideration of the themes of this book, are readily transferable to other sectors of the international service economy.

Tom Baum

Acknowledgements

This volume has existed, as an idea, for a number of years. The development of the idea is due, in many respects, to discussions and interactions with colleagues in CERT, Ireland, the University of Buckingham and elsewhere. That it has actually reached publication is due, in no small measure, to the hard work and enthusiasm of my contributors. Aspects of my own chapters draw from my doctoral studies at the Scottish Hotel School, the University of Strathclyde and I would like to acknowledge the guidance of my supervisors there, initially Dr John Heeley and, latterly, Professor Carson L. Jenkins.

Finally, without the support and encouragement of my wife, Brelda, the project would have foundered a long time ago.

Part One
Human Resources in Tourism –
Macro Perspectives

1   Human resources in tourism: an introduction
Tom Baum

An overview

To state what is, perhaps, the obvious, tourism is about people. For once, we are talking about a cliché that does encapsulate both common sense and reality and it is one that should never be far from the minds of those who have an involvement with tourism, whether from a business, administrative or academic viewpoint. First, tourists as customers or clients or economic statistics are people and, consequently, are subject to the vagaries of behaviour, demand, decision-making and response that cannot be wholly predictable or anticipated. Nor should they be. Second, in common with many other labour-intensive service-based industries, the tourism product is about people and is dependent, for its delivery, on the human factor. It is conceivable to visit Stonehenge or the Pyramids or the Taj Mahal or the Great Barrier Reef and to appreciate what they have to offer without assistance, interpretation and mediation from a guide or the support of physical comforts such as accommodation, food or transport, all dependent, for their quality, on the human element. Conceivable, but unlikely and, for most visitors, undesirable. Finally, many tourism products actually include people as an integral part of the experience that they offer, whether they are cast members at Disney locations; traditional dancers and singers in many parts of the world; or, indeed, our fellow guests in a restaurant who contribute to the atmosphere. For most of us, the experience of tourism is about more than the physical sensation of eating a good meal, sleeping in comfortable beds, travelling in safe and efficient aircraft or viewing magnificent natural scenery or man-made artefacts. It is also (and frequently primarily,

This chapter draws upon my chapter 'Human resource issues in tourism', published in Donald Hawkins, and Brent Ritchie (eds) (1991) *World Travel and Tourism Review*, vol. 1, CAB International, Wallingford, Oxford. The permission of the publishers for this is acknowledged.

about contact with the people who contribute to the actual experience, whether through being an integral part of the location – city dwellers in Manhattan, bazaar vendors in Istanbul, ceremonial dancers in Bali etc. – or as direct contributors to the actual product delivery and experience, as guides, cabin attendants, receptionists, chefs, craft demonstrators or the myriad of other professions and activities that, collectively, go to make up the global tourism industry. This notion that, when purchasing the tourism product the client is also, in a sense, buying the skills, service and commitment of a range of human contributors to the experience that they are about to embark upon, is crucial to much of the ground that is covered in this book. It is also frequently forgotten by those responsible for the development, packaging, marketing and delivery of tourism products. The central role of the human factor in the attainment of service quality within tourism companies is a key theme within the first of V. S. Mahesh's two chapters on 'Human resource planning and development'.

My personal experience of interviewing young people for both employment and educational opportunities in tourism has shown that their motivation is frequently guided by somewhat idealistic notions, by the desire to travel, to work in an expanding industry with an exciting future but, above all, 'to work with people'. Often, they are none too sure exactly what this entails but they do know that their job satisfaction will be through human contact in their employment and by helping others to enjoy and benefit from the contact and assistance they can provide. This desire, naive and unstructured though it may be, forms the raw material of human resources through which tourism, as a global industry, fails or succeeds and is the basis for the investment, through education, training and development, that is crucial to business success in all tourism industries.

This book is about this tourism resource, the human resource through which the quality of a country's or a locality's tourism product, natural or fabricated, is 'mediated' to the customer, client or guest. The industry is already well served by a range of books that look at human resource issues, primarily within the hospitality industry, but there is little doubt that the principles they contain transfer on to the broader tourism canvas. A number of these books are included in the bibliography to this chapter. What they have in common is an approach that starts with a focus on the requirements of those in management in the industry, and their responsibilities for the human resources (HR) within the company. In these texts, the work of the manager in the human resources area may be considered from a functional point of view, looking at the range of HR tasks with which a manager might expect to become involved (Boella, 1987; Tanke 1990; Riley 1991). Headings in this context, include:

- Analysis of the labour market
- Job design
- Recruitment
- Selection
- Appointment
- Equal opportunities
- Induction
- Training
- Management development
- Job evaluation
- Salaries and wages
- Incentives
- Fringe benefits
- Labour turnover
- Termination of employment
- Grievance and dispute management
- Industrial relations
- Employment law
- Personal administration
- Technological administration of personnel

Alternative approaches, drawn from wider study of psychology, also feature, looking at broader issues relating to people at work (Lockwood and Jones, 1984; Riley, 1991) and the application of transactional analysis techniques within the HR function (Martin and Lundberg, 1991). A final approach combines elements of the other two but includes an additional element, with considerable emphasis on placing the tourism/hospitality industry within the wider labour or manpower market (Hornsey and Dann, 1984).

This book takes, as its starting point, the macro tourism environment, internationally, nationally and more locally and looks at the range of issues that affect the effective utilization of human resources within the tourism industries. Thus, put simply, the approach within much of the human resource literature is one that starts at the level of the company and moves, to a limited extent, towards the consideration of wider issues that do have an impact on operations at the company level. This book starts at the other end of the continuum and focuses on matters such as human resource research and planning at a national level; the development of educational and training systems for tourism; and the relationship between growth in the tourism industry and the labour market. However, there are clear implications of many of the 'macro' issues for the work of the personnel or human resource manager within the individual company.

The 'macro' issues are considered in two main ways. The first six chapters of the book and the Conclusion (Chapter 17) concentrate on tourism from a wholly international perspective and draw on material from a number of local, national and regional sources. The purpose of these is to look at:

- The human resource concerns that have applicability at an inter-national level (Chapter 1).
- The role of service excellence within the human resource develop-ment arena (Chapter 2).
- The use of effective human resource planning and development models in tourism (Chapter 3).
- Understanding the tourism labour market and its relationship to vocational education (Chapter 4).
- The vital requirement to establish effective information systems about human resources at national and local levels and how to put such systems in place (Chapters 5 and 6).
- How the diverse human resource planning, research, educational and training strands, considered within the previous chapters, can be drawn together to provide a coherent and integrated framework for human resource planning and development at a 'macro' level (Chapter 17).

The second approach within the book is through the use of national case studies, and Chapters 7–16 cover ten examples of how human resource concerns are managed in Africa, Asia, Europe and North America, written by experts based in and familiar with particular countries within these regions. All but two are based on actual countries: Yvonne Guerrier considers the island of Bali in Indonesia, because of its unique tourism development and cultural features within that country, while Michael Conlin takes a regional perspective within the Caribbean, illustrating the principle of cooperation between small island nations in the human resource field. The use of case study material, in this context, inevitably generates questions about choice and, in particular, the absence of certain countries from the list. The main constraints here are those of space and the availability of suitable contributors, familiar with the countries in question. To a certain extent, any major omissions have been remedied by reference to relevant information about a diversity of further locations in the general chapters. However, the purpose of the case studies is not to be representative but, rather, to illustrate different approaches to dealing with the diversity of human resource issues that exist within inter-national tourism. These case studies, therefore, can act as stimuli for those concerned with similar or related concerns elsewhere.

The centrality of the human element to tourism has already been discussed. It is also important, at the onset, to recognize the diversity that exists, within all major tourism industries, in terms of:

1 The various sectors that make up the industry.
2 The wide range of jobs and employment categories which exist within the industry.

One of the problems, in considering various sectors that go to make up tourism industries in all countries, and the nature of employment within them, is inherent in the nature of the industry itself, primarily that there is no single centre of production. As Parsons indicates, tourism

> cannot be isolated from other activities by looking at the goods or services it produces. It is better regarded not as an industry in itself but a consumer activity of which the effects on employment are dispersed across an uniquely wide range of industries and activities. (Parsons, 1987)

Consequently, precise sectorization is difficult and considerable variation may be evident between countries, depending upon the emphasis that is placed on aspects of the tourism product. Locations where the focus of the tourism product is on sun, sea and sand geared towards the mass package tour market will have a supporting tourist industry that is very different in business structure, ownership and size to an industry that is built around meeting the requirements of specialist groups, interested in fine art or theatre. Furthermore, while in some countries, especially within the developing world, tourism products are for the virtual exclusive use of the international tourist – resorts in the Maldives are a case in point – and even limited local use is very unusual, by contrast, many tourism facilities in developed countries are shared between the international tourist, the domestic tourist and the local resident – pubs in Ireland and shops in Singapore are good examples of this mixed use. One example of the various sectors of a tourism industry can be seen in a study based on the Irish tourism industry, where nine main sectors were identified:

Sector	*Constituents*
1 State organizations	Government departments, Bord Failte (the Irish Tourist Board), regional tourism organizations, CERT (the training agency), SFADC (Shannon Free Airport Development Company), Uaras na Gaeltachta (the development agency responsible for Irish speaking areas), local government

2 Access transport	Airlines, sea carriers
3 Internal transport	Car rental, coaches, caravan hire, rail and bus services, internal air and boat services, taxis
4 Accommodation	Hotels, guest houses, town houses, country homes, farmhouses, camping and caravanning, self-catering accommodation, youth hostels
5 Tourism facilitation	Customs and immigration, Aer Rianta (the airports authority), docks and harbour boards
6 Dining and entertainment	Restaurants, pubs, cabarets, theatres, cinemas, festivals, TV and radio
7 Leisure/recreation/ activity	Cabin cruising, horse-drawn caravans, golfing, fishing, historic houses, national parks, shopping
8 Tourism services	Incoming tour operators, tour operators and travel agents, youth/student organizers
9 Other services	Banks, bureaux de change, local tourism companies and cooperatives (CERT, 1987)

The wide variety of sectors which characterizes most tourism industries inevitably results in a very diverse range of jobs in terms of their technical demands, their educational requirements, their location, their conditions and the kind of person that will be attracted to employment in them. It is virtually impossible to list all the employment categories within a typical tourism industry and even were this possible, the outcome would not be of significant value, owing to the diversity of businesses, in terms of size, markets and operations, that exists within any one category. Thus, a hotel manager may well be responsible for a property that ranges in size from ten to 2000 bedrooms, with consequent differences in business volume, turnover and staffing. Standard job classifications, such as the *International Standard Classifications of Occupations (ISCO)* (ILO, 1988) and the *Standard Occupational Classification (SOC)* (HMSO, 1990) provide limited information on the jobs that exist within the tourism industry. The SOC document, for example, includes the following designations that have a significant tourism orientation:

- Hotel and accommodation managers
- Restaurant and catering managers
- Publicans, innkeepers and club stewards
- Entertainment and sports managers

- Travel agency managers
- Airline pilots
- Receptionists
- Receptionist/telephonists
- Chefs
- Waiters, waitresses
- Bar staff
- Travel and flight attendants
- Railway station staff
- Housekeepers
- Hotel porters
- Kitchen porters, hands
- Counterhands, catering assistants
- Cleaners, domestics

This classification reflects just a proportion of the wide range of positions that exist within tourism and testifies to one of the main weaknesses in general, non-tourism-specific analyses. This inadequacy is one of the motivations behind Chapter 3, which offers a methodology to develop an alternative and relevant tourism employment classification.

Key human resource issues in international tourism

The country case studies in this book, as well as regular perusal of tourism trade publications in virtually any major tourism destination country in the world, give a clear indication of the pre-eminent concerns of professionals within the industry for human resource matters. The discussion is one of reiteration and repetition, with the same themes emerging, albeit with significant local or cultural modification, world wide and within both developed and developing economies. These 'universal' themes, which feature consistently in the case studies and also feature in Michael Riley's chapter on labour markets include:

- Demography and the shrinking employment pool/labour shortages.
- The tourism industry's image as an employer.
- Cultural and traditional perceptions of the industry.
- Rewards and benefits/compensation.
- Recruitment, retention and staff turnover.
- Education and training, both within colleges and industry.

- Skills shortages, especially at higher technical and management levels.
- Linking human resource concerns with service and product quality.
- Poor management and planning information about human resource matters in the tourism industry.
- The tendency to develop human resource policies, initiatives and remedial programmes that are reactive to what is currently happening rather than proactive to what is likely to occur.

One of the underlying problems, with respect to human resources in tourism from a 'macro' point of view is linked to the status and consideration given to these issues within overall tourism policy development and planning. The growth of tourism since 1945 has tended to focus attention, mainly, on concerns of product development and marketing and this model has been replicated as each new tourism destination has emerged to international significance. Thus, priority has, invariably, been given to the building of hotels, airports, roads and other facilities and to attendant marketing campaigns. This commitment to product and market-related planning has been, and continues to be, very significant in terms of both public and private sector investment. This reflects the general optimism which surrounds international tourism, which looks forward to the year 2000 with considerable confidence and in an environment of decreasing world tensions and economic and travel liberalization.

To a certain extent, this optimism is clouded by what will be, arguably, the main challenge facing tourism, world wide, during the next decade, that of human resources. A report prepared by Horwath and Horwath, on behalf of the International Hotel Association in 1988, pinpoints three key issues, all in the human resource domain, which the international hotel industry faces during the 1990s (IHA, 1988). These are

- The availability of labour
- Monitoring and motivating labour
- The provision of training opportunities

The IHA study acknowledges that it is necessary to classify these concerns on a geographical and economic basis; however, such classification focuses more on the detail of cultural, social and economic variation and does not negate the overall worldwide pattern with respect to these issues. The national case studies in this book pinpoint both what is common and what appears to be country-specific. For example, availability of labour is an issue in both Canada and India but in the former it is of concern in the absolute sense of too few available personnel whereas, in India, it reflects shortages in specific skills areas.

Despite considerable international homogeneity, with respect to human resource concerns in tourism, general models of response to these issues are not clearly discernible. In other words, countries appear to go about dealing with the concerns in a manner that is locally determined rather than through the application of common principles. Each country or region appears to adopt policies and provision which have their roots in local traditions, cultures and systems. Traditionally, common approaches, between countries, to the planning and organization of human resources in tourism have only been evident in limited and fairly specific situations. The diversity of systems described within the case studies is evidence of this. However, there are an increasing number of initiatives, particularly in the area of training and accreditation, that have been instituted on a transnational basis and this situation has been assisted by the growth of multi-national companies, demanding common qualifications and human resource practices.

This picture of diversity between countries contrasts with the far more general approaches which can be identified with respect to product development and marketing in tourism. It is possible to speculate that this difference, with respect to common practice, exists because human resource issues are, generally, inward-looking, to and at the indigenous population, local structures and policies, whereas marketing and product development, with limited histories and traditions, perceive their focus to be outward-looking at a common international market, albeit with distinctive sub-market segments. A further and, arguably, the main determinant of this status situation is the fractionalization which characterizes the coordination and provision of human resource policies, planning and implementation for tourism in most countries. On the one hand, the private sector of the industry (not withstanding operations in the few remaining planned economies), in most countries, is highly fragmented, an amalgam of small to large businesses, providing a range of diverse products and meeting the need of differing markets. As a consequence, their human resource requirements are varied. On the other hand, public sector involvement, in the area of human resources, may be subject to the involvement and control of a number of different public agencies as well as some overlap with private sector responsibilities. By contrast, the number of agencies and companies involved in, for example, the area of tourism marketing tends to be rather less and their functions much more clearly defined. While the pattern varies from country to country, in the human resource field, the bodies involved may include:

- The various industry sectors, through their representative bodies as well as at individual company level (especially large state-owned or multinational companies such as airlines and hotels)
- National (state) education providers
- Private educational institutions
- Specialist training agencies
- National employment, labour or manpower agencies
- A range of government departments (which may include Tourism, Employment, Education, Industry, Productivity etc.)
- Social partner organizations, especially trade unions
- National, regional or local tourist agencies

This situation is further complicated by the fact that these diverse agencies do not, necessarily, fulfil the same roles in different countries and that these roles certainly do change over time. One of the features of the situation in the United Kingdom since 1979, for example, has been a significant reallocation of responsibility for training in tourism from the public to the private sector, reflecting similar developments within all sectors of the economy. As a consequence, training support for the hotel and catering sector, for example, traditionally an area where there has been considerable state assistance through the Hotel and Catering Training Board, is now left much more to the private sector.

The varied relationship between national tourism organizations and responsibilities for training for tourism further illustrates this point. The selected extract from the World Tourism Organization's report *Aims, Activities and Fields of Competence of National Tourist Organisations* (1975) shows that the relationship can be one of total management of the training system at one end of the spectrum through to a limited policy/information collection role at the other (Table 1.1). While this information is very out of date, it is, in fact, the only type of its kind available. Although partial up-dates have been undertaken by the World Tourism Organization, the information is not comprehensive or comparable. While this represents an indictment of information collection in this field, the broad picture presented remains valid.

The interaction of the varying agencies and interests in the area of human resource planning and management in tourism inevitably produces a response, in terms of national policies, plans and structures which closely reflects the local environment and is, in many respects, dedicated to the requirements of that environment. This has considerable merit in that it should ensure that education and training, in particular, are relevant to local industry needs and can be related to systems that operate within other vocational sectors. However, at the same time, there is a danger that this parochialism acts as a barrier to

Table 1.1 *Responsibilities of selected national tourist organizations for tourism vocational training*

Country	Functions 1	2	3	4	5	6
Algeria	+		+			
Argentina	+	+	+	+	+	+
Australia	+		+	+		
Austria	None					
Bahamas		+	+			
Belgium			+	+	+	+
Brazil	+	+	+	+		
Bulgaria	+	+	+	+	+	+
Canada	+		+	+	+	+
Chile			+			
Egypt		+	+	+	+	+
France	None					
Ghana	+		+	+		
Greece	+	+	+	+	+	+
Hong Kong			+	+		+
Hungary	+		+	+		
Ireland	None					
Jamaica	+		+			+
Kenya	+	+	+	+	+	
Malaysia	+	+	+	+		
Malta	+		+			
Mexico	+	+	+	+	+	+
New Zealand	None					
Pakistan	+	+	+			
Peru	+					
Poland	+	+	+	+	+	+
Portugal	+	+	+	+	+	+
Singapore	+		+	+		
Spain		+	+	+	+	+
Thailand			+	+		
Tunisia	+	+	+	+	+	+
Turkey	+	+	+	+	+	+
United Kingdom	+	+				+
United States	None					
Zambia	+			+		+

Key:
  1 = Determination of manpower and training requirements
  2 = Granting of fellowships
  3 = Formulation of training programmes
  4 = Organization of vocational training courses, seminars
  5 = Establishment of hotel and tourism schools
  6 = Reception of trainees
Source: WTO, 1975

international cooperation and the transfer of ideas and practices between countries. Thus, while small segments of human resource provision for tourism may have relatively universal transferability, the development of national systems has not evolved with such benefits as a priority.

Perhaps more seriously, failure to take a macro or coordinated view of the human resource considerations and how they link to all other elements within tourism development can lead to neglect and duplication and, possibly, can have major business impacts on tourism within a region, country, locality or business. By way of illustration, a good example of this comes from Singapore where the 1988 *Product Development Plan* was one of the most ambitious, sophisticated and exciting of its kind (STPB, 1988). It covered issues such as urban regeneration, theme park and resort development and cultural, artistic and events programmes as well as focusing on infrastructure, accommodation and other support facilities. Much of the plan was subsequently implemented. Nowhere, in the plan, was any reference made to the inevitable human resource implications of such ambitious developments within an already tight labour market or to the consequences for human resources of growth projections for tourism to the country at that time, in the order of 15% per annum. Subsequent realization of this significant gap has resulted in some measures to upgrade tourism education and training for tourism in Singapore. However, as a general axiom, effective human resource strategies require considerable lead time in order to support tourism development and, ideally, should be in place well before the bulldozers and diggers move in. The Singapore illustration is by no means an isolated example. Cases have been reported at the individual property/ business level in locations such as Hawaii, the Florida Keys and Queensland in Australia, where new developments in relatively remote, low population density areas reached opening without evident HR research or planning. As a result, serious human resource and skills shortages posed a significant threat to service quality, customer satisfaction and, ultimately, to profitability. The principle at stake here, that of incorporating human resource considerations into product and marketing development, applies, therefore, at both the macro and micro levels.

Despite the situation where human resource concerns are frequently separated from other areas of tourism development, administration and management, employment or labour market factors feature strongly within the stated tourism policies in most countries. In some cases, this factor may be the dominant concern, as is the case with the Republic of Ireland in its policy since 1987. Viewed from an economic perspective, most countries promote tourism in the context of objectives that give priority to balance of trade, foreign exchange and employment criteria. The varying emphasis given to these within broader national policies depends upon the strength, structure and balance of the economies in question. Thus, in Germany or Japan, while the actual value of international tourism may be fairly significant, it is, in relative terms, dwarfed by the scale and value of other industries. Therefore, the economic and, consequently, the employment significance of tourism is not accorded priority. By contrast, island economies in the Caribbean or the Indian Ocean are dominated by tourism and are very vulnerable to fluctuations in global or regional travel patterns. The immediate and fairly drastic effect of the 1991 Gulf War on the whole economy of the Maldives was a direct result of tourism dependency in that country. Between these extremes, most destination countries recognize the economic significance of tourism, including the employment component and this, therefore, features strongly within stated policy documentation. In a study made in 1988 encompassing 107 national tourism organizations (of which 49 provided very detailed responses), the determinants of tourism policies were identified and ranked as follows:

1 To generate foreign revenue/assist balance of payments
2 To provide employment – nationally
3 To improve regional/local economy
4 To create awareness about the country
5 To provide employment regionally/locally
6 To support environment/conservation
7 To contribute to infrastructural development
8 To create international goodwill

What this study demonstrates is the prominence of human resource considerations in the framing of national and local tourism policies. The prime motives, however, do show some variation. As is shown in Walsh's chapter on Ireland, a direct contribution to what was seen as unacceptable levels of adult and youth unemployment was central to the Irish tourism policy for the period 1987–1992, which took as a central objective the doubling of tourism arrivals in order to increase employment by 25,000. As the case study in Chapter 16 shows, implicitly, the same objective to reduce unemployment, although not so overtly stated, is represented in the United Kingdom where government responsibility for tourism was, until recently, vested in the Department of Employment. However, even this scenario has considerable regional diversity. UK policy is particularly concerned to disperse tourism activity, and consequent employment, to areas of economic disadvantage at the expense of traditional and congested tourism areas, especially London.

An alternative perspective on the association between tourism policies and employment is found in countries where there is an actual shortage of both skilled and unskilled labour. Both Hong Kong and Singapore have booming tourism economies and encourage this growth for, largely, economic reasons. At the same time, the labour market, in both city states, is very tight and this concern is one that is becoming more and more prominent within economic planning. In Hong Kong, as is evident in reading Vincent Heung's case study, the tourism industry could utilize up to three times the number of skilled personnel than its current recruitment level. Thus, priority in these locations is not so much on growth in overall tourism employment as on increasing productivity in the industry and ensuring more effective management and utilization of labour within tourism. This imperative has, potentially, great significance. Both Hong Kong and Singapore have developed tourism industries on the basis of a well-marketed reputation for quality and highly personalized service. This is in evidence through the awards won by hotels such as the Mandarin in Hong Kong and the Shangri-la in Singapore and by airlines such as Cathay Pacific and Singapore Airlines. Increasingly tight human resource environments may lead to technological alternatives to personal service and a loss of market competitiveness in this respect to other countries in the region, such as Indonesia and Thailand. Similar labour market pressures are emerging in other countries, notably Korea, Malaysia and Taiwan, where the rapid growth of competitor industry sectors, especially electronics, is applying ever increasing pressure on developing tourism industries.

The final model is represented by many developing countries where there is no absolute shortage of labour but where there are significant limitations in the availability of the appropriate skills for tourism and other service industries. This is a growing concern in our case study countries of India and Kenya but also in a variety of other significant tourism destinations. In these countries, national labour objectives seek to maximize the productivity of the skilled workforce while, at the same time, increasing the overall pool of skilled personnel from which tourism can draw.

National tourism policies make the basic assumption that investment in human resource development for the industry, which is an integral component of employment generation, has direct and exponential benefit to the industry. This is assumed to apply both to investments by government, in initial education and training, and to that of the private sector, through in-company development programmes. This assumption is implicit in policies that seek to encourage the growth of tourism as a means of generating employment.

However, there are certain problems with this argument, which centre on skills attrition out of the industry. Such attrition may be internal to the country in question, from, for example, hotel reception positions to front-line administration posts in other industries or from management in tourism into leadership roles in other service or manufacturing sectors. This process can be clearly seen in the continuing high rate (in some case over 50%) at which hotel school graduates, in the United Kingdom, leave the industry during the first year after graduation. This process can be seen at work in many European countries and in North America as well as in Hong Kong and Singapore. Alternatively, this process of attrition may represent an actual skills drain out of the country into tourism industries elsewhere. Malaysia has, traditionally, lost skilled tourism personnel to Singapore; Ireland has and continues to face a similar loss to the UK, mainland Europe and the USA; India has lost personnel to the Middle East and a variety of other locations; while tourism personnel from Hong Kong have emigrated to a variety of countries in Europe, North America and Australasia. Such international mobility from country to country and similar trends within countries (from country to city) is a process that is likely to increase as labour shortages grow and barriers to employment abroad come down. The role of valid, predictive information systems is crucial if such trends are to be countered at a local or national level.

Responding to the issues

Examples of policy responses to the diversity of human resource issues in tourism are illustrated through the national case studies in this book, which show how both public and private sector responsibility can contribute as solutions to some of the identified problems. The case studies suggest responses and strategies that could be adopted elsewhere. They may be classified as:

- Individual business related
- Local
- National

To these may be added a further category, namely

- regional (i.e. transnational)

which Michael Conlin's chapter on the Caribbean illustrates. Examples of such responses at the level of the **individual business** abound. They may include:

- Localized recruitment campaigns, targeted at specific groups of potential employees, for example married women
- Local transport, accommodation and child-care schemes so as to attract employees who may, otherwise, be unable to work for the company
- Flexible rosters and shifts in order to meet employee needs
- Enhanced benefits packages
- Changes in product, designed to reduce labour costs, often involving reducing service levels and job de-skilling
- The use of technology as part of labour-saving initiatives
- Enhanced in-house training programmes.

Local initiatives are, frequently, the result of collective employer action, through industry organizations or under the sponsorship of public agencies. They can be self-help, as would be the case with the proposed (but not so far delivered) local hospitality training centre for the London Docklands, designed to meet local industry needs through skills training or retraining of local people. An alternative model, which utilizes public monies, is the establishment of a dedicated training centre to meet the skills needs of new theme parks near Paris by AFPA, the French adult training agency. A third model is where local industry pressure and representations persuade government agencies to make specific, local training provision – examples from Ireland come to mind as illustrations of this process.

National initiatives take a variety of forms and feature action at both the public and private sector level. At a 'macro' level, the influence of both may be evident. In Ireland, as Mary Ena Walsh shows, the establishment of CERT, in 1963, as the agency responsible for manpower planning and training in tourism, reflected such a joint initiative. The agency's wide remit in the area of human resource research and planning, training facilities development, programme design and training funding and provision illustrates a strategy designed to anticipate human resource needs within a predominantly small business tourism industry. This approach allows for the pro-active anticipation of change in the volume of business, skills profiles and demographics among other things and represents a national tourism manpower model which is under review in a number of other countries. A key component of this model is the information collection process, utilizing the direct survey method, which is considered in Chapter 5. Other forms of national initiatives can also be identified. Countries with a strong tradition of skills emigration in the tourism field – Ireland and Singapore are examples – have instigated major 'return home' campaigns through relevant industry associations and government agencies.

Substantial investment in training facilities by large companies to meet their national and, in some cases, international human resource needs, is a growing trend. Good examples are Forte Hotels' Management Academy and the facilities of McDonald's and Disney. These are by no means isolated. Both Taj and Oberoi in India have developed hotel schools that provide courses leading to accredited awards. Plans for a mega international resort in Desaru, West Malaysia (while currently in abeyance), included a major tourism training centre as an early component within the development. Likewise, a recent craft training centre initiative by Inter-Continental and the UK-based Hotel and Catering Training Company is designed to overcome Inter-Con's skills shortages in Australia. This trend, while currently mainly based within the hotel and restaurant sectors, is one that is likely to spread and extend, both geographically and throughout the various sectors of the tourism industry.

Regional or transnational initiatives frequently mirror national responses in kind but transcend boundaries, often because small countries, with limited resources, are involved. Within the private sector, common human resource policies and transferable training programmes are increasingly common in larger multinational companies, notably in the hotel sector, where the facilitation of staff mobility within the company is one clear benefit. The Taj Group of Hotels, from India, have made the transfer of technology, service standards and key personnel a central requirement within their investment in Asian republics of the former Soviet Union. Disney, for reasons that are more product-related, have replicated their American human resource approach, with some modifications, in their Japanese and European projects. Beyond individual companies, a good example of regional cooperation is described by Michael Conlin in relation to the Caribbean, where the collective Hotels Association has been at the forefront in organizing cooperative training and work to agree common curricula and qualifications in the hospitality field. A similar initiative is that funded by the European Community in South-East Asia, the ASEAN Tourism Training Project, which includes the objective to establish compatible but separate hospitality training systems within all six countries of the Association of South East Asian Nations (Brunei, Indonesia, Malaysia, the Philippines, Singapore and Thailand). The European Community, itself, provides an alternative model where transnational cooperation is designed to harmonize qualifications and skills within the Community so as to facilitate labour mobility.

A crucial and often neglected component of the responses to human resource issues in tourism, at the company, local, national and regional level, is that of the information or data which guides decision-making.

Indeed, it is arguable that one of the main reasons that issues such as

- Skills shortages
- High labour turnover/attrition and
- Perceived gaps between educational provision and industry needs

take such positions of prominence is because necessary research studies and data collection systems have not been put in place. As a result, what should be predictable and manageable through pro-active planning, becomes an issue of debilitating consequence to the tourism industry, whether an individual company or a whole country. Chapters 5 and 6 recognize the vital importance of valid, current and comprehensive information to the management of human resources in tourism and address two key methodologies for its collection. At the company level, the use of modern, computerized personnel systems is a contribution to this, especially in relation to career tracking and succession planning. On a wider plane, the use of different techniques for estimating employment and related human resource concerns is discussed and particular attention is given to one particular methodology, that of the direct industry survey, which is a flexible, multi-functional approach to the collection of information about human resources in tourism.

The final chapter of this book is intended to bring together the main themes of, in particular, the first three chapters and of the case studies, especially the ways in which human resource issues in tourism are managed. The focus is on the development of a comprehensive, integrated and cohesive framework for human resource development for tourism, which can be analysed and modified for application within tourism industries at a local, national or transnational level.

References

Boella, Michael (1987) *Human Resource Management in the Hotel and Catering Industry*, 4th ed, Hutchinson, London.

CERT (1987) *Scope of the Tourism Industry in Ireland*, CERT, Dublin.

HMSO (1990) *Standard Occupational Classification*, HMSO, London.

Hornsey, T. M. J. and Dann, D. (1984) *Manpower Management in the Hotel and Catering Industry*, Batsford, London.

International Hotel Association (1988) *Hotels of the Future: Strategies and Action Plan*, Horwath and Horwath, London.

ILO (International Labour Office) (1988) *International Standard Classification of Occupations*, ILO, Geneva.

Lockwood, Andrew and Jones, Peter (1984) *People and the Hotel and Catering Industry*, Cassell, London.

Martin, Robert and Lundberg, Donald (1991) *Human Relations for the Hospitality Industry*, Van Nostrand Reinhold, New York.

Parsons, D. (1987) Tourism and leisure jobs: a statistical review. *The Service Industries Journal*, 3(7).

Riley, Michael (1991) *Human Resource Management*, Butterworth-Heinemann, Oxford.

STPB (Singapore Tourism Promotion Board) (1988) *Product Development Plan*, STPB, Singapore.

Tanke, Mary (1990) *Human Resources Management for the Hospitality Industry*, Delmar, Albany.

World Tourism Organization (1975) *Aims, Activities and Fields of Competence of National Tourism Organisations*, WTO, Madrid.

2 Human resource planning and development: a focus on service excellence
V. S. Mahesh

Introduction

In many countries, the growth of tourism, as an industry, is severely limited by the lack of adequately trained personnel. Where the industry has developed in spite of this constraint, the quality of service provided to the visitor has frequently been the casualty. Inordinate delays at airports, horrendous experiences in rail and road transportation, unpleasant stays in hotels, are commonly attributed to inadequate systems and facilities when the central problem is actually one of a lack of professionalism in the approach to human resource planning and development (HRPD). The next two chapters consider HRPD at both the macro and the micro level within the global tourism industry, utilizing case material from real situations in the tourism industry.

At a 'macro' level, issues relating to educational infrastructure, government role in the facilitation of training and apprenticeship programmes, creation of quasi-commercial educational/training centres, and industry–government–educational institute interaction will be considered. These will be cast in a 'macro' model that has been developed and implemented within one Third World tourism economy.

At an individual, organizational level, a 'micro' model will be suggested that could be adopted by individual organizations in the tourism industry, whether an airline, hotel, travel agency or a restaurant. By adopting this model, companies can effectively plan for, procure, train and empower their human resources. The 'micro' model suggested in the next chapter is, primarily, a self-help one that allows for amalgamation with whatever infrastructure already exists within the company or location. It is a model that has, in fact, been implemented, successfully, in a variety of locations, ranging from busy metropolises and capital cities to small towns and places that could be described as the 'back of beyond'.

Managing 'Moments of Truth'

Before we commence a discussion of the HRPD model, it is necessary to consider two central features, common to all sectors of the tourism industry, that is the concept of 'Moments of Truth' and its relationship to the attainment of service excellence in an organization. Jan Carlzon, President of Scandinavian Airlines System, defines a Moment of Truth (MOT) as any interaction between a customer and an organization, which leads to a judgement by the customer about the quality of service received by her or him (Albrecht and Zemke, 1985). Research studies suggest that in all service organizations (and thus, in all parts of the tourism industry) over 95% of MOTs take place between customers and front-line staff. More importantly, these MOTs occur beyond the eyes and the ears of management, in other words, a tourist's assessment of a vacation is critically dependent upon how she or he has been treated by airline ticketing staff, customs officials, taxi drivers, hotel receptionists, waiters, tour guides and retail trade sales attendants. Almost all such MOTs occur away from the visible presence of airline, hotel or travel agency management.

What makes this even more of a difficult problem is the estimate that less than 5% of negative MOTs (or potential complaints) are actually reported by customers. This situation is compounded by the fact that most hotel companies report that less than 3% of cards left in rooms for completion are actually filled in by customers. To sum up this problem:

- More than 95% of MOTs occur through direct interactions between front-line staff and customers.
- Almost all of these are beyond the eyes and ears of management.
- If these MOTs are negative experiences, there is a less than 5% chance of their being reported to the management by customers.
- Hence, how does a management ensure positive MOTs for customers?

The underlying question, then, is, 'Are human beings capable of doing their job correctly, willingly and with a smile, when they know that their management is most unlikely to be able to see or hear them, let alone hear of their failure to do so?' Two initial responses to this question merit consideration. First, the place of what is described as the 'Pygmalion Effect' is of importance. Research evidence suggests that people's behaviour is in direct response to the expectations of significant others, in this case management – in other words, a kind of self-fulfilling prophecy is seen in operation. Thus, if the expectations of management for particular front-line staff are positive, the likelihood of this expectation being met will be increased. If the anticipation is of poor performance, then this, too, is more likely to be delivered. The second response relates to the nature and determinants of quality service within the tourism industry. We will consider this in a little more detail.

A service culture as the key to effective HRPD

The tourism industry, world wide, prides itself on its customer focus, on the place that is accorded to service excellence in company image-building, ranging from promotional material in all formats through to strategic business documents. While the approach may vary, the essential theme is the same, emphasizing that the needs of the customer are the prime determinants of how a company is organized, always assuming that profit criteria are met. Indeed, current wisdom is that caring about the customer, far from being a debit factor on the balance sheet, can be an important contributor to profit. The top rating achieved by well-known oriental hotels and airlines, for example, is largely attained as a result of their recognition of this fact. This theme is central to Feargal Quinn's argument when he describes the business environment that he strives to achieve:

> A company where all the key decisions are based on an over-riding wish to serve the customer better. A company where everyone in it sees serving the customer as their only business. (Quinn, 1990)

This theme is also central to the thesis expounded by Karl Albrecht and Ron Zemke in their book *Service America* (1985). They quote Warren Blanding, editor of *Customer Service Newsletter*:

> The trend toward consumerism, the changing competitive climate and the recent recession all have forced companies to reexamine their relationships with customers. As a result, customer service has become a strategic tool. It used to be regarded as an expense. Now it is seen as a positive force for increasing sales – and for reducing the cost of sales. (1985, p. 9)

Before going any further, we need to consider some of the features of the service sector, within which tourism is located, because these greatly influence both how we attain service excellence and the role that HRPD plays within it. The basic features of services are very different from those of the manufactured product. Understanding this distinction is important since it has a significant bearing on the management of an organization in the service sector as against one in manufacturing. Albrecht and Zemke (1985) highlight several of these distinctions.

- Sales, production, and consumption of a service take place almost simultaneously while there is usually a long lead time between production and sale of a product.
- A service cannot be centrally produced, inspected, stock-piled or warehoused – it is usually delivered where the consumer is, by people who are beyond the immediate influence of the management.
- A service cannot be demonstrated, nor can a sample be sent for customer approval in advance of purchase.
- A customer receiving the service generally owns nothing tangible once the service has been delivered – the value is frequently internal to the customer.
- A service is frequently an experience that cannot be shared, passed around or given away to someone else once it is delivered.
- Delivery of a service usually requires some degree of human contact – receiver and deliverer frequently come together in a relatively personal way.
- Quality control over a service requires monitoring of processes and attitudes of staff.

To this list, I would add two other critical differences:

- Unlike a bad product, bad service cannot be replaced – at best, one can be sensitive to customer dissatisfaction and recover the situation with such remarkably good service that the customer may both forgive and forget the bad service just received.
- It is both difficult and undesirable to attempt to overstandardize service (despite strong moves in that direction in the tourism product area) – the more spontaneous and custom-built a service, the greater its value in the customer's eyes.

These features are implicit in the discussion that follows and also in the HRPD strategies that are discussed in the next chapter.

Achieving optimum customer care or service excellence requires investment, planning and management of a similar order and magnitude to that necessary for any other aspect of skills or knowledge development. Arguably, indeed, the requirement for investment in training and other forms of support and assistance in the customer care domain is greater than in other fields and this is evidenced by the growing number of tourism companies that recruit young entrants on the basis of their 'soft skills', in the certainty that any technical skills requirement can be met, relatively easily, in-house. This is done because of the large cost savings which the recruitment of effective customer-orientated front-line staff can entail. A negative consequence of the success of much customer handling training, within tourism education programmes, is the level of staff 'poaching' by other service sector companies.

Effective customer care is about more than training staff in smiling, pleasant manners and complaint handling. Good customer relations comes from a total management culture within a company. This point is well illustrated in research undertaken by Gail Cook Johnson in Canada. Cook Johnson (1991) analysed the results of a large number of employee opinion studies in the United States and Canada and, on the basis of the cumulative data, was able to extract the management and cultural characteristics of companies that were categorized by both employees and customers as:

- **Service Leaders** – on average, 92% of employees and customers rated these organizations as consistently very good in their service – the top 25% of the sample.
- **Service Average** – on average, 79% of employees and customers rated service as consistently very good – the middle 50% of the sample
- **Service Problems** – in these organizations, only 62% of employees and customers rated service as consistently good – the bottom 25% of the sample.

The key characteristics of companies identified as 'Service Leaders' in this study, all relate to the application of the principle of empowerment to all employees. According to Cook Johnson, empowerment is manifest in the way that companies:

- Are highly focused and consistent in everything they do and say in relation to employees
- Have managers who communicate with employees
- Facilitate, rather than regulate, their employees' response to customers
- Solicit employee feedback about how they can do things better
- Stress the importance of teamwork at each level of the organization, and
- Plan carefully the organization's recruitment and training needs

Cook Johnson concludes by describing these companies, in contrast to the lesser service orientation of other organizations, as 'flatter' in structure with less emphasis on hierarchy and formal intra-company relationships. 'More distinctively,' she claims, 'Service Leaders can be recognized for

- their unfailing commitment to service principles
- their investments in people to ensure staffing competence
- a management philosophy which stresses communication, a pro-active orientation and employee feedback, and
- a dedication to teamwork.' (Cook Johnson, 1991)

Cook Johnson's research gives a fairly comprehensive picture of the factors that distinguish a good, service-orientated company, excellent in the eyes of both customers and employees. Similar conclusions can be found in the work of Sarah Mansfield (1990), who identified four key principles in the development of customer care within companies. These are:

1 Customer care 'starts at the top', meaning that commitment to the principle of customer care must emanate from senior management levels within an organization. Successful management 'is not only about the right management style but also an attitude, ethos or culture of the organization which overrides the management techniques used, such that in the absence of other instructions these values will dictate how an employee will behave'.
2 'Customer care involves everyone' within the organization. It is not just about front-line staff. The contrary view 'only serves to reinforce the electricians' or administrators' opinion that the standard of service they give in support of the front-line staff is not important. How can cleaners do the right job unless they fully appreciate their customers' needs and the importance of their role? High standards of customer care cannot be achieved by ignoring seasonal, part-time or voluntary staff who represent the face of the business to many customers.'
3 'Care for your staff and they will care for your customers.' Too often organizations look first to the customer, whereas the emphasis should be placed on the staff. 'Improving the experience of the staff encourages a better service and a better experience for customers. More customers are obtained thereby improving the climate in which management and staff work. Investment and greater professionalism follow success and the cycle of achievement is reinforced.'
4 'It's a continuous process', meaning that 'customer care is not a quick fix project but a long term plan.'

A similar scenario is painted in analysis presented by Zeithaml et al (1990). Their reported research is based on customer and executive interviews in a number of service sector businesses and identifies five gaps as the key causes of service-quality shortfalls. The significance of

27

each of these gaps is placed in the context of service quality as a contributor to profitability. The gaps that Zeithaml et al identify are:

- Gap 1: The customers' expectations–management perceptions gap. This gap represents divergence in the perceptions that customers and management have with respect to what constitutes quality in service. While there is considerable confluence in perceptions, discrepancies were identified in the research which suggest that the respective priorities are not always identical.
- Gap 2: management's perceptions–service quality specifications gap. Zeithaml et al rightly note that 'management's correct perceptions of customers' expectations is necessary but not sufficient, for achieving superior quality service'. This gap represents a further concern that emerges from their research; the difficulty that management experiences in translating its understanding of customers' perceptions into service quality specifications.
- Gap 3: service quality specifications–service delivery gap. This gap represents difficulties in translating well-developed service specifications, within companies, into actual front-line performance by employees. The reported research notes that 'the executives we interviewed . . . invariably expressed frustration at the inability of their employees to meet these service performance standards'. The authors go on to acknowledge that service performance gaps can reflect a variety of factors in addition to the establishment of service quality standards; these include poorly qualified employees, inadequate internal systems to support contact personnel and insufficient capacity to serve.
- Gap 4: service delivery–external communications gap. A key determinant of customers' expectations is the external communications employed by service companies through advertising, sales and marketing initiatives. If the promised service does not match reality, customer perceptions are, inevitably, undermined. 'In short, external communications can affect not only customers' expectations about a service but also customers' perceptions of the delivered service.'
- Gap 5: customers' expections–perceptions of quality service gap. This gap derives from the cumulative consequences of the other four gaps; at the same time, this gap itself is one of the key factors within the creation of each of the other four gaps. It is thus presented as, perhaps, the linchpin gap within the Zeithaml model and the one that requires most immediate remedial action within most service companies.

This discussion of the nature, determinants and problem areas of service quality within tourism points clearly to the central role of personnel, at all levels, in attaining levels of excellence in this respect. Developing the service culture, within a company, and within a tourism industry, can be seen as crucial to the success of tourism. I have described, elsewhere, how the notion of service excellence can be imbued within a company's culture, through training and development (Baum and Mahesh, 1992). The answer to the question I posed earlier, as to whether staff are capable of doing their job correctly and willingly away from management supervision and without fear of come-back if they fail to do so, must, then, be an unequivocal 'Yes', and human resource development plans need to give priority to this concern. How this can be undertaken, in practice, will be considered in the next chapter.

References

Albrecht, Karl and Zemke, Ron (1985) *Service America! Doing Business in the New Economy*, Dow–Jones–Irwin, Homewood, Ill.

Baum, Tom and Mahesh, V. S. (1992) 'Developing a system for competitor analysis'. In *Managing Projects in Hospitality Organizations*, (ed. Richard Teare, Debra Adams and Sally Messenger) Cassell, London.

Cook Johnson, Gail (1991) *How Service Leaders Empower their Employees*, Reacon, Toronto.

Mansfield, Sarah (1990) *Customer Care in Tourism and Leisure: Insights*, The English Tourist Board.

Quinn, Feargal (1990) *Crowning the Customer*, O'Brien Press, Dublin.

Zeithaml, V. A., Parasuraman, A. and Berry, L. L. (1990) *Delivering Quality Service: Balancing Customer Perceptions and Expectations*, The Free Press, New York.

3 Human resource planning and development: micro and macro models for effective growth in tourism
V. S. Mahesh

In the previous chapter, we considered the role of 'Moments of Truth' and the attainment of service excellence in effective human resource planning and development (HRPD) strategies by looking at some of the research evidence that has focused on this topic. This approach underpins the development of HRPD models, at both the micro and macro levels, which I have applied in the Indian context. While aspects of the detail may be specific to that country, the principles involved can be generalized to the tourism industries of other countries.

The nine-step HRPD model

With the underlying faith in people's ability to perform well, willingly and voluntarily (given the right environment and management leadership), which we have already considered, the actual construction of the micro HRPD model can now be discussed. The following steps are required:

1 Correctly plan for the requisite number of people required at each level of each category of skill, providing for expansion, attrition and internal developmental needs.
2 Identify alternative sources from where people can be recruited, ranging from fully trained and experienced people who could operate directly on the job, to new entrants who require appropriate training before commencing work.
3 Set up appropriate, cost-effective recruitment systems.
4 Set up effective induction and training systems to cater for every source of recruitment.
5 Identify and make available the requisite number of trainers to operate these systems.

6   Install an effective personnel administration system to take care of those recruited.
7   Set up a discipline management system whereby all employees are prepared to accept basic norms of discipline at work.
8   Create a collaborative climate for industrial peace so that customers are not in the least aware of the unavoidable tensions that are likely to occur in any management–employee relationship.
9   Set up a team of human resource professionals who have the requisite professional and personal skills to ensure continuous monitoring and improvement of the integrated HRPD system described above.

A 'back of beyond' application of the micro model

To understand the nine-step micro model for HRPD in action, let us first consider the example of how human resources planning and development was undertaken, successfully, in a single hotel. The example taken is one of a small, 34 bedroom hotel, established by Gateway Hotels and Resorts (a part of the Taj Group of Hotels) in Chiplun, located in a relatively remote and underdeveloped area, half-way between Bombay and Goa in India. Chiplun had no other hotel of a similar standard, nor was there any such hotel within a radius of 150 miles.

The main steps taken for human resource planning and development for Chiplun were:

1   Manpower requirements for the hotel were finalized a full year before opening.
2   With the exception of the positions of hotel manager, the heads of food production, service and rooms division and a temporary training manager, all other positions were to be filled through recruitment of local personnel, following appropriate training.
3   All schools within a certain mile radius of the hotel were visited and graduating students were told what a hotel is all about, and what kinds of jobs and careers were available. Given the orthodox and, primarily, rural background of the local community, the very concept of a hotel was so unfamiliar that this first communication was far more complex than would have been the case in an urbanized, more developed region.
4   After considerable persuasion, designed to overcome local prejudices against the hotel and catering industry in general, interviews were set up and a tentative shortlist of candidates was prepared. As most of the candidates could speak only their local

dialect and had no knowledge or experience of the hotel industry, the criteria for selection were restricted to personality, ability to smile, the ability to contribute to teamwork (demonstrated through games participation), average intelligence and physical fitness.

5   Among those selected, there were many who had difficulty in communicating to their parents or guardians what they had been selected for; in these cases the hotel manager and the training manager visited the homes in order to help communicate with the parents.

6   Those finally selected were put through a rigorous medical examination to ensure that only those in perfect health were hired. This process also helped to communicate the high priority given to health and hygiene by the hotel company.

7   Commencing with the very simple (in this case, the use of forks and knives as the local population were unfamiliar with these), the very raw and inexperienced recruits were educated and trained in different aspects of hotel work. With the objective of facilitating easy job rotation and mobility, many were trained as multi-skilled employees, for example, a resort attendant being one who could work as a room boy, gardener, waiter or utility assistant.

8   Within 6–8 months of joining, most of the employees were adequately trained for the opening of the hotel; for example, those trained in kitchen work could not only prepare a range of basic dishes but could also complete a portion control format and an itemized cost sheet.

9   In anticipation of possible attrition, a number of supernumerary staff were recruited and trained and, in the event, this provision proved vital as a number of staff did leave before the hotel opened.

10   Internal systems for grievance management and counselling were established, wages formalized and all personnel administration systems were in place from the onset so that potential causes of labour unrest were anticipated and minimized.

11   The training manager was withdrawn only after all systems had been established and the small management team was in position with a fully trained staff. For the first two years, thereafter, central support was provided in the area of industrial relations and associated personnel concerns but, in all other respects, the hotel was able to function independently in the human resource domain.

In sum, an island of efficiency was created in under one year, employing local, 'raw' labour who were trained and developed within a highly professional HRPD framework. The self-fulfilling prophecy, in terms of the expectations of high performance from the local population, was realized in this example as was the validity of giving primacy to service as opposed to technical potential at the time of recruitment. Finally, the value of a well organized and formalized approach to HRPD was validated. Both financial performance and customer feedback data for the hotel confirm these assertions.

A similar approach to HRPD has been implemented successfully, within the same company, in capital cities such as New Delhi and Colombo, where both the local infrastructure and the experience and potential of recruits was very different from the rural situation. By restricting the number of senior positions to be filled by those with working experience – to form a nucleus around which to build the rest of the team – and maximizing the number of positions that could be filled by new personnel recruited with sufficient lead time to allow for proper training, even the human resource needs of large hotels can be comfortably met. The dependence on the external educational, training and tourism industry environment is, thus, minimized and, at the same time, the hotel is able to benefit through the development of a homogeneous team of like trained personnel. I have given a more detailed description of this system at work elsewhere (Mahesh, 1988).

The macro, country-wide model

So far, we have considered what an individual organization can do in order to plan effectively for, recruit, train and retain the human resources that it requires. This has been viewed purely within the degrees of freedom and constraints applicable to the individual company. However, if a country as a whole wishes to professionalize its approach to HRPD, much can be done that may support the growth of its tourism industry. That growth can be generated and sustained only with the support of sufficient well-trained and motivated people at all levels should not require reiteration.

Below is presented the outline of an HRPD plan which was prepared for implementation in India at a time when that country was committed to the growth of its international tourism arrivals by a factor of 2.5 during the following seven years. The outline of the model is presented in sequence in order to facilitate application elsewhere.

1 *Human resource availability at the commencement of the planning period*

The first task, within the project in question, was to assemble all existing statistics on manpower in the tourism industry for the 'base' year of the exercise, in this case 1988. In most countries, the availability of reliable and up-to-date statistics about tourism employment in anything like the required detail is unusual and what is accessible must be treated with some caution. As a result, a number of assumptions and extrapolations may be required. In this case, although the project was undertaken in 1988, acceptable manpower statistics were only available for the year 1981. These figures were updated, on the basis of a number of assumptions derived from the growth in international arrivals and domestic tourists during the period in question. These assumptions included the following:

- Within the accommodation, food and air transportation sectors, an increase in manpower of 7% per year.
- Growth in employees within the taxi sector of 5% per year in order to recognize the movement towards luxury tourist coach travel.
- Increase in railway manpower by 4% per year in order to reflect additional track kilometres laid during the period.
- An increase of 8% per year in the bus transportation, retail, tourism administration and travel trade sectors.
- An increase in manpower employed within the entertainment and recreation sectors of 10% per year, to reflect the competitive nature of this segment of the industry and the clear growth trends in evidence.

The human resource distribution for the year 1987–8 was, thus, estimated for all the main sectors of the tourism industry and this is shown in Table 3.1.

2 *Projecting human resource requirements*

Given the estimated 1987–8 figures, projections were made of the human resource requirements up to the year 1994–5, on an annual basis, based upon the following methodology and assumptions.

- **Planning for productivity improvement** By 1995, sufficient human resources in all categories of all industry sectors would be required to meet the demands of 3 million international tourists, as against a 1987 figure of 1.48 million. A parallel growth in the domestic

Table 3.1 *Human resources distribution in tourism and allied sectors, 1987–8*

	Managerial	Supervisor technical	Clerical	Skilled	Unskilled	Others	Total
1 Accommodation and food	0	4193	1381	7644	7302	508	21 029
1.1 Approved sector	0	2051	660	2480	1325	218	6734
1.2 Unapproved sector	0	1076	562	2444	1972	35	6089
1.3 Supplementary accommodation	0	–	–	–	1492	–	1492
1.4 Restaurants	0	1066	159	2721	2513	255	6714
2 Transport	0	2189	2200	4811	2169	341	11 709
2.1 Airways and airport	0	322	358	515	256	34	1486
2.2 Taxi trade	–	–	–	652	259	–	912
2.3 Railways	0	1388	1314	1041	1104	276	5123
2.4 Bus transport	0	35	113	1180	289	31	1648
2.5 All other transport	0	443	415	1422	260	–	2541
3 Retail trade	0	226	3090	0	1030	0	4345
4 Entertainment	0	0	0	0	0	0	0
5 Tourism admin. and travel trade	0	226	333	244	200	0	1003
Total	0	6834	7004	12 700	10 700	849	38 086

tourism market was also projected. Accounting for productivity improvements through the introduction of computer technology, simplification of work procedures, improved telecommunications and better utilization of resources, the assumption was made that the human resource requirement would increase by approximately half of the growth in business. It was estimated that, while business would increase at an average of 14% per year, the growth in clerical and unskilled staff, those most vulnerable to the changes outlined above, would be only 4%, and skilled and supervisory/management personnel would increase by between 9% and 10% per year. In Table 3.2, rows marked 'E' (denoting expansion needs) in each of the five sectors represent these quantitative assumptions. It will be noted that where particular levels are inappropriate to a sector, they have been omitted, for example, no clerical category is provided with respect to the entertainment and recreation sector.

• **Planning for attrition** Owing to the international nature of the industry, and the high degree of contact between front-line staff and clients, the tourism industry suffers from a high level of staff turnover (attrition). In this plan, this was catered for by assuming an 8%

Table 3.2 *Expansion/promotions and turnover assumptions, categorywise and sectorwise*

	Managerial	Supervisory/ technical	Clerical	Skilled	Unskilled and others
Accommodation and food					
E	9	13	4	9	4
P(out)	–	13	5	5	8
P(in)	(13)	(5) + (5)	(7)	(1)	
T	8	8	4	5	4
Transport					
E	9	9	4	9	4
P(out)	–	6	7	4	5
P(in)	(6)	(7) + (4)		(5)	
T	5	8	8	8	4
Retail Trade					
E	11	11	11	–	11
P(out)	–	5	5	–	3
P(in)	(5) + (5)		(3)		
T	3	3	3	–	3
Entertainment and recreation					
E	11	–	–	11	11
P(out)	–	–	–	2	2
P(in)	(2)			(2)	
T	3	–	–	3	3
Tourism admin. and travel trade					
E	9	13	4	9	4
P(out)	–	10	4	4	8
P(in)	(10)	(4)	(4)	(8)	
T	8	8	8	8	4

E, Expansion of strength as a percentage of current strength.
P(out), Provision for promotions out of level as percentage of current strength.
P(in), Provision for promotion into level from lower categories *after* sufficient development inputs.
T, Provision for attrition (or, manpower turnover) as percentage of current strength indicating possible loss due to retirement, death, emigration to other countries, inter-sectoral movement etc.

turnover rate among certain staff levels while at the unskilled grades, the rate was kept at 3–4% to account for normal resignations, retirements, death etc. This assumption may appear somewhat low to those working in the tourism industry of a developed economy but is valid in the context of a developing country. In Table 3.2, rows marked T (for turnover) give these assumptions by industry sector. Again, it will be noted that the attrition rate, for the retail, entertainment and recreation sectors has been projected as very low when compared to the other three, more internationally competitive sectors, which are prone to suffer from higher attrition rates.

• **Maximizing internal development and growth** It is imperative that internal development and growth, within any organization, are maximized. In the service sector, in particular, only a contented and well-motivated staff will ensure customer satisfaction. One factor that has a major impact on staff morale, as has already been noted, is the extent to which provision is made for their development and growth. A commitment to this policy by all relevant parties is a requirement for the operation of a plan such as this. As such, internal movement, within the organization, from one category to the next within the hierarchy, was provided for, thus reducing the need for direct recruitment of staff at more senior levels. In Table 3.2, the rows marked P(out) (promotion out of a category) and P(in) (promotion into a category) respectively denote the percentage of each category planned for promotion from one category into the next. To take the case of supervisory/technical staff in the transportation sector, the figures (7) + (4) shown against P(in) correspond to the 7% of clerical staff and the 4% of skilled staff to be promoted, if suitable, each year. This is indicated by arrows connecting the respective figures.

• **Recruitment plan as a derivative**   After accounting for expansion and attrition needs, and providing for promotions out of and into the various categories, the resultant recruitment plan was derived. Using the accommodation and food sector as an example, Table 3.3 shows how this process worked in practice for the year 1988–9.

Table 3.3 *Accommodation and food sector: calculations to arrive at net promotion and recruitment action in 1988–9 and resultant strength at end of year 1988–9*

	Managerial	Supervisory/ technical	Clerical	Skilled	Unskilled	Others
I Position in 1987–8	27 033	28 546	26 562	140 264	87 761	6111
II Expansion needs:						
%	9%	13%	4%	9%	4%	4%
n	2433	3711	1062	12 624	3510	244
III Provision for promotion out of level:						
%	0%	13%	5%	5%	8%	8%
n	0	3711	1328	7013	7020	488
IV Provision for attrition:						
%	8%	8%	4%	5%	4%	4%
n	2163	2204	1062	7013	3510	244
V Provision for promotion into level	(3711)	(1328) (7013)	(939)	(6569)	–	
VI Recruitment action (=II+III+IV−V)	885	1364	2514	20 079	14 042	978
VII Position in 1988–9 (=I+VI−III− IV+V)	29 466	32 257	27 624	152 888	91 271	6355

• **Yearly plans for internal development and recruitment** Using the same assumptions for each year, annual plans were derived, quantifying the numbers of personnel that would need to be recruited and the numbers requiring further development in order to be eligible for promotion, up to the year 1994–5. As examples, the plans for 1989–90 are given in Table 3.4 (for promotion) and Table 3.5 (for recruitment).

Table 3.4 *Human resource distribution in tourism and allied sectors: promotion in 1989–90*

	Managerial	Supervisory/ technical	Clerical	Skilled	Unskilled	Others	Total
1 Accommodation and food	27 033	28 546	26 562	140 264	87 761	6111	316 277
1.1 Approved hotels	4579	13 961	12 699	45498	15 927	2 619	95 283
1.2 Unapproved sector	11 618	7325	10 808	44 835	23 700	426	98 712
1.3 Supplementary accommodation	4485	–	–	–	17 934	–	22 419
1.4 Restaurants	6351	7260	3055	49 931	30 200	3066	99 863
2 Transport	17 087	33 467	30 217	147 133	41 710		6552 276 166
2.1 Airways and airport	1641	4923	4923	15 753	4923	657	32 820
2.2 Taxi trade	–	–	–	19 949	4987	–	24 936
2.3 Railways	8493	21 230	18 045	31 845	21 230	5308	106 151
2.4 Bus transport	173	534	1549	36 086	5566	587	44 495
2.5 All other transport	6780	6780	5700	43 500	5004	–	67 764
3 Retail trade	31 030	4064	55 672	–	30 922	–	121 688
4 Entertainment	1225	–	–	23 275	1750	–	26 250
5 Tourism admin. and travel trade	2000	2000	8000	5600	2400	–	20 000
Total	78 375	68 077	120 451	316 272	164 543	12 663	760 381

• **Summary of projections** The use of this model resulted in the estimate that the number who would need to be recruited, within the tourism industry, would increase from 104 018 in 1988–9 to 173 525 in 1994–5. Of this number, those in skilled categories and higher levels would account for about 75% each year, or an average of about 100 000 per year at these levels. These are the levels where either college education and training or in-company training investment are required. The breakdown for this 100 000 was as follows:

1	Managerial/entrepreneurial	3300
2	Engineering/technical	5000
3	Kitchen/restaurant	17 000

Table 3.5   *Human resources distribution in tourism and allied sectors: recruitment for 1989–90*

	Managerial	Supervisory/ technical	Clerical	Skilled	Unskilled	Others	Total
1 Accommodation and food	816	1942	2615	22 215	14 603	1017	43 208
1.1 Approved hotels	138	950	1250	7206	2650	436	12 630
1.2 Unapproved sector	351	498	1064	7101	3944	71	13 028
1.3 Supplementary accommodation	135	–	–	–	2984	–	3120
1.4 Restaurants	192	494	301	7908	5025	510	14 430
2 Transport	419	1379	5971	29 565	5639	886	43 859
2.1 Airways and airport	40	203	973	3165	666	89	5136
2.2 Taxi trade	–	–	–	4009	674	–	4683
2.3 Railways	208	875	3566	6399	2870	718	14 636
2.4 Bus transport	4	22	306	7251	753	79	8415
2.5 All other transport	166	279	1126	8741	677	–	10 989
3 Retail trade	1507	857	10 712	0	5835	0	18 910
4 Entertainment	190	0	0	3617	272	0	4079
5 Tourism admin. and travel trade	145	124	1331	1082	399	0	3081
Total	3076	4302	20 629	56 479	26 749	1903	113 137

4	Pilots	100
5	Taxi and bus drivers/conductors	9600
6	Entertainers	3000
7	Railways	14 000
8	Skilled and supervisory staff	28 000
9	Clerical staff	20 000
	Total per year	100 000

Besides providing 100 000 new trained staff at the above levels each year, an additional 45 000 existing staff would need to receive tailor-made development in order to equip them for promotional responsibilities. In addition, existing staff at all levels would also require on-going retraining and constant motivation. Thus immediate and effective investment in the creation of further training and development facilities was pinpointed by the plan as essential.

Proposed action to meet recruitment and developmental needs

Having arrived at the estimated number that the tourism industry would require through the establishment of the quantitative framework on the basis of the above process, it was now necessary to propose the steps that would be needed in order to meet these targets. In other words, the plan also contained proposals relating to the necessary steps that would have to be taken, by what date, how and by whom, in a way that would allow the problem of human resource availability to be tackled in a qualitative as well as a quantitative way. In making recommendations, at this stage, it was essential, first, to review the existing educational and training infrastructure in the country in question.

As an aside, at this point, it is worth while to note that a wide range of jobs in the tourism industry, probably the majority, can be filled by providing short, pre-employment training to those who have limited secondary or equivalent schooling. What is primarily required from potential employees in the tourism industry is the ability to smile naturally; to be pleasant with other people, customers and colleagues alike; to be hardworking; to be clean, presentable and hygiene conscious; and to be able to work as part of a team. There are an enormous number of young people with these qualities in most countries who, having passed school or college with insufficient grades to enter higher education or the more preferred professions, are seeking career opportunities. The availability of such manpower is the basic premise around which the macro HRPD model has been built. This premise alone allows most countries the potential rapidly to overcome the problem of availability of well-trained human resources for the tourism industry.

Returning to the plan, this premises was central to the review of existing educational and training provision, which focused, in particular, on the potential of educational provision outside of formal tourism-related education and training. As a result, a number of recommendations were presented and these are outlined in their original form.

• **Managerial and entrepreneurial needs** Existing management institutions as well as the major universities in the country should have separate departments or areas of study specializing in the tourism/hospitality/service sector disciplines. With the global shift from manufacturing to service economies, this change in emphasis is, in any case, desirable. Graduates and postgraduates specializing in these areas will provide the entrepreneurial impetus as well as the management expertise that is required for the rapid growth envisaged throughout the service sector, not least in tourism. Existing hotel management schools in India, of which there are four of international quality and a further 12 of intermediate standard, should be encouraged to offer postgraduate specialization in management; so as to increase further the pool of management expertise. All institutions offering such education should also be encouraged and assisted to convert their programmes into modular ones suitable for practising managers in the tourism industry. The key here is flexibility in terms of the timing and duration of these programmes. The tourism industry is well suited to support modular development of this nature, because it allows for the creative combining of practical experience and theoretical knowledge. The seasonal nature of the industry can also be advantageously utilized in this manner.

• **Engineering/technical** There is an oversupply of degree and diploma graduates in engineering in the country in question. Therefore, this requirement, in tourism, can readily be met by providing relatively short-term development programmes within the place of employment. If required, engineering colleges could also be encouraged to offer specializations in the necessary areas.

• **Kitchen and restaurant manpower** This is likely to be the most critical problem within these recommendations, as the existing sources of training supply only about 4000 trained personnel per year, including those apprentices trained by industry within the government supported programme. Thus, the requirement is to meet an estimated shortfall of 13 000 trained staff per year. It is recommended that the following actions be taken immediately to cope with this shortfall.

(1) Enhance the scope of the apprenticeship scheme, currently subsidized by government, by doubling the intake of those participating establishments. At the same time, provide adequate funding to the industry to cover costs, improve instructional quality, with a stronger customer service orientation, and upgrade the system of monitoring on-the-job training so as to reduce abuse of this area by the industry. These steps should be designed to generate a further 2000 new entrants into the industry as well as improving the quality of manpower from these sources.

(2) Operate the existing craft catering institutes on a double training shift in order to double their output of this critical manpower category. At the same time, admissions criteria require amendment so as to put greater emphasis on personality and customer-orientated criteria. Leading hotel and restaurant companies should be encouraged to 'adopt' specific craft catering institutes, providing both financial support and relevant expertise for the development of the institutes. The colleges should also move to modular course provision so that practising executives and crafts personnel from the industry can

further develop their expertise. The institutes should also open financially independent restaurants and bakery shops, open to the general public, thus generating extra revenue, giving practical exposure to the students and, last but not least, providing an excellent means through which to promote the institute in the local community. (The model of the Singapore Hotels Association Training and Education Centre's hotel and restaurants merits consideration.) These steps should lead to the generation of a further 2000 trained new entrants through the college system. In addition, this strategy will contribute to upgrading the skills of those already in the industry.

(3) To assist small restaurants as well as budget and one- and two-star hotels, and to enhance the employability of school leavers, it is recommended that a new model of 'pre-employment training centres' is established. The target should be to open five of these centres per year, over the six-year period. Each facility should, ideally, have provision to teach 40 kitchen and 40 restaurant students at a time. Operating two shifts and running modular programmes of four months each, as many as 480 students can attend basic, preparatory programmes in each centre per year. By establishing five such centres each year, the supply of semi-skilled manpower in this critical category will increase by 2500 per year.

(4) Ethnic food is becoming popular throughout the world and is one factor in tourist destination choice. It is recommended that a National Culinary Institute is established, on the lines of the Culinary Institute of America in the United States. Through this school, which would require full industry support, the objective should be to enhance the status and skills of the ethnic chef to the level enjoyed by the exponent of French cuisine. As a starting point, the target should be 100 graduates per year. However, of greater significance is the potential of the school to influence the development and interest in ethnic and regional cuisine.

(5) There is an oversupply of graduates from universities in general, non-vocational disciplines, who are seeking employment. It is recommended that selected groups of these graduates be enrolled on rigorous two-year programmes of education and training, in order to prepare them for supervisory and junior management positions in the kitchen and food service areas. These programmes should involve extensive placement within approved establishments, with some financial incentives to companies to participate in the scheme.

These five inter-connected recommendations should contribute to bridging the shortfall of 13 000 envisaged in this crucial category.

- **Pilots** Even though the target number appears to be relatively small, on an annual basis, the costs and duration of pilot training are such that this category requires careful consideration. Furthermore, it is possible that attrition, among pilots, may be rather greater as a result of external factors, notably predictions of a worldwide skills shortage in this area. The attractions of working for overseas companies, offering higher remuneration, may be difficult to counter. To be self-reliant in this important category, the airline industry should be supported to develop a local training facility, over and above that in existence for the military (from where many civil pilots are recruited).

• **Taxi drivers** While the requirement of 3000 taxi drivers per year does not present a major problem in the quantitative sense, complaints about the courtesy and knowledge of taxi drivers are common. Only those who have passed a rigorous test, to be re-taken at regular intervals, with respect to hygiene, appearance, safety, courtesy and local knowledge, should be licensed to work in the tourism sector.

• **Bus/coach drivers and conductors** The problem here is similar to that of taxi drivers and equivalent measures are required. A modular programme of training, covering the main areas of courtesy, hygiene, safety and product knowledge, could be organized by either the industry association or by the government tourism department.

• **Entertainers** With growing tourist interest in areas such as folk and ethnic arts and entertainment, there is a need for government support to revive, preserve and support these art forms. Owing to lack of financial support, many artists are, currently, changing to other vocations. It is recommended that regional centres be established in order to provide support, training and quality management of the traditional entertainments area.

• **Manpower for railways** As the railways is a single, government monopoly organization in the country in question, the HRPD requirements need to be established by the company itself, utilizing the micro HRPD model described earlier. However, while doing so, emphasis should be given to ensuring that the entire organization looks at itself as being in the service business rather than just in transportation. Tourists' complaints are, generally, about lack of courtesy by staff, delays and deviations from schedule, poor hygiene, inadequate catering and poor safety. These require consideration when planning the training of staff.

• **Other skilled and supervisory staff whose roles centre on direct customer contact/relations** This is the largest category of manpower required, although they are located in a number of businesses. They include such a range of staff as retail salespersons, hotel receptionists, telephonists, ticketing staff, tour guides, airline cabin crew and customs officials. As people who are responsible for creating positive Moments of Truth for tourists, their selection and training are critical components of the entire HRPD model. From the vast numbers of young people who graduate from schools and colleges each year, it should be feasible to select the required 28 000 who have the naturally pleasant disposition required for work as front-line staff. Modular programmes of not more than two weeks could be conducted at suitable times to provide for their basic training, utilizing existing teachers outside of their normal teaching commitments. This will provide the basis for further development through incompany training once the students find positions in the industry. In addition, school and college curricula could be amended in order to include introductory front-line and communications skills training.

• **Computer-literate clerical staff** A similar approach to that suggested under the previous heading may be adopted, in order to meet the requirement for 20 000 staff per year. Again, short-term, modular programmes should be used as the precursor of further training in industry.

• **Creation of a Tourism and Hospitality Resource Centre (THRC)** Such a Centre is required in order to support and initiate developments in tourism and allied areas. The Centre should:

1 Provide expert assistance to small businesses in facilitating development in areas such as operational standards, training, automation, computerization, management, marketing, project planning and implementation.
2 Advise small businesses with regard to their interface with support services such as equipment maintenance, transportation, the retail and travel trades.
3 Assist the existing and new educational institutions in development and sharing of training materials, including audio-visual aids, translation into regional languages and curriculum development.
4 Provide and conduct training programmes in basic hygiene, courtesy, safety and related areas to small businesses, the taxi trade, police, customs officials and other front-line staff at airports and similar travel centres.

Such a centre would require grant aid from government and support from the various industry sectors. The centre should be judged by its ability to provide effective dissemination of information about education and training techniques within tourism. The role played by the training agency CERT in Ireland is the recommended model for this centre.

• **Developmental efforts within organizations** As has been already pointed out, over 40 000 people per year require development support through focused, tailor-made programmes, so that they can be given additional responsibilities. The larger corporations in the tourism industry, who undertake outstanding work in this area, should be recognized so that they become role models for other companies. While the modular training programmes proposed for all new entrants can be utilized in support of this objective, smaller organizations will mainly depend on the assistance of the proposed THRC for expert trainers and training materials.

• **Industrial relations** The consequences of industrial disharmony, within the service sector generally, and tourism specifically, can be cataclysmic and have an immediate effect on customer satisfaction with the whole tourism product of the country. Hence, ensuring a healthy and peaceful industrial relations climate is essential for the survival of the tourism industry. Government initiatives and legislation are required to reduce confrontational practices and to ensure that employee relations operate on a positive and supportive basis.

• **Leave the implementation to human resource management (HRM) professionals** In order to implement all the above recommendations, while sensitively adapting them to changes in the environment, to opportunities and to threats that will, inevitably, arise in the future, a team of specialist staff will be required. Technical knowledge, whether in travel management, tourism administration or French cuisine, will not be sufficient in order to implement an HRPD programme of this nature. Expertise in human resource management will be essential in order to ensure an effective translation of this plan into action.

Summary and conclusion

In both this chapter and Chapter 2 we have seen that making a tourist's Moments of Truth positive and memorable, in other words the attainment of service excellence, is not an easy task. It cannot be ensured by 'scientific management', automation or through traditional principles of manufacturing management. The solution lies in the enlightened principles and methods of human resource management, firmly rooted in a belief in the potential of the individual employee and in the contribution of all staff to the attainment of service quality. This is easier said than done. Since the beginning of the century, when Henry Ford, Frederick Taylor and the scientific management school began to leave their indelible stamp on the expectations and behaviour of management, the front-line employee has been frequently undervalued. Despite acknowledgement of the Hawthorne effect and the work of humanists such as Maslow and the management specialists that he influenced, McGregor and Herzberg, most managers have continued to behave in a manner which suggests little change from the early years of the century. As behavioural scientists supported their beliefs by extrapolating their conclusions from experiments with rodents to the industrial setting, it is hardly surprising that the dominant view of the employee is one of a person who is dishonest and unreliable, requiring constant supervision and manipulation.

The best organizations, in service industries, have begun to change this approach to management with conspicuous success. Organizations such as Disney and Marriott in the United States, British Airways, Superquinn in Ireland, France's Club Med chain, the Mandarin Oriental group in the Far East, and the Taj Group of Hotels in India are testimony to this change. These organizations have proved that true excellence in customer service can be achieved only through an enormous faith in human drive for seeking perfection at work, backed by a managerial system for empowering the front-line who deal with customers. In these organizations, the stop watch and control systems of the industrial model are slowly giving way to freedom-centred, human resource specialists.

With less than a 5% chance of seeing, overhearing or even having reported the customers' Moments of Truth, managers committed to enhancing the growth of tourism in their country, quantitatively and qualitatively, must accept the premises of the Pygmalion Effect and the professional capabilities of HRM specialists to put that effect into positive use . . . in the form of billions of positive Moments of Truth for the visiting tourists.

Reference

Mahesh, V. S. (1988) Effective human resource management: key to excellence in service organisations. *Vikalpa*, **13**(4).

4 Labour markets and vocational education
Michael Riley

Introduction

Any review of labour issues in tourism is likely to produce a list that looks something like the following:

- The movement of labour from the land to tourism
- Vocational education versus direct entry training
- Cultural differences in learning
- The replacement of skilled expatriates by local people
- The contribution of tourism to employment
- Deficits in labour supply
- Immigration
- Education–industry relations
- Cost–benefit analyses of vocational education
- Indigenous culture and tourist culture

Most, if not all of these issues are related in some way to the performance of the labour market and its relationship to vocational education.

Often a government authority of some form addresses these problems through a broad strategy. Whether such strategies come in the form of employment projections, educational plans or training strategies they often mistakenly assume the labour market to be static in character and consequently fail to take advantage of some dynamics. Tourism labour markets are almost invariably dynamic in nature and it is not recognizing this quality that can frustrate the objectives of formal strategies. The word 'almost' is deliberate because there are examples of bureaucratically constricted labour markets but these exceptions only go to illustrate the thrust of the arguments used here, which are, that strategies addressing labour issues in tourism must accept the dynamics of labour markets and turn them to the advantage of the strategy. Where a static market is found, incentives should be used to revitalize it into the dynamic mode. Whether or not the market is totally 'free' or restricted in some way by institutional strictures, the basic economics and structure of the industry remain the same and it is from these factors that the pressures in the labour market emanate.

Very roughly, the dynamic characteristics of labour markets are conspicuously high levels of inter-firm mobility, equally conspicuous mobility in and out of the labour market itself, perhaps less visible, but more significant, occupational mobility and a high level of upward mobility. This latter characteristic is augmented by direct access careers competing with the products of vocational education. This creates its own dynamics. With so many of the jobs being unskilled or semi-skilled in nature tourism often finds itself awash with newcomers with the consequent burden carried by on-the-job training. Because there are so many occupations in tourism it is possibly not prudent to talk of only one market. Certainly there are wide ranges of pay between occupations and within occupational groups yet one dynamic feature cuts across this view – occupational mobility is fairly strong and tends to weld the occupational markets together.

These, and other dynamics in the labour market come about because of certain fundamental features of the industry itself. Probably the most universally applicable of these are:

- The small unit structure of the industry.
- Constant fluctuation in consumer demand across large and small time periods.
- The transferability of skills between organizations.
- Occupational rigidity within organizations, i.e. people don't change occupation within organizations except for promotion.
- The high proportion of unskilled, relatively easily learned jobs with low pay attached to them.
- High skilled jobs require mastery of complexity rather than depth of knowledge.
- Unsocial hours are a key factor operating on the border between tourism labour markets and other markets displaying similar income characteristics.

As will be seen shortly, the net result of these features is a tendency for the industry to be low paid and display constant pressures to maintain low pay. This feature has repercussions for vocational education.

Not all tourism industries or even sectors within it display all the fundamental features listed above, but most of them display some and it is how they work together to create dynamic forces in the labour market that is important here.

Labour markets and vocational education: a human resource management conceptual framework

In order to understand the relationship between labour markets and vocational education it is necessary to work through a conceptual model. One simple way of conceiving the relationship is to see the nature of jobs producing different labour market characteristics for different jobs, with technological change intervening occasionally to change both and with economic performance of the industry being the main determinant of the demand for vocational education.

It is more complicated than this. The argument here is that the key to understanding labour market dynamics (and therefore the pressures on vocational education) is the mode of human resource management applied within firms. The mode is the outcome of two critically significant variables:

- The nature of the jobs; particularly the degree of organizational specificity/transferability.
- The economic imperatives of managing a unit, particularly the degree of uncertainty of demand.

The mode of human resource management can be expressed in terms of two extremes of internal labour market with the assumption of a continuum between them. Figure 4.1 illustrates the alternative conceptions (Riley, 1991).

[Strong]	[Weak]
[Structural features]	[Structural features]
<ul><li>Specified hiring standards</li><li>Single port of entry</li><li>High skill specificity</li><li>Continuous on-job training</li><li>Fixed criteria for promotion and transfer</li><li>Strong workplace customs</li><li>Pay differentials remain fixed over time</li></ul>	<ul><li>Unspecified hiring standards</li><li>Multiple ports of entry</li><li>Low skill specificity</li><li>No on-job training</li><li>No fixed criteria for promotion and transfer</li><li>Weak workplace customs</li><li>Pay differentials vary over time</li></ul>

Figure 4.1 *Dimension of internal labour markets. Including the mode of human resource management reconstructs the conceptional framework shown in Figure 4.2*

The significance of the internal labour market mode is that it sustains the characteristics of the external labour market, for example a weak internal labour market simply uses a secondary, unstable market and maintains it in that state and this relationship is shown in Figure 4.2. In

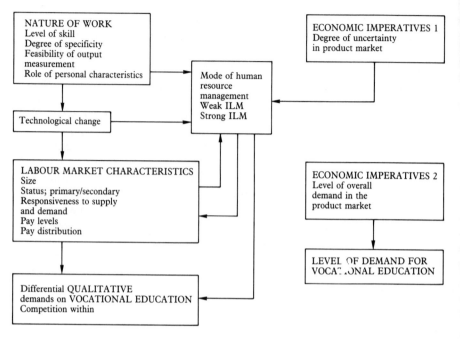

Figure 4.2   *A model of the relationship between type of work, labour markets and mode of human resource management*

Figure 4.2, note the two-way influence of labour market characteristics, mode of human resource management and qualitative demands on vocational education. In the normal way, the influence of economic growth is on the demand for vocational education.

A number of suggested propositions follow from this framework:

The weaker the internal labour markets then:
- Pay levels will be low and attraction to vocational education reduced
- The greater will be the dependence of the industry on vocational education to provide skills
- The greater will be the range of skills required from vocational education
- The harder it will be to match courses with jobs and careers

The stronger the internal labour market then:
- The more specific and qualitative will be the demands on vocational education
- The easier it will be to match courses with jobs and careers

To examine the usefulness of this conceptual framework it would be appropriate to see how the dynamic processes it contains operate in a particular defined industry. What follows is an example from the hotel industry.

A model of hotel labour markets

The purpose of any labour market model would be to identify and differentiate the behaviour of the market's participants, that is, both employers and workers, and be able to explain the measurable activities of the market itself, such as: pay levels, differentials, patterns of mobility, segmentation, levels of employment and market size. It will be argued here that two primary influences on all these activities are, the nature of the skills involved, and the stochastic nature of consumer demand for services. As the price of labour is considered to be the market mechanism, every contributing element or variable will be described in terms of its influence on the rate of pay. The description begins with the construction of a model of the skill structure of the hotel industry after which the discussion turns to the likely conditions of supply and demand for labour in the light of the stochastic nature of demand from consumers. The final section presents an integrated model and identifies the key relationship on which it depends and the dynamic which it produces.

A skill model

The construction of a skill model is in three stages, each with its attendant problems. The first stage is actually to describe and differentiate skills. The problems here are:

- Hotels employ a large range of occupations and skills
- Occupational titles only describe a typical skill not a level of skill: the term 'cook' conveys only an activity
- Skills levels overlap other sectors of the industry
- There is a problem drawing a line between what is skilled and unskilled

To tackle these problems it is necessary to unhinge the concept of skill from the mask of occupation. To do this an occupational classification has to be represented by a skill classification. This means an arbitrary definition of skill must be used. The work of the UK Hotel and Catering Industry Training Board (HCITB) is helpful here. They used a skill classification of four tiers of management, supervisory, craft and operative. The definition used to differentiate skilled from unskilled was whether or not vocational education was required for the job. In other words formal education roughly defined skill. Unskilled work could be learned solely on the job, skilled could not. While managerial and supervisory were obviously skilled, craft would be dependent on the level and operative was clearly semi-skilled or unskilled (HCITB, 1984). The fact that all parts of the classification can be learnt on the job, as the market shows, does not devalue the classification.

The second stage is to estimate the proportion of skilled to unskilled per unit. The problem here is whether it varies with the size of the unit. The only starting point is the occupational structure of each unit; how uniform is it? There is a similarity in the finding of studies which suggest that the proportion of occupations is roughly the same in different hotels (Knight, 1971; HCITB, 1984; Walsh, 1987). If these proportions are then translated in a skill classification using the four tier system, then the first triangle shown in Figure 4.3 becomes the second.

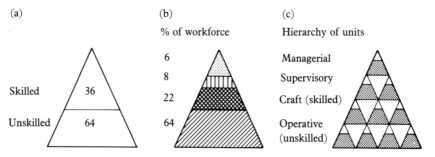

Figure 4.3   *Skill proportions*

Does this proportion vary with size? There is a prima facie case for suggesting that it does not. While the number of unskilled maids rises with size, large hotels tend to have more function rooms and employ more chefs. The more elaborate the cooking the more washing up! Here skill breeds unskilled work. In other words, hotels are like sets of Russian Matrushka dolls, the same whatever the size.

What the second triangle in Figure 4.3 does not capture is that there must be gradations of skill within the skill category. This is the final stage and is supported by conceiving a hierarchy of units with the proportions in each unit remaining the same, but the skill categories rise in absolute term as the hierarchy ascends (the third triangle in Figure 4.3). The suggestion here is that the industry is structured in a hierarchy of consumer standards which represent a hierarchy of skills. Riley (1991) argues that the hierarchical structure of skills works with two other factors to create **a skills accumulation system**. The other factors are, first, the existence of an absolute limit to which each unit can teach – once its standards have been mastered there is nothing more – and second, the assumption that little attempt will be made to retain staff. The result of this constellation of structural factors is to impel those workers with a desire to accumulate skills to use mobility to do it. All staff, from managers through to young commis chefs, would use the hierarchy as a vehicle for learning by experience. In other words, the hierarchy of units forms the basis of a skills accumulation pattern. Such a hierarchy places responsibility at the top to maintain standards. It is important to understand that the top of the hierarchy has an influence well beyond the unit of immediate responsibility. *It influences the whole learning system.* This is not without social significance where expatriate skilled labour holds this high ground.

Notwithstanding the accumulation of skills, one obvious point stemming from the skill proportions is that the main thrust of training is the on-the-job training of unskilled labour. However, it is somewhat too easy to dismiss the importance of this fact. There must always be a capacity to train unskilled workers but the label 'unskilled' is deceptive. By and large, hotel work is not single task monotony. It is a bundle of low level tasks requiring a degree of self-organization. Some instruction is always necessary and because personal attributes count even in the most mundane job there will be variations in performance. Furthermore, much of what has to be learned is culturally determined. The implication here is that there are bound to be differences in learning rates of unskilled jobs.

Two further important aspects of the skill model are the implication of surplus supply and whether productivity is related to job tenure. First, by far the strongest message as regards influences on the rate of pay is that the high proportion of unskilled work is likely to create surplus supply in the external labour market, exerting a downward pressure on the rate of pay. However, it is one thing to say that a high proportion of unskilled jobs lead to a market surplus but quite another actually to have it. For one thing, other industries may also be in the market for unskilled labour, and for another, high levels of organizational mobility can *create the appearance of a deficit when a surplus actually exists.* Second, unskilled work always carries the burden that, if productivity does not improve with tenure, then there is very little reason to reward seniority which is yet another downward pressure on pay.

The skill model carries a number of implications for levels of pay:

- Skill proportions create a tendency towards surplus supply in the market.

- The nature of tasks creates individual differences that fuel a competitive market.
- The structure creates an incentive for mobility to accumulate skills.
- There is little incentive to reward seniority.

Apart from the obvious point that people can learn from experience on the job as an alternative to education, the important influence of this model on vocational education is through its influence on pay levels.

The influence of the stochastic nature of demand

It is a universal characteristic of hotels that there will be short-term variations in demand. This produces the need to make adjustments in short-term labour supply if labour costs are to be controlled. The commonest approach is to set up a buffer consisting of part-time workers, casuals and overtime and bonus incentives for full-time staff. Productivity in hotels is essentially the management of labour supply. The effect of this micro adjustment mechanism is to separate the price of labour from demand. In other words, demand is inelastic.

The effect of this is twofold. First, the very necessity to control labour costs through adjusted labour supply puts a downward pressure on basic pay rates. Second, the tendency towards inelasticity throws the emphasis back on the general supply conditions which themselves contain a downward pressure (the surplus). The organizational impact of this need for flexibility is to encourage weak internal labour markets designed to take in and train newcomers but to make no attempt to retain people. In itself a weak internal labour market will, in conditions of surplus supply, keep pay low but when in conjunction with functional or occupational rigidity within the unit it has an additional influence on segmentation in the external labour market. While it is understandable that skilled occupations would exhibit occupational rigidity, what is noticeable about hotels is that it applies to unskilled occupations as well. The effect is to produce segmentation of the unskilled market. Because people cannot change occupations within the unit, they have to try outside where the surplus makes it harder. Since they move around in the same job, the segmented market forms. The stochastic nature of demand is less influential on skilled occupations, which are therefore not subject to its particular influence on pay.

A question arises as to whether it can really be true that demand is inelastic. In the long run it could be argued that more people would be employed the lower the pay. This suggests that there may be a relationship between the level of pay in the market and the *need to make micro adjustments*. In other words, when labour is so cheap it is worth employing enough people to cope with any level of fluctuation in demand and simply absorb the cost. This suggests that labour markets may be differentiated by two modes of operation: labour supply adjustments – no labour supply adjustments. Sometimes these worlds collide! What happens when excessive guest–staff ratios meet a labour market deficit?

It is not uncommon to see forecasts of labour shortages coinciding with excessively generous use of staff to provide service. In other words, there is the expected relationship between the price of labour and its usage, i.e. the cheaper the more is employed. However, it does not appear to work as effectively in reverse. Hoteliers hang on to their high guest–staff ratios while simultaneously suffering from a deficit of labour supply without being tempted to raise pay. Malaysia and Singapore offer good examples of this phenomenon.

The skill model and the nature of consumer demand taken together

So far it has been suggested that the proportion of unskilled work is responsible for surplus supply which depresses the level of pay and that the need for short-term adjustment shows the same direction of influence. However, they are not discrete concepts – they work together. As it is easier to adjust the supply of unskilled labour than that of skilled, *it is always in the interests of management to deskill*. The ever-present fluctuation in customer demand creates an ever-present incentive to deskill. It is worth reiterating Alpert's point that the unskilled and skilled have a relationship in the absence of capital substitution (Alpert, 1989).

Taken together, the skill model and the propensity of employers to use adjustment mechanisms to meet fluctuating consumer demands produce a number of influences on the rate of pay.

- The likelihood of a surplus supply of unskilled labour
- The need for short-term adjustment in labour supply
- The opportunities to deskill labour
- Mobility for those wishing to learn or advance, encouraged by the hierarchical structure of the industry
- The supply of skilled labour from vocational education
- The transferability of skills, allowing workers to emigrate to other markets without loss of material benefit
- A lack of incentive to reward long service as productivity is not related to job tenure

55

For the most part these influences exert a downward pressure on the rate of pay. Only a genuine deficit could work the other way and even that would have to cope with technological substitution. In effect only *a deficit in conjunction with rising consumer expectations* is likely to exert a real upward pressure on the rate of pay.

The influences on pay differentials are:

- Levels of service – pay differentials are created by skill differentials which follow directly from levels of service demanded by consumers.
- Functional or occupational rigidity, apparently operating for both skilled and unskilled labour. If people are forced out on to the external market, segmentation reinforces the differentials.
- For all types of work personal effort and character actually count, producing individual differences.
- Different training and education duration for different occupations.

To understand the importance for vocational education of these essentially economic arguments about pay it is necessary to focus on how they distribute *managerial value and attention* between the *unskilled and the skilled*. The argument here is that the mode of people management in hotels is devised for managing unskilled workers.

The economic argument for favouring the unskilled rests on the proportion of skilled to unskilled workers in the unit. As long as the proportions favour the unskilled, the overall mode of employee management will tend towards a weak internal labour market. The value of skilled workers would exceed that of unskilled workers only if, on the one hand, skilled workers contributed more to revenue than the unskilled or, on the other, if the proportion of skilled exceeds that of unskilled to the degree that the skilled contribute more to marginal revenue than the unskilled. What really matters is additional productivity, and given the proportion of skilled to unskilled, the productivity of the unskilled is the crucial economic factor. This is why hotel managers concentrate on unskilled labour and don't go out of their way to retain skilled staff. In a very real sense the 'periphery' *are* the core.

What really emerges from this analysis is that the *labour economics of the unit are in conflict with skill development*. Put in a structured way, the interests of the unit and the interests of the industry conflict. Because of the higher proportion of unskilled staff in the unit, who contribute more to the marginal revenue product than the skilled staff, it is in the interests of management to increase their proportion in relation to the skilled. Thus, in purely economic terms management of the unskilled is more important than the skilled. The effect of this on the industry as a whole is to throw the burden of skill development on to vocational education and individual mobility on the lines of the skill model advocated here.

Some important conclusions from the example

This example of a labour market illustrates four factors which are significant to vocational education. These are:

1 The tendency towards lower pay
2 That the economics of the unit is incompatible with the development of skills
3 That as a consequence of (2) the responsibility for skill development falls heavily on vocational education and individual mobility
4 The crucial factor in differentiating labour markets is the behaviour of the buyers in the market; that is, management behaviour

Three components of the process are directly relevant to vocational education:

1 The output of vocational education competes with direct entry workers.
2 Impressions of low pay affect the recruitment into vocational education.
3 The objective of 'good fit' between educational products and existing occupations may not be as beneficial as it at first seems.

The fact that most skills are easily learned, are transferable between employers and that advancement is a matter of mastering complexity rather than overcoming specific knowledge hurdles means that, at least in theory, a person can build a career from an unskilled beginning to reach the top. This umbilical link between the unskilled and the skilled has the effect of lowering the rate of pay of the skilled. It is to the disadvantage of the entrant from education. This downward pressure on the rate of pay greases the ladder for the direct entrant but gives a poor impression of pay for the industry as a whole and therefore frustrates the intentions of vocational education to get better entrants into its courses.

Invariably there is pressure upon education to mount courses that are relevant to the needs of industry. It is possible to be sympathetic to this idea without ignoring the danger inherent within it. If there is dynamic occupational mobility *within the labour market* but occupational rigidity *within the organization*, as appears to be the case, then 'good fit' between courses and specific occupations helps students to get jobs but contributes to their low pay because the industry's need for flexibility is being met by the market and not by flexible use of multi-skilled labour within the organization. Such flexibility within the organization could lead to lower employment levels but higher pay.

The coupling or decoupling of skills and occupations lies at the heart of the industry–education debate. Coupling makes it easier for young people to get jobs but decoupling, with the intention of raising the general level of human capital, might encourage better utilization of labour which might in turn lead to higher pay.

Modes of human resource management revisited

In the example given above the overwhelming mode was very weak internal labour markets. However, not only is it a matter of degree, it is perfectly possible to have more than one mode within the same industry or organization. The key factor here is the continuity of knowledge between the bottom and the top of an organization. If it is possible to learn from the bottom upwards and simply take on greater degrees of complexity, then it follows that such a career path would exist. In the example given it does. If, however, there is a **point of discontinuity** then flow from the bottom to the top will be interrupted and discrete career paths will exist. The importance of this discontinuity is twofold. First, the break cuts off the salaries of skilled people from those of unskilled, and second, it may well be in the interests of the organization to keep those skilled staff, in which case a separate strong internal labour market is worth while. The greater the strength of the internal labour market, the higher will be the qualitative level of input from vocational education.

Strategies, plans and markets

It was suggested earlier that national or regional level strategies on tourism manpower fail to take enough notice of labour market dynamics. It is undoubtedly true that where labour markets are constricted by comprehensive legal industrial relations systems, high levels of unionization and approved qualifications, then grand strategies will be facilitated by such institutionalization. The comprehensive schemes suggested by Pollock and Ritchie (1990) are a good illustration of well-thought-out conceptions which could easily be undone by labour market dynamics.

What is being advocated here is not the abolition of planning and strategy in this area but that such planning should take on board the approaches advocated by Psacharopoulos (1991). He argues for a greater faith in the past and the present in predicting the future. We need to know more about what produces the present situation. What are the underlying processes, market dynamics, well-worn channels? The use of tracer studies to uncover mobility patterns, key occupations and the role of incentives is advocated as necessary ground building for strategies. Even a casual study of the tourism industry suggests that pay differentials and skill differentials are not too synchronized. *Rabid occupational mobility lives with occupational rigidity to the detriment of everybody except the market.* Such idiosyncrasies can easily undermine rational plans. The argument here is that tourism planning needs to know more about these matters and take account of them in the planning process. Labour market analysis precedes manpower planning is the message, and that the behaviour of managers holds the key to the process at work in the markets.

References

Alpert, W. T. Y. (1986) *The Minimum Wage in the Restaurant Industry*, Praeger, New York.

HCITB (1984) *Manpower Flows in the Hotel and Catering Industry*, HCITB, London.

Knight, L. B. (1971) *Patterns of Labour Mobility in the Hotel and Catering Industry*, HCITB, London.

Riley, M. J. (1991) *Human Resource Management: a Guide to Personnel Practice in the Hotel and Catering Industry*, Butterworth-Heinemann, Oxford.

Pollock, A. and Ritchie, J. R. B. (1990) Integrated strategy for tourism education/training. *Annals of Tourism*, **17**, 568–85.

Psacharopoulos, G. (1991) From manpower planning to labour market analysis. *International Labour Review*, **130**(4), 459–74.

Walsh, T. (1987) Pay and employment in Great Britain? Private sector with particular reference to the hotel catering and retail industries. PhD Thesis, University of Bath.

5 Collecting and using information about human resources in tourism – the direct survey method
Tom Baum

Introduction to tourism information collection

Planning and development, in any sphere of business or government, is dependent upon valid, reliable and quality information. The absence of such information, whether it is quantitative (statistical) or qualitative (non-statistical), means that the basis of decision-making will be seriously impaired and will depend upon impressions, hunches, beliefs or, at worst, prejudices. As a result, the decisions that are made may well be flawed, with significant consequences for the business or administration concerned. This generalization is true of the tourism industry as it is of any other, in both the public and private sectors.

It is fair to say that in most areas of business and administration, the power and value of comprehensive information are well recognized. As a result, the argument that we are moving into an age when information is becoming the most powerful and valuable commodity available to those involved with the decision process, cannot really be disputed. The impact of increasingly sophisticated information management by business and government is readily identifiable by us as consumers and citizens in the form of direct marketing, database access, use of financial services, and immigration and police control to identify but a few examples. Furthermore, the increasing sophistication of the technology that is available to managers and administrators means that range and speed of access to key information about both the micro and macro environment are greatly superior to what they were in the past and this is evident in the extent to which successful companies build their operational, financial, marketing and human resource strategies around the use of technology for information and management purposes.

Tourism, as an industry sector, world wide, is not renowned for the quality and optimal use of its information sources although there are clear indicators that this situation is gradually changing. Providing a driving force behind this change are the multi-national tourism companies, in particular the airlines. The rise of computerized reservation systems (CRSs) is a textbook example of how information technology can be used as a marketing tool. CRS, which began as a simple way to automate airline ticketing in the 1960s, has evolved as a powerful marketing tool, which already has a major influence on passenger choice and on airline competition. The new generation of CRS (currently reducing in number so that, perhaps, three major systems will survive in Europe and the United States) will extend far beyond simple airline activity in providing an integrated travel information and reservations service to users, including hotel, car hire and leisure options. The future of companies which choose to remain outside of the CRS may be adversely affected. Other examples of the use of information technology within tourism include integrated management systems within most major hotels and related businesses and the development of public access tourism information systems, such as the English Tourist Board's ETNA project.

One of the problems with tourism and the collection and management of information that relates to it is that of its diverse nature. Raymond Bar-On, in his wide-ranging, seminal text *Travel and Tourism Data* (Bar-On, 1989), identifies ten features of the industry (not all of them unique to tourism) which influence the quality of information that is available about tourism. These are worth reproducing here.

1 The large numbers of market segments with differing characteristics which will each be affected in different ways by changes in the overall tourism environment: these include international and domestic tourists and other travellers, from different socio-economic backgrounds and on journeys of different purpose and type.
2 A variety of types of accommodation and transport, whose supply is relatively inelastic in the short run (though some substitution is possible when demand exceeds supply for a particular type of service) and whose long-term profitability is essential to maintain and improve standards of service.
3 Strong changes throughout the year and between years, due to the high seasonality demand in many destinations, to changes in underlying tastes and to interruptions due to unusual events (such as an exhibition, the Olympic Games or a terrorist outrage). There are peak days around holidays and weekends, on which excess demand, congestion and over-booking may be major problems.
4 The transient character of tourism and the 'perishability' of

unused supply (rooms, aircraft seats etc.) which cannot be stored for later demand.

5   The sale of individual products or services at a variety of different prices. For example, a hotel room will be sold at different rates depending on the season (and even on the day of the week) or whether the guest books as an individual or in a group. An airline seat will be sold at different prices depending on the time of year and the booking restrictions imposed.

6   Demand is affected by a very wide range of influences including events, habits, promotion and publicity, as well as by economic variables such as prices, exchange rates, incomes and the socio-demographic and 'psychographic' characteristics of the tourists themselves.

7   Control of the industry is diffused, with many different national, regional and local government and public and private enterprises responsible for developing tourism and supplying the appropriate transport and other services. Their activities may not be well coordinated.

8   The provision of new tourism facilities and the promotion to develop new markets require a relatively long lead-in time, whereas the factors affecting demand for a specific product may change very rapidly and at short notice.

9   Large investments in tourism facilities are often required, including allocation of land and the training of human resources who may not be employed continuously, with the attendant risks of over- or under-supply.

10 The sheer size of the industry, with the strong competition from tens of other countries, hundreds of resorts and thousands of programmes for international and domestic tourists, is itself a challenge.

To Bar-On's ten features, I would add one further element which requires consideration and, certainly, impacts upon how information about tourism is analysed. This is

11 The varying relationship between international and domestic tourism in different countries. In developed countries, such as those in Western Europe and the United States, it is true to say that the international and the domestic tourist use, broadly, the same facilities and visit similar locations. Florida resorts do not differ, significantly, in what they offer American and European visitors. However, in developing countries, the same is by no means true. The overlap, in terms of product and facilities, between international and domestic tourist demand in India and

Malaysia, for example, is very limited, although gradually increasing.

This complex environment may well account for the relatively immature (in terms of scope, depth and quality) nature of research which has been undertaken in the tourism industry, when it is compared with other sectors. Philip Pearce, in an excellent analysis of this problem within the Australian context (Pearce, 1989), highlights the rapid 'roller coaster' growth of the industry from relative insignificance to substance over a short time frame, with the consequence that the contributions of research, with its facility for reflection and projection, and the use of data and other information, have tended to be sidetracked and undervalued. Bar-On also states that 'the scientific study of tourism and tourism management are relatively new subjects' (Bar-On, 1989). The somewhat low academic status of tourism, within major institutions of higher education, is further testimony to the immaturity of serious research in this area.

Bar-On's analysis (1989), while referring to the management of statistics and data in tourism in general, has direct and equal relevance in the specific context of human resource information. Bar-On also identifies ten special problems that occur in the preparation of statistics about tourism. These are

1 The need to identify and separate 'tourism' activities and expenditures from other recreational and business activities of individuals, and to identify the tourism receipts from other receipts in establishments or service organizations which provide services both to tourists and others, such as local residents.
2 The conceptual and practical problems of identifying and measuring the tourism revenue of a country, a resort or region, and 'tourist' behaviour: the tourist who buys an inclusive (package) tour is unaware of the way its price is split between carriers, hotels, tours or travel agents or between several different destinations. In addition to consumption expenditures there may be capital expenditures on second homes, recreation vehicles and equipment which may not be recognized as being tourism-related.
3 The large volumes involved. There are hundreds of millions of visitors crossing frontiers in the course of a year and tens of thousands of accommodation establishments in many countries.
4 The simplification or elimination of documentation and of formalities at frontiers, banks and exchange bureaux, to facilitate tourism, which, while highly desirable for the tourist and the government, reduces the sources available to the statisticians.

5   The difficulties in collecting reliable data from all relevant individuals and establishments, or from appropriate samples, taking into account poor levels of response to inquiries; the great variability between such units and the problems of sampling from the flow of travellers over time (some important groups being relatively small), and in collecting data in a variety of languages and currencies.

6   The special problems in sampling tourism phenomena and tourists over time and space and even in sampling tourist establishments, since listings are often incomplete. But for economy and speed it is frequently necessary to use sampling techniques, rather than to attempt to collect and process all data required on a 100% basis.

7   Hotels and other organizations may be obliged to report certain data, but the coverage of establishments and the content of their reports may be incomplete, because of their desire to avoid tax obligations, for example.

8   The difficulties in collecting statistics from unregistered accommodation, e.g. households who rent out a room or youngsters who camp wild, or on currency exchange outside the banking system.

9   The very detailed data which are required about different periods (peak days, weeks, months) and about different geographic areas (destinations, areas of origin, routing) and types of travellers.

10 Some data which are collected for administrative purposes, for example counts of entries by tourist visa holders, may be adequate for an administrative purpose but provide misleading information for tourism purposes, if for example only a few nationalities require visas to enter a certain country.

Bar-On's analysis provides a very comprehensive and realistic assessment of the difficulties involved in reliable information collection about the tourism industry in general. It is interesting to note that these problems are, by no means, new. As early as 1933, F. W. Ogilvie, writing what must have been one of the earliest books of its kind, *The Tourist Movement: An Economic Study*, noted the confusion that existed at the time, with respect to classifying who were and were not tourists. Different countries adopted different standards and varying approaches to the collection of data. The work of the International Statistical Institute from 1927 onwards, in which Britain declined to participate, attempted to bring some uniformity to the fledgling tourist industry but with limited success (Ogilvie, 1933).

Human resource information in tourism

To this point, we have been considering some of the issues pertaining to access to valid, reliable and quality information about tourists and the tourism industry in general. What is true in relation to tourism in general is equally, if not more, applicable with respect to the human resource field. It is arguable that all the difficulties and constraints that apply to tourism are of some relevance to human resource matters and that, over and above these, there are a further series of concerns that derive from the position which human resources adopts, straddling the tourism, education, training and labour market environments. The range of human resource-related information that is available and of value to the planning and development process in tourism is considerable. It includes information relating to:

- Local and national demographic trends
- Local and national employment and unemployment patterns (general)
- National and local employment patterns in tourism by sector and skills level
- Actual and predicted changes in tourism employment by sector and skills level
- National and local education and training programmes in colleges and elsewhere
- International, national and local educational and training needs of tourism industry sectors
- Trends in the skills and technical requirements of tourism industry personnel
- Individual company personnel records
- Company career tracking systems
- Company succession planning systems

This and related information is essential for the planning and development of effective human resource systems for the tourism industry in any locality, country or region, focusing, in particular, on recruitment, education, training and career development. In line with the macro tourism environment emphasis of this book, the concern, here, is with information that facilitates analysis and description of human resources at an industry-wide level.

The main focus of information collection in the human resource area at the macro level has, traditionally, been on studies which derive from mainstream labour market and economic studies and, in essence, focus on the association between overall tourism performance (the numbers and expenditure of visitors) and employment, at the macro level. This approach, while of value in the context of broad-sweep planning and investment policies, does not provide much descriptive assistance to the variety of agencies and professionals, in tourism, education and training, with an active interest in this area.

In general, information about the human resource environment within a local, national or regional tourism industry must be culled from a variety of sources, and modified in order to conform with tourism industry requirements. In many instances, such information is collected for other purposes, as part of non-tourism specific studies. Base data about employment, in tourism, is normally available through reference to multi-industry labour market studies, under-taken by official agencies on a periodic basis. These statistics are of varied quality and reliability and frequently suffer from problems of currency, both in terms of when they were most recently up-dated and, perhaps more seriously, in relation to when the categories and parameters in use were defined in order to construct the base data for the statistical model. This means that relatively current information is frequently channelled into categories and designations that were defined, maybe, 20 or more years earlier, when the economic, social and, above all, the tourism industry structure was very different from the contemporary situation.

While many of the difficulties arise from the general deficiencies in tourism data collection outlined earlier, the most immediate problem that faces the human resource planner in tourism is the frequent absence of an identifiable and defined 'tourism' category within mainstream statistical sources, whether relating to economic per-formance, output or growth, foreign revenue earnings, or employ-ment information. Strands of tourism-related activity are frequently found under general 'services' headings, for example, but this broad banding includes activities ranging considerably beyond conventional interpretations of tourism. Thus, key performance trends within the service sector may either totally mask the picture with respect to tourism or, on the other hand, may actually be driven by it! Alternatively, tourism may be split between a number of independent categories, such as 'hotels and restaurants', 'transportation' and 'retail'. Thus, extracting the real tourism picture becomes a matter of inference and intelligent guessing, backed up by some specialist studies or analysis. This problem, in relation to tourism employment, is further compounded by inadequacies in official classifications of occupations, which are neither comprehensive (a significant number of tourism occupations are omitted) or specific (some categories apply both within tourism and in other industries). Useful examples of documents where these problems are evident include *The International Standard Classification of Occupations (ISCO)* (International Labour

Office, 1988) and the United Kingdom's *Standard Occupational Classification (SOC)* (HMSO, 1990).

A further matter of concern, in the human resource area, is the extent to which direct, indirect and induced employment are taken into consideration. Direct employment concerns those whose work falls directly within one or other of the tourism subsectors identified in Chapter 1, although this employment may be part-time, seasonal or partial (a full-time job in which only part of the working time is allocated to tourism-related work). Indirect employment relates to work undertaken in a support sector, not directly involved in tourism itself. This may be agriculture (providing food for the tourist) or utilities operations (ensuring electricity and water for the tourist). Induced employment is that created as a result of the tourism multiplier effect, whereby earnings from tourism (whether wages, profits or dividends) are respent in the economy and further jobs are sustained as a result. This chapter, and indeed the major part of this book are concerned with direct employment, representing the 'real' human resources within tourism. However, the other elements cannot be underestimated or ignored in a consideration of this subject.

The enumeration and analysis of the human resource environment within any tourism industry is tempered by the problems which Bar-On discusses and, specifically, those of categorization and definition that I have referred to above. Given these caveats, there are, essentially, two major approaches through which to provide estimates and descriptions of the extent and nature of employment within tourism industries. The first may be termed the 'top-down' macro approach, whereby broad-based, generally econometric data are utilized in order to derive and infer information about specific aspects of the tourism industry labour environment. Aspects of this approach are considered in some detail by John Fletcher in Chapter 6, in the context of input–output analysis. The second 'bottom-up' micro approach takes the industry itself as the starting point, in terms of information collection, and extrapolates these data upwards into the broader economic and labour environment. This is my concern in this chapter.

The direct survey method

The direct survey method is a practical approach that can be adapted to a variety of uses and on differing scales to meet specific needs at local, national or regional levels. The method, if conducted on a significant and multi-sectoral basis, is likely to generate comprehensive quality information about tourism employment and related human resource issues, especially relating to education and training. It can form a very flexible and adaptable data base from which prediction and planning of labour market, education and training trends can be monitored and interventions mounted as a result. The approach does not, however, make allowances for the impact of indirect or induced employment within tourism and this aspect is considered in greater detail in Chapter 6. The direct survey method is widely used in collecting relatively precise and valid data for planning and development purposes and is frequently undertaken on an occasional basis. In many developing tourism environments, the approach is adopted as part of donor aid projects, in order to establish the precise manpower and training requirements of the local tourism industry. This chapter argues the need to undertake studies, using the direct survey method, on a periodic basis, providing up-dated information and also allowing for the monitoring of changes in the workforce and the skills requirements of the industry. The model used by CERT, in Ireland, represents a good example of this approach in practice.

The direct survey method may involve either person-to-person interviews as the means of collecting data or the use of a mailed questionnaire. The former is the preferred approach and will form the basis for subsequent discussion. However, mailed information collection, often in conjunction with other data collection, can prove a useful and cost-effective supplement to the field survey approach.

Unlike approaches that extrapolate and infer information about human resources in tourism from wider economic or employment data, the direct survey method allows for the collection of information under a wide variety of headings, depending upon the particular needs of the study in question. It may enable us to assemble information on areas such as

- The numbers in employment at the time of the survey/in the past/ projected into the future
- Links between employment changes and market/product changes
- Employment by department, gender, age, qualifications etc.
- Full-time, part-time and casual employment
- Information on training and qualifications
- Training needs and priorities
- Course content/curriculum requirements

Before embarking on a detailed consideration of this method it is worth while to summarize its attendant benefits and disadvantages.

Advantages of the direct survey method
- It is comprehensive and wide-ranging.

- It can accommodate the diversity of tourism industry sectors and sub-sectors.
- It can reflect regional and local variation or can focus on a limited area only.
- It can accommodate the impact of both domestic and international tourism.
- It can provide a richness of descriptive data through use of open-ended questions and 'probes'/discussion about particular issues.
- It reflects the 'here and now' situation in the tourism industry.
- It can be up-dated, using an established model, providing for directly comparable data and the consequent monitoring of very detailed trends and developments in the industry.
- It can have useful predictive value, especially in areas such as training requirements and skills needs.
- It can target issues of special concern, for example training needs or attrition rates.

Disadvantages of the direct survey method
- It may result in an element of subjectivity, from both the interviewee and the interviewer and this may affect both the validity and reliability of the data collected.
- It is subject to difficult sampling problems, given problems with defining various sectors of the industry and the need to meet geographical and other sampling concerns.
- Direct responses are, also, sometimes difficult to elicit, either by mail or by personal interview, and this problem is especially true when dealing with small tourism businesses.
- Fieldwork can be time-consuming and frustrating.
- Ideally, it requires specialist interviewers in the field and their training is very important.
- It is, generally, expensive to conduct.

The direct survey method can involve a number of crucial stages, which are summarized here.

(1) Define survey objectives

One of the virtues of the direct survey method lies in its flexibility and suitability as a vehicle to collect a diversity of data. This can also be a weakness in that, without careful definition of the survey's objectives, there is a tendency to attempt to collect too much data, some of which may not be central to the main purpose of the study. This will confuse both respondents and those charged with data interpretation. Survey objectives may include

- To estimate current employment and structure
- To monitor historic employment changes
- To estimate projected employment changes
- To estimate the impact of seasonality on employment
- To estimate the extent of part-time and casual labour
- To estimate the extent of family labour
- To identify skills and departmental structures
- To identify skills and labour shortages
- To estimate labour turnover
- To identify recruitment 'black spots'
- To identify recruitment strategies and sources
- To estimate the extent of 'multi-skilling' within employment, i.e. the extent to which employees operate within more than one operational department
- To identify the level of trained staff within the business
- To identify the source of training (internal, external)
- To identify the extent of in-house training
- To evaluate the impact of training
- To identify skills and curriculum deficiencies within training
- To identify curriculum content guidelines
- To identify product, technical and market changes which impact on human resource requirements in the workplace.

(2) Define survey parameters

Parallel to the statement of survey objectives, and probably an integral part of them, is the definition of survey parameters, in other words what the survey will encompass in terms of, for example, the sectors within tourism that merit or demand inclusion, the geographical area to be included and the timeframe that will apply to information sought. The variables that require consideration may include, first, sectors and sub-sectors of the tourism industry. This will vary from location to location and may depend on local custom and definitions but can incorporate a number of separate categories, all requiring independent survey, namely:

- Hotels
- Guesthouses/bed and breakfast establishments
- Other serviced accommodation
- Self-catering accommodation
- 'Fine dining' restaurants
- Fast food or local eating establishments
- Bars/pubs
- Clubs and leisure facilities

- Attractions and theme parks
- Heritage sites
- Arts and cultural facilities
- Retail outlets
- Travel/tour operators
- Tour guides
- Access transport companies
- Internal transport companies
- Vehicle hire companies
- Tourist information and facilitation centres
- Government tourism agencies
- Educational/training providers

A second variable will be geographical parameters for the study, whether it is local as in incorporating a single resort or town; based on the state or some other sub-national administrative unit; national; regional; or involving a combination of all or some of these in order to facilitate cross-geographical comparison. Good examples of these various categories include a study of hotels and restaurants in Gwent, South Wales, conducted on behalf of the Newport Chamber of Trade Tourism Interest Group; national surveys, incorporating a local and county dimension, within CERT's Irish studies; and the transnational studies conducted in South-East Asia as part of the EC funded ASEAN Tourism Training Project.

Timeframe parameters represent a third variable. It is necessary to decide whether studies should cover one or more years, both in historic and predictive terms.

(3) Identify survey population and sample

Identification of the parameters for the survey provides the basis from which the actual population and subsequent sample are drawn. Preparing a valid population is not necessarily an easy task. In the case of hotels there may be few problems if, say, a full list of registered establishments is held, as is the case in Ireland where a business may not style itself a hotel unless it is registered. However, this is not always the case; in Singapore, for example, the Tourist Promotion Board (STPB) only recognizes establishments with over 50 bedrooms for marketing purposes but this does not constitute a legal definition. Listings of smaller establishments are not readily available. This is also a major problem with respect to many other sub-sectors, especially those involving smaller businesses. It is a problem also with regard to sectors such as retail and restaurant operations, which may cater, largely, for local needs; populations may need to be drawn on the basis of prime tourist locations, omitting businesses serving primarily local needs. The author adopted this approach during a 1989 study of the Singapore tourism industry, eliminating establishments in postcode areas outside of the main tourist belt. Various guides, registers and directories as well as other official and unofficial sources may be required from which to prepare the various population lists. Where these sources do not exist, it may be necessary to construct a listing from telephone directories and other sources. Local and tourism industry knowledge, combined with pragmatic common sense are indispensable in the preparation of such lists. It is very important in the compilation of populations that the data are fully up to date and revision is essential prior to repeat surveys.

The actual survey sample is drawn from the defined population(s). The sample size and the proportion of the population that this constitutes will be influenced by a number of factors, including: the objectives of the survey; geographical and structural variation within the population (for example, the need to represent urban and rural tourism locations as well as various grades of hotel); and available resources. It is very difficult to be prescriptive about sample size, although statistical requirements do influence minima or, rather, affect the validity of information drawn from very small samples. Political considerations may also dictate use of a rather larger sample than is statistically necessary. A reasonable guideline is to aim for a 5% sample of a relatively large population, where this is 1000 or more; however, a larger sample will enhance the value of information relating to any sub-grouping within the sample. Small populations will require different treatment and 50% or even greater sampling may be required. Reserve lists, to cater for inevitable drop outs, are also a good idea. Sampling procedure should be random in so far as is possible, based either on alphabetical listings or on use of random numbers, either machine or chart generated.

(4) Decide survey methodology

The direct survey method allows for a number of methodological variations in terms of how data are collected and this will influence the preparation of the actual survey instrument. The main options include

- A mailed survey
- A structured interview
- Group discussions or focus groups, involving a number of partici-pants from the sector under survey
- An open-ended, unstructured interview or discussion

In addition, the first three approaches may consist of open and/or closed questions, depending on the nature of the information sought. The final approach is, generally, based on open, free-flow questions and prompts.

The actual approach adopted will depend on the situation at hand, notably resource factors, especially the quality of the interviewing personnel and time constraints. Survey field workers who are familiar with the local tourism industry and can relate, at a professional level, to the interviewee, are likely to generate information of a far greater quality than is the case with normal general market research personnel.

Experience suggests that individual interviews, combining both 'open' and 'closed' response options, provide the most effective, valid and in-depth source of information. It may be that different sectors of the industry demand somewhat different methodologies, because of the size of the sector, geographical or other considerations. In many countries, for example, the number of major businesses involved in the internal transportation sector, within tourism, is very limited, perhaps to one or two airlines, a railway corporation and a miscellany of other land carriers. Thus, the approach, in catering for this sector, may demand techniques that aim to describe the main employment and training features of the operation(s) rather than provide the basis for statistical amalgamation with the findings from other interviews.

(5) Prepare draft instruments

The actual instrument(s) employed for the survey will take shape as a result of decisions about the study objectives, its parameters and the samples and methodologies to be used. Thus, instruments design must follow consideration of all of the above matters. The structure and type of questions presented will depend on the method of delivery, whether verbal or written, as well as the anticipated responses, verbal, 'open' or 'closed'. The means and resources available for the analysis of data may also influence question presentation in that dependence on manual or computerized means will influence how the survey instrument and its questions are prepared and presented. Actual question design should follow normal good practice with respect to clarity, ambiguity, brevity and similar considerations.

(6) An optional role for industry

The various stages in preparing a direct survey of employment and training, within tourism, can be undertaken in relative isolation of the potential target group(s), the tourism industry and its various sub-sectors. Methodologically, this presents no problems. However, one of the benefits of this method over the rather greater remoteness of econometric techniques is the opportunity to operate in tandem with private and public sector tourism interests, both in conducting the survey and in interpreting the data. This process is enhanced through carefully managed contact with the industry and its representative groups in the lead up to the survey and the involvement of a group of key industry leaders in an ad hoc, advisory capacity during the preparatory stages, execution and analysis of the work. The benefits, in terms of the ownership of the results, that accrue from this process more than outweigh any incumbrance.

(7) Train the field workers

The value of competent, qualified and industry-familiar field workers has already been mentioned. They are of value not least because they will be in the best position to maximize the possibilities of more open-ended questions and to pursue potentially valuable lines of discussion with respondents at a credible level. Experience has demonstrated, amply, the benefits that can arise from such 'beyond the questionnaire' discussion. This said, training remains an important feature of the preparatory process, so that procedures are relatively standardized and all those involved with the study are fully briefed as to its purpose, scope and methodology.

(8) Prepare survey administration

Tight and efficient administration (and, indeed, management) is essential to the execution of a survey involving a significant number of appointments with, frequently, small businesses during their operational periods and in geographically dispersed locations. Holding respondents to agreed schedules can present quite a challenge in itself. Careful consideration of the administrative procedures that are required before, during and after the actual survey is essential to its effective operation.

(9) Piloting the survey

Good survey practice, prudence and a concern for ensuring a well-trained survey field force all demand that initial piloting of the survey instrument(s) is conducted prior to finalization of the survey. This should involve real trial interviews, mailings or group exercises so that both the content of the instruments and their delivery methods can be evaluated and modified, as necessary.

74

(10) Conducting the survey

Given appropriate consideration of (1) to (9) above, the actual conduct of the employment and training survey should prove to be the most straightforward element within the process. Flexibility and prag-matism are essential at all stages during the conduct of the study, so that unanticipated changes to the sample or instruments can be accommodated as and when necessary.

(11) Analysis and interpretation of the data

Data analysis is a crucial component within the survey process and, ideally, requires a combination of manual and electronic support in order to maximize the value of the information collected. Standard data analysis packages are readily available to process quantitative data, although the depth of statistical manipulation undertaken should reflect the needs of the study rather than the capability of the technology! Qualitative information requires rather more subjective and professional handling and assessment. There is a natural tempta-tion to shy away from full analysis and interpretation of 'open' question responses because they present information that is rather more subjective and more difficult to handle. Yet, at the same time, these data can prove to be the richest and most useful to planners and developers within the human resource field and, therefore, should not be neglected.

Interpreting the findings of a direct survey of employment and training, within a particular tourism industry, inevitably involves a far wider range of interests than is the case with the alternative methodologies discussed. The detail and richness of the information that this approach can generate provide food for a diversity of public and private sector bodies involved with the industry and its various sub-sectors – the labour market, education, training – as well as central and local government interests. Thus, an approach to data interpreta-tion which involves as many interested parties as possible, is essential if the investment of the direct survey method is to be justified.

(12) Up-dating of the model

The completion of one direct survey of employment and training within a tourism industry (or sector), provides the base data from which to plan immediate interventions and to predict future trends. This process is considerably enhanced if this database is regularly up-dated and refined in order to reflect changing trends within the tourism industry as well as within the wider human resource environment. Comparison with previous findings is one of the most effective indicators of change. Thus, replication of a direct industry survey provides the most effective means whereby to monitor and predict change. It is a common weakness of this approach (of which a number of international funding agencies are guilty), that such replication is not undertaken. The survey serves as a one-off barometer of the human resource environment but no thought is given to the future and, in some cases, subsequent studies are constructed without reference to previous work and the value of comparison. Replication, however, cannot afford to be a rigid process but should be undertaken flexibly in order to accommodate additional sub-sectors or questions/information areas of particular but new importance. The timing of up-dates is discretionary but a five-year cycle, involving a major survey in years 1 and 5, with an interim up-date in year 3, is not an inappropriate model to adopt. This is, broadly, the approach adopted by CERT in Ireland.

Conclusion

This chapter has considered the importance of quality, valid and reliable information to those involved in human resource planning and development for tourism, along with some of the problems inherent in the collection of such information. The direct survey method has been described in some detail and a step-by-step guide to its implementation provided. This may be considered alongside John Fletcher's assessment of input–output analysis and employment multipliers which follows in Chapter 6.

References

Bar-On, Raymond (1989) *Travel and Tourism Data*, Euromonitor Publications, London.
HMSO (1990) *Standard Occupational Classification*, HMSO, London.
International Labour Office (ILO) (1988) *The International Standard Classification of Occupations*, ILO, Geneva.
Ogilvie, F. W. (1933) *The Tourist Movement: an Economic Study*, King, London.
Pearce, Philip, (1989) Research and the tourism industry. *At the Centre*, Newsletter of the Centre for Studies in Travel and Tourism, James Cook University of North Queensland, no. 1/2.

6 Input–output analysis and employment multipliers
John Fletcher

Whenever there is a change in the level or pattern of exogenous expenditure, an economy will be subject to its economic impact. That impact will manifest itself in a variety of forms; changes to the level of local income, employment, government revenue and, where applicable, changes in the net flow of foreign exchange. It is important to understand the impact on employment of such expenditure changes for a number of reasons. At the establishment level it is vital to be able to forecast future labour requirements, particularly if the employment changes relate to skilled or qualified staff who may not be readily available. At the industry level, employment forecasts are useful for devising sound education and training programmes. Finally, at the regional or national level, knowledge of employment effects can assist both in maximizing the utilization of the available labour force (particularly when there are several potential development options competing for scarce funds), and for project evaluation. Indeed, government agencies responsible for encouraging and fostering economic development often place great store in the value of the employment multiplier associated with potential projects.

The objective of this chapter is to examine the application of input–output analysis to the estimation of local employment multipliers. It begins by briefly reviewing the technique of input–output analysis and then examines the assumptions incorporated into the model with respect to the employment functions and looks at some of the more recent modifications that have been developed to improve the performance and reliability of the derived employment multipliers.

Unlike alternative partial equilibrium models used to estimate multiplier values (such as *ad hoc* multiplier models), input–output analysis is a general equilibrium approach to examining the structure of an economy, its dependencies and the economic impact of exogenous changes in final demand.

The multiplier concept

The multiplier concept is based upon the nature of production and the purchase of intermediate goods and services within the production process. Each sector in the economy will, to varying degrees, employ labour in order to produce its output. If the number of persons employed by a firm is divided by the total output of that firm, labour/output coefficients (or ratios) can be calculated which show a crude relationship between the level of output and the number of people that would have to be employed in order to produce that output.

The direct effect

When guests staying at a hotel settle their account, they are responsible for the employment of some proportion of the staff employed by that hotel. This is known as the direct effect. However, the multiplier concept involves not only a direct effect, but also an indirect and induced effect. To see how these latter two elements come into play consider the hotel guests who have just settled their bill.

The indirect effect

In order to provide the services and goods to these customers, the hotel has had to purchase goods and services from a variety of suppliers within the local economy – building maintenance; food and beverages; electricity; water; advertising and promotion; banking and insurance; auditors; and so on. Each of the suppliers of these goods and services will employ staff and, thus, be subject to an employment/output ratio. Additionally, these firms, in order to meet the demands from the hotel, must purchase goods and services and some of these will be supplied by firms located within the local economy. These additional firms will also employ staff and be subject to an employment/output ratio. The sum of all of the employment effects generated by the indirect expenditure of the hotel is known as the **indirect** effect.

The induced effect

Finally, the induced effect must be considered. When the hotel guests settled their account, part of that money would be used to pay wages, salaries and distributed profits (the **direct** income effect). In the same way, the firms that are subject to increased demand as a result of the hotel's activities, will also pay some of their increased revenue in the form of wages, salaries and distributed profits (the **indirect** income effect). So too will these firms' suppliers pay out some of their increased revenue in the form of wages, salaries and distributed profits (also **indirect** income effects).

Thus, it can be seen that the level of income in the local economy will increase as a result of the initial tourist spending. Some of this increased income will be saved, some will be spent on goods and services provided by firms outside the local economy (imports) but the remainder will be spent on goods and services provided within the local economy and this will stimulate economic activity yet further, and be responsible for additional employment generation (the **induced** employment effect).

Therefore, employment generation takes place on three levels, the direct, indirect and induced effects. The employment multiplier estimates the change in the number of full-time equivalent job opportunities (FTEs) associated with a change in either the level or distribution of tourist expenditure. It may be expressed in terms of the number of FTEs generated by a unit of tourist expenditure. It is clearly of importance to planners and policy-makers to be aware of the employment impact of any change in tourist expenditure. This is particularly true in developing countries which may be endowed with an abundance of labour and where the employment effects of development may be of greater or equal importance to the income effects.

The estimation of these effects can be undertaken by a variety of models, such as base theory models, *ad hoc* multiplier models and input–output models. The latter model, because it is a generalized equilibrium model, provides the most detailed and reliable method of analysis and is discussed below. Those readers interested in the development and comparison of the various models should see Fletcher and Archer (1991).

Definition of an employment multiplier

Employment multipliers show the direct, indirect and induced effect of one additional unit of final demand upon the level of employment. Employment multipliers may also be expressed in terms of the ratio of direct to direct plus indirect plus induced employment effects. However, from a forecasting and policy point of view, it is clearer to express the employment multiplier as the ratio of employment opportunities created per unit of tourist expenditure.

Input–output analysis

Input–output analysis can be used to estimate all three effects of a change in tourist expenditure on the level of employment. The modelling procedure is a compromise between the general theory of economics and its practical application. Wassily Leontief is tradition-ally referred to as the 'father' of input–output analysis, but in reality the seeds of this type of analysis can be traced as far back as 1758, with the publication of Quesnay's *Tableau Economique* (Phillips, 1955). Quesnay's work provided the foundation for the development of input–output analysis by focusing attention upon the concept of general equilibrium and inter-sectoral relations. Leontief's contribu-tion to the development of input–output analysis was to modify the basic theory and concepts put forward by Quesnay and consolidated by Walras, and to make it practicable from an empirical point of view. The end result was a model that was particularly attractive as a means of studying the various impacts associated with a change in final demand (Leontief, 1936).

It is hard to understand how easily Leontief's original model gained acceptance. It was simple to the point of naivety and it contravened many of the established economic theories of production. However, the model had many advantages over the relatively complex neo-classical models of that time and Leontief's method of analysis is now widely used in Eastern, Western, developed and developing economies alike. Before outlining the simple Leontief model, it is useful to draw a distinction between what is known as the input–output table and the input–output model.

The input–output table

The input–output table is similar to a set of national (or regional) accounts. One major difference between national accounts and input–output tables is that where the former tends to concentrate upon the various aspects of final demand, the input–output table focuses attention on the flows of transactions between the different productive sectors which make up the economy. This is why the input–output table is often referred to as the transactions table.

The input–output table can be sub-divided into five quadrants:

- 1 **Quadrant A** is a matrix of inter-industry transactional flows. The economy is disaggregated into homogeneous productive sectors and the rows of quadrant A represent the sales of intermediate goods and services from each sector to each other sector of the

Quadrant A	Quadrant C
Quadrant B	Quadrant D
Quadrant E	

company. Therefore, the columns of quadrant A show the purchases that each sector makes from each of the other sectors.

- **2   Quadrant B** is a matrix of primary inputs for each of the productive sectors listed in A. For instance, the rows of quadrant B will represent factors such as wages and salaries, profits, taxation and imports. Therefore the columns demonstrate the purchases of each of these factors by the productive sectors listed in A.

- **3   Quadrant C** is a matrix of final demand. The columns of this quadrant will represent the purchases of the government, households, capital and exports, from each of the productive sectors. By definition, the rows of quadrant C show the sales of each of the productive sectors to each category of final demand.

- **4   Quadrant D** is a matrix which shows the purchase of primary inputs by each of the categories of final demand. For example, goods which are imported for re-export would be entered in the import row of the export column in quadrant D.

- **5   Quadrant E** is a matrix which shows the number of employees in each of the industrial sectors. In its most simple form the matrix may be a single row vector, showing the total number employed in each sector. However, more sophisticated tables provide for an employment matrix which distinguishes between employees according to their sex, skill levels, nationality and whether they are part-time, full-time or seasonal in nature.

The transactions table may be described algebraically as:

$$X_i = \sum_{j=1}^{n} X_{ij} + Y_i \tag{1}$$

where,

X_i = the total output of the ith industry

X_{ij} = sales of industry i to industry j

Y_i = final demand for industry i

The input–output table is an extremely useful tool for gaining insight into the structure of the economy, but it is not an operational model. In order to convert the input–output table into an operational model, it is necessary to modify quadrants A and B of the transactions table into what is known as a 'technical coefficients matrix'. This is achieved by dividing the various cells which make up an industry's column of purchases by the corresponding column total. In this way each column consists of cells which now show the proportion of inputs purchased from each of the other industrial sectors (intermediate goods and services) and primary inputs. The columns will now all sum to 1.

The employment matrix (Quadrant E) is also treated in a similar manner. Each cell of an industry's employment matrix is divided by the total output of that industry to yield employment/output ratios.

Having constructed the coefficients table from quadrants A and B, it is necessary to transform it again into what is referred to as the Leontief inverse, or the inverted technology matrix. This is a table which shows the **direct plus indirect effect** of a change in any category of final demand. The Leontief inversion is only applied to the Quadrants A and B shown in the diagram above.

Using simple matrix algebra:

Let,

I = the identity matrix (equivalent to 1 in simple algebra)

A = an $n \times n$ matrix of technical coefficients

X = an $n \times 1$ vector of gross output

Y = an $n \times 1$ vector of final demand

then,

$$(I - A) X = Y \tag{2}$$

which can be written as,

$$X = (I - A)^{-1} Y \tag{3}$$

where $(I - A)^{-1}$ is the inverted technology matrix.

This provides the researcher with the foundation of the input–output model. If the inverse matrix is then multiplied by a matrix, or column vector of changes in tourist expenditure, the model will estimate the direct and indirect impact of these tourist expenditure changes on employment, income, government revenue and import levels throughout the entire economy. If the household income and consumption row and column are included in the inverted matrix, then the results will estimate the direct *plus* indirect *plus* induced impact of these changes in tourist spending.

In order to estimate the level of employment generated by a given level of output the model is:

$$L = E (I - A)^{-1} T \tag{4}$$

where,

L = the number of full-time equivalent job opportunities (FTEs)

E = the employment matrix

T = the tourist expenditure matrix

and the change in employment (ΔL) generated by a change in tourist expenditure ΔT will be:

$$\Delta L = E (I - A)^{-1} \Delta T \tag{5}$$

where E is an $1 \times n$ matrix of employment coefficients.

Limitations of the model

The major limitations of input–output analysis for the study of employment effects are a result of the rather restrictive assumptions incorporated into the model's structure.

For instance, it is assumed that the relationship between employment and output is linear and homogeneous. That is, should the demand for one sector's output increase, then it is assumed that additional labour will be employed in exactly the same ratio as that already used. In other words, the model uses average coefficients to predict the effect of marginal changes. Furthermore, if the model is constructed in such a way as to differentiate between the sex, skill levels, nationality etc. of the labour inputs, the model assumes that such a distribution of employment will continue as a result of a marginal change in demand.

For there to be a linear relationship between employment and output, it means (a) that all of the labour, prior to the increase in demand, is fully utilized and this would make it impossible for the firms to respond to an increase in demand without hiring additional units of labour; (b) that there are no economies to large scale production; and (c) that there are surplus units of labour which can be hired if the need arises.

Assumption (a) is unrealistic, most firms would be able to meet increases in demand for its output, in at least the short term, by improved utilization of its labour force, either through reorganization or adopting an overtime scheme. Firms are unlikely to take on additional units of labour until they feel that the increase in demand is permanent. However, it is possible to build threshold limits into the employment matrix which would allow limited changes in final demand to take place without the resultant effects on the level of employment. Once these threshold levels are passed, then the full effect of the change in final demand is applied to the employment matrix.

The adoption of assumption (b) violates marginal theories of production that have been accepted since the writings of Adam Smith. Large scale production often leads to increased specialization and greater capital intensity which, in turn, allows greater productivity levels of labour. This limitation can, to some extent, be circumnavigated by careful disaggregation of the economy. That is, distinctions can be made between firms of different sizes in order to proxy a marginal coefficient matrix. Such distinctions can also be made between new technology firms and old technology firms in order to reflect a marginal response for technological change. However, such refinements are often expensive in terms of data requirements and may make the modification impracticable.

Assumption (c) suggests that there is always a surplus of labour waiting to be employed. Although this may often be true in both developed and developing countries, when particular skills are required it is quite conceivable that labour shortages might occur. This limitation can be overcome by the construction of a restrictions matrix (see Wanhill, 1988; Fletcher, 1989).

The restrictions matrix sets limits on a cell-by-cell basis. The cell may be fully restricted which means that any further increase in demand for that type of labour unit can only be fulfilled by importing employees from outside the region, it may not be restricted at all which means that the full employment effect will be recorded, or it may be partially restricted to allow some satisfaction of the increase in demand before the need to import labour arises.

Conclusion

It has been shown that the technique of input–output analysis is well suited to the study of the employment effects associated with changes in final demand. There are also significant limitations to the use of this technique in estimating employment effects. These limitations can be overcome, but at a price! The technique of input–output analysis is an expensive one in terms of its data requirements. Even the most basic model requires detailed data that are unlikely to be available without undertaking a specific business expenditure survey. The adoption of refinements to overcome the model's inherent limitations increases the data requirements still further, and adds significantly to the construction costs. However, even the basic input–output model provides a level of analytical power that cannot be matched by alternative methodologies.

References and further reading

Archer, B. H. and Fletcher, J. E. (1989) The tourist multiplier. *Teoros*, **7** (3), 6–9.
Archer, B. H. and Fletcher, J. E. (1990) *Multiplier Analysis*, Les Cahiers Du Tourisme, Series C, No. 103, April 1990.

Fletcher, J. E. (1989) Input–output analysis and tourism impact studies. *Annals of Tourism Research*, **16** (4), 541–56.

Fletcher, J. E. and Archer, B. H. (1991) The development and application of multiplier analysis. In *Progress in Tourism, Recreation and Hospitality Management* (ed. C. Cooper), vol. 2, Belhaven Press, London.

Kuenne, R. E. (1954) Walras, Leontief and the interdependence of economic activities. *Quarterly Journal of Economics*, **68**, 323–54.

Leontief, W. (1936) Quantitative input and output relations in the economic system of the United States. *Review of Economics and Statistics*, **18**, 105–25.

Leontief, W. (1966) *Input–Output Economics*, Oxford University Press, New York.

O'Connor, E. and Henry, E. W. (1975) *Input–Output Analysis and its Applications*, Griffin's Statistical Monographs, No. 36, Charles Griffin and Co., London.

Phillips, A. (1955) The Tableau Economique as a simple Leontief model. *Quarterly Journal of Economics*, **69**, 136–44.

Pigou, A. C. (1929) The monetary theory of the trade cycle, *Economic Journal*, **39**, 183–94.

Sadler, P. G., Archer, B. H. and Owen, C. (1973) *Regional Income Multipliers*, University of Wales Press, Cardiff.

Wanhill, S. R. C. (1988) Tourism multipliers under capacity constraints. *Service Industries Journal*, **8**, 136–42.

Part Two
Case Studies

7 Australia
Kenneth Wilson and David Worland

Introduction and background

Australia experienced major changes in its hospitality and tourism labour markets during the 1980s, the direct result, but not exclusively because of the dramatic increase in international tourism to Australia. International tourism is now big business in Australia. It has emerged in the 1980s as a big earner of foreign exchange (more than A\$4.3 bn in 1989, with an annual rate of growth of 32.7% between 1985 and 1989, according to the Bureau of Tourism Research, 1990b) and now rivals some of the more traditional and established Australian industries in the contribution it makes to the economy. Even given the difficulties associated with the domestic airline pilots dispute of 1989, the revaluation of the Australian dollar and the current economic recession, tourism looks set to continue as an important contributor to the Australian economy.

The full magnitude of the recent rapid growth in international visitor arrivals can be fully appreciated by referring to Table 7.1, which provides data on inbound tourism between 1983 and 1990. Several factors have been identified by Faulkner and Poole (1989) as contributing to the dramatic growth in inbound tourism visits during this period:

1 The Australian dollar was substantially devalued in 1983 following the move by the Australian government to float its currency in world markets and this devaluation made the Australian tourism product considerably cheaper than it had hitherto been at that time.
2 A far more successful marketing effort of Australia as a tourist destination was undertaken in the 1980s, particularly in North America and this complemented the increased awareness of Australia resulting from the success of Australian films and entertainers in world markets.

Table 7.1 *Major inbound tourism growth markets, 1983–8 and 1988–90*

	Short-term arrivals of overseas visitors		
Country of residence	*No.* *1983* *('000)*	*Average annual* *% change* *1983–8*	*Average annual* *% change* *1988–90*
China	2.3	51	21.6
Japan	71.8	37	18.3
Scandinavia	12.5	32	−7.3
Taiwan	5.6	28	14.4
Thailand	5.0	26	11.4
Austria	3.5	21	2.7
New Zealand	225.0	19	−11.4
Asia excl. Japan	132.7	18	6.3
United States	140.4	18	11.5
Europe excl. UK/Ireland	115.4	17	0.9
South-East Asia	83.7	16	7.3
UK/Ireland	152.7	12	2.7
All countries	943.9	19	−0.5

Source: Australian Bureau of Statistics, Cat. No. 3401.0

3   A massive investment in the Australian hospitality industry and tourism sectors improved the quality and quantity of facilities and services available.
4   Major international-standard events such as the America's Cup in 1983 and 1987, the Adelaide Grand Prix, Expo and the Australian Bicentennial in 1988, focused world attention upon Australia.
5   Acts of terrorism in Europe and disasters such as Chernobyl reduced confidence in traditional tourism markets, which favoured the relative safe destination of Australia.
6   Australia had novelty value as a destination for seasoned travellers who had already visited traditional destinations.

Other factors, particularly relevant to inbound tourism from Asia, may also be included:

7   The growth in income levels and living standards in the developing economies of Asia has produced new entrants into tourism markets in Australia's region of the world.
8   The growth in Australia–Asia trade has placed Australia as a tourist destination in the minds of Asians.
9   The marketing, during the 1980s, of educational opportunities in Australia for Asians at the secondary and tertiary level has had a spillover effect on tourism as families visit relatives studying in Australia.

10   The effects of the Gulf War and conflict in Europe redirected tourists away from that geographical area.
11   The increase in air fare price competition, principally directed to stimulate traffic during the world recession has made flights to Australia affordable for more travellers.

The evidence on which of these items are the most important is scant. In the only econometric study published so far, Poole (1988) found that income and the real devaluation of the Australian dollar after deregulation were the most important determinants of the increase in inbound arrivals. These findings are important when we consider that both these determinants are generated by factors outside Australia. In particular, the income elasticity of tourism has important implications for the promotion of the Australian tourism product in overseas markets.

Table 7.1 emphasizes the rapid growth of tourism from Asia. It remains problematic how important Asia will be as a source of inbound tourists relative to Europe, North America and New Zealand. Although incomes are growing faster in Asia than elsewhere they are growing from a much lower base than the relatively high incomes of Europe and North America. The kinds of tourists attracted from these different markets are also important issues. Is it volume of tourists alone, or is the value of the tourist service the key in encouraging overseas visitors? If the Australian tourism product turns out to be more income-elastic than price-elastic then value and volume might move together but the evidence from Poole (1988) is sufficiently inconclusive for the development of marketing and promotion policy.

During the last couple of years of the decade, the growth in inbound tourism was severely curtailed by the recession. The overall average annual change was negative (0.5 percent) in 1988–90 and this compared to an average annual rate of growth of 19% from 1983 to 1988. Generally, Asian countries retained their position as the most rapidly growing sources of tourists for Australia (see Table 7.1). Indeed, in 1990 Japan became the largest source of visitors to Australia.

A different story of tourism demand can be told for domestic trips. Data published in the *Domestic Tourism Monitor* shows a virtually static situation for domestic travel during much of the 1980s, hovering around 45 million trips annually.

It is unclear what exactly overseas visitors are coming to Australia to see, but there can be no doubt that natural attractions such as the Great Barrier Reef, Uluru (formerly Ayers Rock) and the Australian 'outback' generate significant tourism. The protection of these natural assets is inevitably an issue and the relationship between tourism and conservation is politically sensitive, but the role of conservation should

91

not be understated; international tourism, in particular, benefits from conservation. If the natural environment is not maintained properly tourism will inevitably suffer.

While Australia's population tends to be centred in its major cities of Melbourne, Sydney, Adelaide, Brisbane and Perth, many of the major natural attractions are located in remote areas and this creates particular human resource problems for the tourism industry. The remoteness adds to the cost of tourist facilities and infrastructure such as hotels, casinos and roads and although these facilities do not of themselves generate the tourism, they are a necessary part of the delivery of the tourism and hospitality service. These difficulties are particularly apparent in the relevant labour markets, where, inevitably, such an increase in international tourist arrivals has had an effect.

The labour markets

From the above analysis we can see that the increase in demand for tourism services in aggregate during the 1980s was attributed to inbound tourism and hence the concomitant increase in the derived demand for labour needed to provide those tourism and hospitality services has generated its own specific labour market difficulties and shortages. A number of surveys have been undertaken which provide useful insight into some of these difficulties. The Bureau of Tourism Research (BTR) undertook a major survey of the hospitality industry during 1988 and asked respondents about their labour market experiences in 1987; a stratified random sample of 15 000 establishments was selected from the Australian Bureau of Statistics (ABS) register of businesses. Questionnaires were despatched to firms in the following Australian Standard Industrial Classifications (ASIC) industry classes: 9231 cafes and restaurants; 9232 hotels etc. (mainly drinking places); 9233 accommodation units; 9242 licensed golf clubs; 9243 other licensed clubs. The survey results are published in *Hospitality Industry Labour Force Survey 1988* by the Bureau of Tourism Research (BTR) (1990a) and complement other survey work by Charlesworth (1983), the Department of Labour (1986), Wilson and Worland (1987), Worland and Wilson (1988) and the Industries Assistance Commission (1989) which provide data that form the basis of our analysis.

The Industries Assistance Commission (IAC) (1989) characterized the hospitality workforce as follows: 'It is relatively lowly paid, poorly trained, lowly unionised and very mobile. There is significant casual employment. Many employees work part-time, many are young and a large proportion female. Many have more than one job' (p. 82). The

BTR (1990a) provides information on the numbers of establishments and employees sector by state in 1987. The employment figures cover all paid staff including working proprietors. More than 271 000 people, out of a total labour force of 7.6 million, were employed in the hospitality industry in 1987 in approximately 23 000 establishments.

As in most parts of the world, the Australian hospitality industry is characterized by fluctuations in the pattern of demand occurring on a daily and weekly basis, and also on a seasonal basis. We would therefore expect the derived demand for labour to be affected accordingly. BTR (1990a) provides data on peak and low season employment in the hospitality industry sector by occupation. Wilson and Worland (1987) also found marked seasonal variations in employment and their findings that casual and part-time employment are the employment categories most affected by seasonality are confirmed by the BTR survey. Both studies found that casual and part-time employment are the employment categories most commonly used to satisfy seasonal and peak demands. Before continuing, it may prove useful to clarify exactly what casual and part-time employment mean in the Australian context.

Pay and conditions of work

One of the unique features of employment and wage determination processes in Australia is the role played by wage-fixing tribunals at either the state or federal level. These tribunals make 'Awards' which specify minima on pay and conditions of employment and are legally binding on employers and employees alike. The Awards covering the four main sectors of the hospitality industry (cafes and restaurants, hotels etc., accommodation and licensed clubs) are consistent in their application of 'penalty rates' (bonus rates of pay) for employment outside non-standard hours of work and their definitions of part-time and casual employment. We have surveyed all relevant Awards covering the four sectors of the hospitality industry and found very little difference in the way they define part-time and casual employment.

Generally speaking, the definition of part-time in the Awards contrasts markedly with the definition of casual. Casual employment connotes an employment relationship where there is no tenure and where there are premium rates of pay in lieu of normal employee benefits (e.g. sick and recreation leave). The employment of casuals provides employers and employees with considerable flexibility in the pattern and hours of work. The part-time employment category is rather less flexible; the pattern of hours of work is specified in the

93

Award and part-time employees receive the benefits, pro rata, that accrue to full-time employees.

As labour market phenomena, full-time, part-time and casual are clearly distinct. The concepts part-time and full-time connote a far more formal relationship with the major difference between the two being the number of hours worked. This is clearly contrasted with the casual concept which is a far less structured employment relationship, particularly in respect of the pattern of work. There is more similarity between the concepts full-time and part-time, save for hours worked, than there is between part-time and casual where the number of hours of work is the only labour market characteristic the two concepts share. Casual employment, in particular, tends to be important in all sectors of the hospitality industry and Wilson and Worland (1987) found that not only is it used to satisfy peak load and seasonal demand, but it is also used as a buffer to changing labour requirements and tends to be the type of labour chosen in the first instance when employers need to expand their workforces. They also found that its use had increased during the 1980s.

Why has casual employment become so important in the hospitality industry? On the supply side increased female and teenage participation in the hospitality workforce occurred during the 1980s while at the same time there was both an increase in and a change in the demand patterns for the services and goods offered by the hospitality industry, particularly desiring non-standard hours which is more readily delivered by casual employees.

Penalty rates

Another interesting feature of employment in Australia's hospitality industry is the existence of 'penalty rates' of pay for overtime and work during non-standard hours. As in most parts of the world, the Australian hospitality industry is characterized by a pattern of non-standard hours of employment. These 'penalty rates' of pay are a contentious issue in Australia with many employers calling for their abolition and claiming that they are a constraint on employment.

The existence of penalty rates, it is argued a priori, will have a damaging effect on labour demand in two ways. First, there is a scale (or output) effect where the derived demand for labour will be lower than it would otherwise be because the final product will be more expensive. Second, there is a substitution effect where capital will be substituted for the now more expensive labour.

However, there is little evidence to show that either of these effects has had a significant impact upon employment in the hospitality industry. Ahlburg and Schumann (1986) investigated the relationship between penalty rates and employment in Australia and found no support for the contention that there are adverse employment effects associated with penalty rates. Given that the elasticity of substitution of capital for persons is even more limited in the hospitality industry than it is elsewhere in the economy, this limited substitution effect is likely to be complemented by a minimal scale effect; the point being that a significant reduction in penalty rates will, in all likelihood, have very small employment-creating effects.

It is also worth noting that Dawkins (1985) found that, although penalty rates contributed 12–15% of the wages bill for firms in the hospitality industry compared to an all-industry average of 5.8%, non-standard hours of employment were continuing to grow during the 1980s.

Turning to the supply side, the following question is relevant: to what extent does the existence of penalty rates increase, unnecessarily, the supply of labour for non-standard hours of work? This question has been addressed by Dawkins, Rungie and Sloan (1986), who conclude that the existence of penalty rates may well induce a greater supply response than is required for the hospitality industry at non-standard hours, particularly given the increased participation of married women and teenagers. Their conclusions, though based on a small sample of somewhat anecdotal responses, confirm the views of Wilson and Worland (1987) that the increased participation of married women and teenagers is more related to a desire for part-time work, with the extent of the part-time response influenced only at the margin by the substitution effect.

It is problematic what would happen to employment if penalty rates were either abolished or reduced, but the evidence suggests that there could be a very modest increase in labour demand at non-standard hours, while labour supply may be slightly reduced. We might therefore expect a very slight upward pressure on the ordinary hourly wage rate with an uncertain effect on employment.

Labour shortages

With respect to recruitment, the Bureau of Tourism Research survey (1990a) reveals a number of difficulties in recruiting employees, experienced by respondents. The BTR found that 18% of all establishments in the hospitality industry experienced some difficulties in recruiting staff. Also, more than 50% of establishments which experienced recruitment difficulties felt one reason was 'too few people with the right skills/experience'. Further, 4% of restaurants recruited staff from outside Australia while overseas recruitment was almost zero in the other three sectors.

The Industries Assistance Commission (1989) also found evidence of skill shortages in the hospitality industry though they are not dramatic and do not necessarily indicate a need for policy adjustment. Traditionally skill shortages have been filled by a range of policies including government assisted training and immigration. Some continuing long-term shortages exist for highly skilled chefs and the IAC argues that this is due in part to insufficient differences in wage levels between general and more highly trained chefs to encourage them to undertake training (1989, p. 83). Generally though, there is little evidence to support the view that there are widespread labour shortages. Nevertheless, the IAC did identify some important inadequacies with respect to training.

Training and training needs

The hospitality industry, in embracing a wide range of services, employs labour from an equally diverse spread of occupations. The range of skills possessed or expected to be acquired by the hospitality workforce covers the full gamut of skills utilized in industry generally although there are differences in the skill composition between various industry sectors and even between firms in the same sector. For instance, the traditional model of a large hotel has a high proportion of unskilled workers many of whom will be employed on fractional time. The hotel job will probably not be their main job and certainly not their career job. However, senior managers within a large hotel are usually graduates (sometimes of a Hotel School), are highly skilled and they occupy career positions within the organization in highly structured internal labour markets. The differences in skill needs within these two groups are reflected in their differing education and training arrangements. Traditionally, a majority of hotel workers participate in little if any education and training while in the case of managers there is considerable emphasis on training and skills enhancement. But the hotel sector is not homogeneous. Within it there is considerable diversity of size and organizational structure from the small sole trader through to the large hotel chain. For the small firm the employment relationship is very informal and it is not uncommon for people who work for small firms to be employed as casual labour. In a small hotel, an individual's skills are enhanced principally through on-the-job-training; the employee learns on the job.

The large hotel chain operation has a more formal employment relationship. Here, the focus on education and training will be different. Larger organizations are more able to incorporate a training objective as part of their organization goals and are more likely to encourage people to undertake skills enhancement through the improvement of qualifications or participation in 'off-the-job' formal skills enhancement programmes.

However, 'off-the-job training' in the main for the Australian hospitality industry has been restricted to the kinds of courses that might be taken by small business in areas of sales, marketing, computer terminal operation and finance. Costs associated with these kinds of training programmes have been a deterrent and only the larger organizations have been prepared to embark upon such training. Smaller operators in need of suitably qualified staff have generally looked for people with experience rather than educational qualifications and they have often 'poached' such people from other operators.

But very recently we have seen an important change. The community and industry response of encouraging education and training in hospitality (and tourism) is partly in recognition of the shortcomings attached to this strategy. Concerns about lack of education and training have been accentuated by the industry conditions that existed through the 1980s – a period of rapid growth in the demand for tourism and hospitality services which led to an explosion in the demand for labour with an accompanying increase in skill requirements.

Although many hospitality skills are relatively easily acquired, either through short courses or on-the-job training, there is still a need for considerable extension of, and improvement in, training opportunities. There is both an industry and community perception that there has been insufficient attention given to the required supportive education and training and this is supported by the available documentary evidence.

On the question of training, the BTR survey (1990a) found that only 21% of establishments in the hospitality industry participated in staff training activities, with 47% of the establishments which employed 20 or more people undertaking training. The hospitality industry must be able to deliver an adequate service with well-trained and professional staff. At present most hospitality employees are semi-skilled, particularly waiters, bartenders, clerks, kitchenhands and cleaners. Only about 20% of the workforce is employed in the relatively more skilled occupations of chef or manager.

The training opportunities that are available can be summarized into the following categories: (i) Australian government programmes; (ii) apprenticeship training; (iii) post-secondary education; and (iv) immigration.

Government-assisted training

According to the Department of Employment, Education and Training (1988) in 1987–8 the Australian government spent $70 million on training and placement activities of direct benefit to the tourism sector, which amounted to 6% of such expenditures. The Department (DEET) operates several labour market and training programmes, including JOBTRAIN, JOBSTART, the Australian Traineeship System, the Skills Training Program, and the Commonwealth Rebate for Apprentice Full-Time Training Scheme and group training schemes. All these programmes are utilized by firms in the hospitality industry and on a per employee basis this sector receives a greater share than any other industry. For example, to be formally qualified as a cook or electrician a person requires a formal period of training en route to a trade certificate. Traditionally entry to such training has been restricted to youth, although more recently, an adult apprenticeship training scheme has been introduced. People entering a trade are indentured to a specific employer who bears some of the costs associated with training and a subsidy is provided by government in the early part of the training period. Apprenticeships are generally of three or four years' duration.

The importance of holding the relevant trade qualifications for performance of work is determined by the degree of prudential supervision undertaken. In some occupations, for example electricians, it is mandatory for workers to hold the relevant licence. In other trades it will depend on the specific workplace circumstances. In large organizations a union will see to it that workers hold the appropriate qualifications and in some cases this is reinforced by government licensing requirements, e.g. certain electrical work requires that the person conducting the work be appropriately licensed. In small organizations, where union surveillance can be rather less rigorous, work which might normally be associated with a certificated person is often done by a person who is not formally qualified. So that, for example, there are many restaurants employing or using the skills of a self-employed chef who does not hold a trade certificate. A variation to the apprenticeship scheme is commonly applied in this industry, namely the indenture of a group of apprentices to a central authority which then allows them to rotate around specific employers.

Apprenticeships are available in commercial cooking, the bakery trades and waiting. Apprenticeships in these trades account for approximately 5% of all apprenticeships in training. However, the annual attrition rate for apprentice cooks is 13.5%, considerably above the average for all trades of 9.9%. The IAC identified the reasons for such attrition, which include high-pressure working conditions, inconvenient hours, and movement to full-time (often better paid) positions before completion of training (1989, p. J7).

An alternative to apprenticeship training is the traineeship scheme that was introduced into the Hotels and Retail Liquor Industry Award in 1987. Employers who engage trainees receive a government subsidy and are able to employ the trainee at 75% of the junior rate. The subsidy also provides them with assistance with the payment of payroll tax and coverage for workers' compensation premiums.

Other training opportunities

As with many industries, it has been common practice for employees in the hospitality industry, particularly among smaller organizations, to develop their skills from experience on the job. Some organizations, particularly large hotels, have developed formal in-house training programmes for induction, basic skill development and supervisory and management training.

The 1980s also saw the immediate shortage of skills being partly addressed by the private sector through short-duration training programmes. Training courses such as those sponsored by industry-based training committees are used to upgrade the skills of people currently employed in the industry; specifically in the fields of hotel/motel reception, restauranteuring and tour guiding. The travel sector, through its travel associations, is upgrading the skills of retail travel agents and is also working towards credentialling people working in that industry, i.e. people working as travel agents may ultimately require a certificate to practise in this field. Private sector management consultants and technical and further education colleges have also expanded their involvement in specialist short courses within the industry.

More recently, a pool of specialist graduates has enhanced the workforces in the hospitality and tourism sectors. The Victoria University of Technology at Footscray pioneered the teaching of hospitality and tourism studies at the degree level and offers two of the 16 programmes currently available in Australia. Both degree pro-grammes at the Footscray campus of the Victoria University of Technology combine formal classroom studies with a structured programme of on-the-job training. Here, students spend the third year of their four-year degree course attached to an employer who is responsible for employing them in as many facets of the business as their education and training will allow. Some employers have used this industry training process as an opportunity to preview the labour

99

market and it is not uncommon for a student to return to their host organization as a part-time employee during the final year of their programme and/or a full-time employee on completion of their studies. By 1989 in addition to the 16 degree programmes there were six postgraduate courses directly servicing the hospitality and tourism sectors.

The long lead times necessary for the introduction of such courses have meant that the supply of graduates has increased quite slowly. More recently, however, the mushrooming growth of courses in colleges and universities has led to an explosion in the number of courses, especially in the field of tourism, and this may lead to an over-supply of graduates in the short term, particularly when it appears to be coinciding with a slow-down in economic activity, the effects of which are likely to spill over into tourism. An economic downturn brings with it specific human resources planning problems, namely the challenge of avoiding the potential labour market wastage that occurs during a downturn. The immediate prognosis is for the slower growth to result in a loss of trained labour to other industries, and it will be important to minimize this flow to prevent a labour shortage when industry demand recovers.

The major provider of formal trade and other training is the Technical and Further Education (TAFE) system with hospitality-based courses operating at approximately 80 TAFE colleges through-out Australia. TAFE colleges offer formal accredited training via diploma, associate diploma, certificate courses, pre-apprenticeship, trade and post-trade courses. As well, TAFE offers a range of short courses in areas including food and drink service, food preparation, commercial cookery, waiting and management. TAFE colleges also offer training in the area of travel and tourism in 30 institutions Australia-wide.

Immigration has always played an important role as a labour market adjustment mechanism in Australia, particularly for the filling of skill shortages. Skilled migrants can enter Australia either via the Occupational Share System (OSS) or the Employer Nomination System. The OSS programme limits the annual number of visas issued to occupations identified as requiring reliance on migration. In 1987–8, about 20% of the total 3300 positions in the OSS were allocated to hospitality occupations. For chefs/cooks the share increased from 4% in 1984–5 to 15% in 1987–8 before falling to 11% in 1988–9 (AIC, 1989, p. J8).

Major recent developments

The picture painted above is one of a dynamic labour market subject to considerable pressures and dynamism through much of the past decade where skills enhancement, education and training have become increasingly important. The changes to education and training imposed on the hospitality industry by the rapid increase in international tourist arrivals has been complemented by two more recent developments with further implications for skills enhancement and human capital development. The first initiative involves the process of Award Restructuring and the second involves a recent Australian government policy change to encourage training at the workplace.

Award Restructuring: skills enhancement within the workplace

A major initiative which will have important repercussions for skill development is the process of Award Restructuring currently being adopted within the community under the aegis of the various industrial tribunals. Award Restructuring is progressing on an award-by-award basis and agreement has been reached in some segments of the hospitality industry on the implementation of this Award Restructuring process.

The need for structural adjustment within Australian industry has emerged as a major agenda item during the past few years and with this has come a recognition that a more efficient labour force is an imperative element of this reform process. Labour market deregulation is an inevitable part of the restructuring process. Although there is disagreement as to the extent of the deregulation, there is nevertheless recognition of the need for change by government, employers and unions. In fact, the peak union body in Australia, the Australian Council of Trade Unions (ACTU), is worth paraphrasing on this point. The ACTU/TDC Mission to Western Europe in 1987 concluded in their report, titled *Australia Reconstructed*, that Australia has a deficient skills base and identified a need to invest in skills to improve the skills base: 'Education and training must be an essential component of long term corporate strategies to maintain and strengthen competitive advantage. Moreover, the need for skill upgrading and adaptability during a working life applies to all levels of the workforce, including management' (Department of Trade, 1987, p. 121).

Although a 'skills crisis' has existed for a long time, the urgency of the crisis is now beginning to be appreciated within the community as part of the wider debate about how to develop internationally competitive industries. The main elements of the crisis rooted in the labour force were perceived by the ACTU/TDC mission as:

- Inadequate skill formation and enhancement
- Inadequate job placement and other labour market services
- Segmentation of the labour market (Department of Trade, 1987, p. 117).

The tourism industry is not quarantined from the effects of these labour market inefficiencies. Indeed, many of the problems are brought into sharper focus when one considers the specific labour market requirements of the tourism industry. The rapid growth of tourism described above and the regional characteristics of much of this growth have created special human resources problems which have in some ways impeded the industry's development.

It has not been uncommon for a resort development to be created within a total 'green field' environment quite remote from any established labour market and this has produced specific human resource problems requiring a unique solution. People involved in the development of tourism facilities have been criticized for not giving sufficient attention to the human resources planning in their project development. The developments have often been totally market-driven without the appropriate attention being given to the kinds of human resources that will be needed for the resort/project. Award Restructuring is a significant initiative consistent with the direction of industry restructuring advocated by the ACTU, employers and government. Reforming the structure of Awards is seen to be a critical part of the process of industry restructuring since the terms and conditions of employment contained in Awards govern labour utilization by an industry. Awards covering workers in the tourism industry, as do Awards in other industries, set down the terms and conditions of employment, spelling out the minimum pay and employment standards. It is common practice for wage rates and terms and conditions of employment to exceed the minima; albeit more likely in some occupational areas than others, for example in the hotel industry chefs are often paid in excess of the Award because of their unique skills and the innate shortage of this kind of labour. Both Wilson and Worland (1987) and BTR (1990a) found evidence of substantial over-Award payments for chefs in particular.

The Award system is criticized by employers because of the perceived reduction in decision-making flexibility caused by such arrangements. On the restrictive nature of Awards, the Business Council of Australia (1989) in its report on enterprise based bargaining units claims: 'It means that for the core conditions of employment, the typical workplace has little or no direct say in the minimum standards it has to comply with' (p. 55). Employers see this perceived absence in flexibility as the major impediment to greater efficiency in the workplace and concomitantly increased international competitiveness. Many of them believe that were they not constrained by a system of minimum Awards, they could become more efficient (and internationally competitive) by reducing labour costs.

The Award system is also criticized because of its lack of vocational focus. Some 40% of people entering the workforce for the first time have no substantial vocational preparation and yet many Awards give no attention to skills acquisition and career progression.

In 1987, the Australian Conciliation and Arbitration Commission recognized the significance of the community awareness and concern about this issue and responded by revising the wage fixation principles to include a principle of structural efficiency. In its August 1988 decision the Commission (1988) articulated this principle as 'Award Restructuring', which specified that future national minimum wages were to be conditional upon the:

> union[s] party to an Award formally agreeing to co-operate positively in a fundamental review of that Award with a view to implementing measures to improve the efficiency of industry and provide workers with access to more varied, fulfilling and better paid jobs. Part of this involved the introduction of an Award Restructuring process, whereby the parties were to make fundamental changes to the Award which would improve the level of efficiency in the workplace. (p. 11)

The Industrial Relations Commission identified a number of measures that could be included as part of that evaluation process, nominating a range of issues that could be addressed including:

- The development of skill-related career paths
- Eliminating impediments to multi-skilling
- Providing an opportunity for more flexible working patterns
- Reducing discriminatory characteristics of Awards

The restructuring process is more advanced in some industries than others. The hospitality industry has been one industry to make significant progress in the process of Award Restructuring. The Australian Hotels Association and the Federated Liquor and Allied Employees Union have reached agreement on the shape of a new Award which spells out the terms and conditions to apply to employees in that industry. The agreement allows for a significant variation to the traditional working hours arrangements, such that the employer (by agreement with the employee) can have greater flexibility in work rostering arrangements, and thus be able to cover busy as well as slack periods more efficiently. Employers in the hospitality industry claim that this will contribute to a major increase in efficiency within the industry.

103

One of the other major changes brought on as a result of Award Restructuring is the development of a career structure based on the level of skill acquired by the individual worker. This skills enhancement approach will be the 'tool of change'; it should provide an opportunity for individuals to move along acceptable career paths within one specific place of employment. This will be a major departure from past practice. Further, it is welcomed by the industry because it begins to address the problem of misdirected training effort under the old order.

The establishment of a linkage between skill acquisition and career progression has created the need for a new approach to training. First, it will be imperative for training to be universally accessible and second, national standards will be necessary to facilitate the efficient movement of labour between establishments.

In the hospitality industry the career paths and associated training regime coming out of the Award Restructuring exercise of 1988–90 grew out of a survey by the National Tourism Industry Training Committee conducted in 1985–88. This survey set about discovering the tasks that people normally undertake in their specific jobs with the purpose of identifying how careers are structured and skills acquired. The study found that most training occurred at the top end of the scale although there is a concentration in the number of jobs at the bottom end. The incidence of training is highest among the five-star hotels although in aggregate they are quite small employers. Very little energy has been directed towards the bottom end of the scale.

In the newly restructured Award there will be four main work classifications representing major areas of work within a hotel. Within each area there will be up to seven levels of skill competence. Rates of pay will reflect the skill competence of the person occupying the job and there will be provision for workers to move up the scale upon improving their level of skill.

Apart from the increase in flexibility that the new Award provides to employers in the industry, it also raises the profile of education and training, such that an employee entering the industry can more clearly see a career path within that industry, progression being conditional upon the individual undertaking skills enhancement programmes during the course of their employment. The industry training arrangements for the Hospitality Industry Award provide for the development of a range of training modules which will give effect to a structured skills formation programme to enable individuals to participate in career progression. Further, such progression can occur beyond the boundaries of a single employer. So a person who has reached a given level of competency will be able to carry the recognition for that competency to other employers within the industry.

Training Industry Guarantee Scheme

A recent response by the Australian government to the shortage of skills in industry generally has been the introduction of a new approach to the responsibility for training. The government has introduced a training scheme that requires all employers to make a financial commitment towards training their workforce. In July 1990 it introduced the Training Industry Guarantee Scheme. This is a scheme requiring employers in organizations that have an annual payroll in excess of $200 000 to commit resources equivalent to 1% of their payroll to the education and training of their workforce. The 'stick' being used to enforce this is a requirement that the uncommitted funds will be collected as a type of rent tax which will then be used to assist in the provision of overall human resources training. The level of financial commitment to training was increased in 1992 to 1.5% of payroll.

This scheme represents a whole new approach to the training of human resources, encouraging employers to commit resources to the training function by contributing to the process of skills enhancement within their own workforce or through a more general financial commitment to industry training.

An indication of the degree of support for this proposal has been the absence of any concerted attempt by employers to sabotage it. Employers have probably been affected by the scheme in one of two ways: one group is already committing at least 1% of payroll to training and has been subsidizing the non-contributors in the past; the other group (the non-contributors) can find little support for the view that they should not take some responsibility for this task. The scheme, while requiring the expenditure on education and training to be authenticated, none the less provides considerable discretion for the employers in the kinds of training that might be undertaken. It is not highly prescriptive as to either the process or content.

Conclusion

The training and management of human resources in the Australian hospitality industry have undergone a major transition over recent years. Part of the explanation for this lies in the growth in demand for tourism services offered within Australia emanating from overseas demand for the Australian tourism product, and the need for the hospitality and tourism industries to respond to that growth and future growth opportunities. The hospitality industry is beginning to see the need for a more sophisticated approach to human resource management and this is being reflected in a new approach to education and training of the workforce.

An additional impact factor has been the change in community attitudes towards training. At the macro level, the issue of labour market adjustment has been placed prominently on the agenda such that restructuring of work arrangements is being initiated on a wide scale, where the evidence indicates that work practices other than the payment of penalty rates are likely to lead to productivity improvements. Thus, in summary, we have seen two very important new initiatives beginning to take effect. First, the Award Restructuring process is beginning to change work practices and lead to better trained and more productive employees. Second, the introduction of the Training Guarantee levy is forcing employers to develop training programmes to enhance skills formation. These two initiatives taken together will have a dramatic impact in coming years in improving the skills of workers in the hospitality and tourism sectors of the Australian economy.

The potential impact on human resources efficiencies within the hospitality and tourism industries of these structural efficiency programmes is enormous. They are expected to produce economies within the labour market as well as changing the total culture of the workplace, impacting particularly upon work practices, attitudes to training, quality of service and productivity. Such changes can be expected to impact markedly on all parts of the hospitality and tourism industries – employers and their representatives, employees and unions and government agencies. The resultant attitudinal changes can be expected to establish additional agendas and adjustment mechanisms in the human resources management area.

Bibliography

Ahlburg, D. and Schumann, P. (1986) Increased penalty rates for overtime and job creation in Australia. *Journal of Industrial Relations*, **28**, 102–8.

Australian Conciliation and Arbitration Commission (1988) National Wage Case August 1988, Print H4000, 12 August 1988.

Bureau of Industry Economics (1984) *Tourist Expenditure in Australia*, AGPS, Canberra

Bureau of Tourism Research (1988) *Tourism Update* 1(1), Bureau of Tourism Research, Canberra.

Bureau of Tourism Research (1990a) *Hospitality Industry Labour Force Survey*, Bureau of Tourism Research, Canberra.

Bureau of Tourism Research (1990b) *Tourism Statistical Review, 1990*, Bureau of Tourism Research, Canberra.

Centre for International Economics (1988) *Tourism Report: Economic Effects of Tourism*, AGPS, Canberra.

Charlesworth, S. (1983) *Employment in the Hospitality Industry* (A report based on a survey of Liquor Trade Union members in hotels, restaurants and clubs in Victoria, Melbourne), Monash University.

Dawkins, P. (1985) Non-standard hours of work and penalty rates in Australia. *Journal of Industrial Relations*, **27**, 329–49.

Dawkins, P., Rungie, C. and Sloan, J. (1986) Penalty rates and labour supply: employee attitudes to non-standard hours of work. *Journal of Industrial Relations*, **28**, 564–87.

Department of Employment, Education and Training (1988) *Training for the Hospitality Sector of the Tourism Industry*, Discussion Paper, AGPS, Canberra.

Department of Labour (1986) *Report of the Inquiry into the Training Needs of the Victorian Tourism and Hospitality Industry*, Department of Labour (Victoria), Melbourne

Department of Trade (1987) *Australia Reconstructed: ACTU/TDC Mission to Western Europe: A Report*, AGPS, Canberra.

Faulkner, B. and Fagence, M. (eds) (1988) *Frontiers in Australian Tourism*, Bureau of Tourism Research, Canberra.

Faulkner, B. and Poole, M. (1989) *Impacts on Tourism of the Disruption to Domestic Airline Travel*, BTR Occasional Paper Number 5, Bureau of Tourism Research, Canberra.

Industries Assistance Commission (1989) *Draft Report on Travel and Tourism*, AGPS, Canberra.

Poole, M. (1988) Forecasting methodology. *Bureau of Tourism Research Occasional Paper No. 3*, Bureau of Tourism Research, Canberra.

Wilson, K. and Worland, D. (1987) *Employment and Labour Costs in the Hospitality Industry*, Research Report No. 1, John Reid Faculty of Business Research Papers, Footscray Institute of Technology, Footscray.

Worland, D. and Wilson, K. (1988) Employment and labour costs in the hospitality industry: evidence from Victoria, Australia. *International Journal of Hospitality Management*, 7(4), 363–77.

8 Bali
Yvonne Guerrier

Bali is an example of a South-East Asian resort with a longstanding
tourist industry which has grown rapidly in the 1980s and early 1990s.
As such, it is a good illustration of the problems faced by countries that
need to develop skilled people fast to meet the needs of an expanding
industry. It is also an island with a strong local culture: traditional
Balinese culture is one of the attractions for tourists. It is also,
therefore, a suitable case study to explore the issue of whether local
culture does and should affect human resource practices even in
international organizations, such as first class hotels.

Tourism in Bali

Despite attempts to attract tourists to other parts of Indonesia, Bali
remains the country's main tourist destination. The number of visitors
to Bali first began to increase in 1969 when the Ngurah Rai International Airport was opened but there was a particularly rapid growth
in foreign tourist arrivals in the 1980s. Indonesia began to plan its 'Visit
Indonesia 1991' campaign in 1989, aiming for an increase of visitors to
Indonesia from 1.9 million to 2.1 million. In fact, this target was
reached in 1990. The Gulf War affected the Indonesian tourist industry
in 1991. However, the situation does now seem to have improved and
figures for tourist arrivals in 1991 do show an increase on 1990,
although not as great as had been hoped.

Tourist development in Bali is largely concentrated in the southern
part of the island, south of the capital Denpasar. There are three main
resorts. Sanur, on the south-east coast, was the site of the first large
luxury hotel developments. The Bali Beach Hotel was opened in 1966.
A tall concrete building, it was widely criticized for the inappropriate-
ness of its appearance (Udayana and Francillon, 1975), although
Rodenberg (1980) argues that the Balinese may have been mainly
opposed to the coming of large scale industrialization which the Bali

Beach symbolized. Nevertheless, subsequent legislation has required that hotels be no higher than the palm trees. Most hotel developments are designed to mirror traditional Balinese architecture and Bali has, at least, escaped the mix of architectural styles and the high-rise hotel development that can be found, for example, in the Thai resorts of Pattaya and Phuket.

The other older development is at Kuta on the south-west coast. Kuta caters largely for the lower-spending mass tourist, particularly from Australia, and is a lively and unplanned collection of small hotels, *losmen* (local inns), restaurants, discotheques and so forth.

When expanding tourist provision in the 1980s, the planners attempted to avoid the mistakes of Sanur and Kuta and limit the negative effects of tourism on Balinese culture. All new international standard hotels were to be concentrated in Nusa Dua, to the south of Sanur. According to Rodenberg (1980, p. 192), 'the primary rationale of the Nusa Dua planners was the minimization of the adverse social and cultural effects of tourism. They wished to concentrate and isolate tourists, like any other industrial effluent, to minimize cultural pollution'. Hotel provision expanded rapidly in Nusa Dua during the late 1980s and early 1990s with the opening of a number of new international hotels, including a Hilton, a second Hyatt for the island and a Sheraton, which have doubled the number of rooms available in the resort.

The planners have not been totally successful in confining tourism to the south of the island. Small scale independent hotel developments are growing in other areas. Ubud, in the centre of the island, is known as a centre for artists and craft work. New hotels have been opening on the north coast of the island, around Lovina Beach and in the east, around Candi Dasa.

Bali has, therefore, had to cope with a rapid increase in tourism but also with several different types of tourism. Travellers were originally attracted to Bali because of its culture, but most visitors now have only a passing interest in such matters (McTaggart, 1980). (There have nevertheless been some attempts to develop cultural tourism in the west of the island around Tabanan.) Gibbons and Fish (1989) argue that Bali now operates a two-tier approach to tourism, attracting a mix of lowerspending tourists who are attracted by budget facilities and also higher-spending, affluent tourists looking for the luxury of the international hotels in Sanur and Nusa Dua. For Australians, Bali is a relatively cheap resort which is comparatively easy to reach. For Europeans, Bali is an exotic long haul destination. Visitors also come from Japan and other parts of South-East Asia. In common with other parts of this region, as local labour is relatively cheap it can be used intensively. Staff to room ratios in four- and five-star hotels are around

1.8:1 and some data suggest they may actually be higher in three- and four-star hotels than in five-star hotels.

The Indonesian context and Balinese culture

In any discussion of human resource management in Bali, it is useful to start with some understanding of the context and culture within which people work. One set of influences comes from the way Indonesia has developed. Indonesia is an extremely diverse country of 1300 islands spread across 3000 miles, with more than 300 ethnic groups and 250 distinct languages. In the years since independence one of the concerns has been to build a unified nation from these diverse cultural groupings. The Indonesian language is one force for unity. Bahasa Indonesia, which is a variant of Malay, became a powerful symbol in the fight for independence and the post-independence years (Grant, 1964). But another unifying force is the Panca Sila philosophy. The Panca Sila, or five principles, are taught to all Indonesians from childhood. They are faith in one God, humanity, nationalism, representative government and social justice. The inclusion of course components on Panca Sila, national resilience, religion and nation- and character-building in the diploma courses run at the Balinese Hotel and Tourism Training Centre demonstrates the importance placed on this philosophy and on Indonesian notions of unity through diversity.

Another notion which has an impact on management culture is that of the *bapak* (or father) manager. Grant (1964) argued that the traditional system of village decision-making through consensus was transferred into management through the notion of bapakism, where the manager will not issue orders until the question has been discussed with subordinates and their agreement obtained in principle. Developing this idea, it can be argued that achieving harmony is a major objective in Indonesian society and that efforts are always made to prevent disturbances and frictions. Although the bapak manager's style is apparently participative, subordinates (who also wish to maintain harmony) will not dare to disagree openly with the manager or make decisions without his prior approval.

Balinese culture has its own distinctive features. McTaggart (1980, p. 457) argues that 'to the Balinese, the survival of their own culture in the face of pressures from their own numbers, from political forces within Indonesia as well as economic and political forces from the exterior, is a primary objective'. Because of Bali's relative geographical isolation, the coming of Islam and inter-island trade that affected Java bypassed Bali and colonial government arrived later (in 1908). Bali remained a Hindu rather than a Moslem country, but with an individual brand of

Hinduism retaining many aspects of earlier religions. Religious activity in Bali is closely associated with artistic activity. Geertz (1967, p. 50) points out that 'aesthetic activity in Bali is an activity pursued by large numbers of people from all segments of the society'. There are small hotels in areas like Ubud, for example, that are owned and run by people who consider themselves to be primarily artists. Obviously the craft work, the dances and the temple ceremonies remain part of the appeal of Bali as a tourist destination.

Most Balinese are members of three types of social unit (Geertz, 1967), one of which is the *bandjar*. The bandjar is a council of heads of households which takes care of ritual duties. It has powers of taxation and can punish backsliders or criminals by means of fines or in the last resort by means of eviction from the village. Religious and aesthetic life on the island centres around temple ceremonies and a series of personal life cycle ceremonies. Balinese are expected to return to their villages to attend these, and they can be frequent.

There is debate about the extent to which tourism is affecting Balinese culture. McTaggart (1980) reports that loyalty to the bandjar remains strong and that since tourism is largely confined to the southern part of the island, many Balinese remain largely untouched by it. In fact, he claims 'the whole Hindu religious and cultural system of Bali is now regarded more positively by the Jakarta government in view of its international renown and its potential to assist the nation's economic effort' (p. 463). However, he was writing more than ten years ago and tourism has expanded fast since then.

From the point of view of human resource management, it is clear that there can be some tension between duty to the bandjar and the demands of work in a large international organization. One tour operator gave an amusing example of the way in which his tour guides reconciled these two sets of responsibilities when he claimed that if the guides were supposed to attend a ceremony on a day they were in charge of Australian tourists (who have a reputation for being bad tippers) they would insist on attending the ceremony. But if their tour party was European or American (known as good tippers), they would happily pay a fine to the bandjar and guide the group.

Meeting the demand for trained staff

In a fast expanding industry such as exists in Bali, clearly one of the problems is that of providing a supply of suitably qualified staff to fill the new jobs that have been created. Twenty years of international tourism may have made the Balinese more familiar with Western culture but it needs to be remembered that for a Balinese to train as a

111

waiter, for example, for an international hotel catering for Western guests he or she needs to learn a whole new food culture as well as acquire a basic command of English and ideally other languages. The process is akin to training a European to wait on Japanese guests in a Japanese restaurant.

The main institution providing vocational training for the hotel and tourism industry in Bali is the Bali Hotel and Tourism Training Centre. Known as BPLP (Balai Pendidikan dan Latihan Parawisata) Bali, it was set up in 1970 with assistance from the United Nations Development Programme and the International Labour Organisation and operates under the supervision of the Department of Tourism, Post and Telecommunications. It started by offering one- and two-year courses in basic hotel trades (food preparation, food and beverage service, house-keeping and reception). The emphasis on basic hotel skills initially was in part a response to the recognition that management courses required expertise that the centre did not have at that time (Bagiarta, 1988). The Indonesian government had also had an unsatisfactory experience of launching hotel management training at the university level without sufficient emphasis on technical skills, finding that graduates from such a programme had difficulties progressing their careers because they lacked basic technical skills (Mappisammeng, 1988).

BPLP, Bali now offers courses at, what is termed, Diploma I, Diploma II, Diploma III and Diploma IV levels and provides courses in tourism and travel as well as focused on the needs of hotels. The Diploma IV courses are a relatively new venture and are designed to equate to a university level education. The centre is based around a campus in Nusa Dua. Students are able to practise their basic technical skills in the teaching restaurant and guest house and through placements in hotels.

With the opening of a number of major hotels in the past few years, BPLP has been hard pressed to keep up with the demand for trained staff. Six-month crash courses have been introduced; courses on the Nusa Dua site are being run over two shifts and classes are also being run in Sanur. One of the implications of the heavy demand for students from the centre is that the classes at Diploma III and IV tend to be relatively small as it is difficult to persuade students of the benefits of further education when they have already been offered a job.

As BPLP aims to provide courses at more advanced levels, another issue is the development of teaching staff who are capable of working at that level. The training centre has sponsored staff on short development programmes and masters level programmes in Indonesia and overseas and encouraged the development of links with overseas institutions. However, obviously such development takes time and resources.

BPLP alone cannot hope to meet all the needs for trained staff in the hotel and tourism sectors, even within the large international hotels. Outside this sector, the *losmen* (locally run guest houses), for example, are largely staffed by people who have been educated to the junior or senior high school level but have no vocational qualifications. Many of the jobs in this type of operation are as general helper and employees are expected to be multi-skilled.

Human resource issues

Labour turnover in the hotel and tourism industry in Bali tends to be relatively low by western standards but obviously the opening of major new hotels fuels movement as people are attracted by what they perceive as more prestigious jobs. In some of the longer established hotels lack of movement may equally be a problem. In a hotel such as the Bali Beach, staff may be found who have not only worked in the hotel since opening but have stayed in the same job. This can pose some problems for managers attempting to introduce change.

The development of management and supervisory skills remains an issue. The large international hotels have the resources to be able to develop their own managers but for smaller independent establishments access to training and development is harder. BPLP can and does play a role here by organizing short seminars and workshops. There is then a dilemma about who should run these workshops. If they are run by local BPLP staff do they have the skills and credibility? If 'experts' are brought in from overseas, can they learn enough about the Balinese situation in a short period to make what they do useful and what follow-up is available?

There is also the question of what management style is likely to work in the Balinese setting, especially in relation to the management of people. The question of whether Western approaches towards management necessarily transfer into different cultural settings is a hotly debated one. Perhaps the best known work on national value systems and the impact these have on management style is by Hofstede (1980, 1985), who defined four dimensions describing differences in values. Hofstede would describe Indonesia as having large power distance values (i.e. accepting that power in organizations is distributed unequally) and weak uncertainty avoidance values (i.e. that people will feel relatively comfortable with uncertainty and ambiguity), leading to a preference for a 'family' style of organization with powerful leaders but few formal rules and structures. He would also describe it as having collectivist values (i.e. a preference for a tightly knit social network in which individuals can expect their relatives, clan or other in-group to look after them in return for their loyalty). This would certainly be in line with the notions, discussed above, of the bapak manager and would suggest that the implementation of certain Western human resource management techniques like open appraisal systems and individually based performance-related reward systems might be somewhat problematic in Indonesia.

Comparisons with experience in other countries

Many of the human resource management issues that have been discussed in relation to Bali can be seen mirrored in other countries in South-East Asia. In Thailand, for example, there has been a rapid growth in new hotel development in recent years and some concern about potential shortages of trained staff. As new hotels open so the labour turnover of existing hotels increases and key personnel, such as good quality local department heads, become difficult to recruit (Lockwood and Guerrier, 1990).

There are a variety of institutions in Thailand providing vocational education for the tourism and hotel industries but the standard of these varies. Again, the shortage of appropriately trained educators has been seen as a problem. As the better institutions could not possibly meet all industry's needs, some sections of the industry became more involved in the training process. The Dusit Thani Group, for example, has opened its own training centre in Bangkok.

As Thailand also illustrates, tourist booms do not necessarily continue forever. There is now an oversupply of hotel rooms and even when concerns about political stability have dissipated, concerns about the environment, AIDS and poor infrastructure may deter potential tourists. In Bali there are fewer problems. However the challenge of the future may be to develop the human skills needed to improve the quality of existing provision rather than to keep pace with the growth in new developments.

References

Bagiarta, N. (1988) The Diploma IV Programme in Hotel Administration: the Experience of Bali. Paper given at the National Workshop on Tourism Education and Training, Bali, October.

Gibbons, J. and Fish, M. (1989) Indonesia's international tourism: a shifting industry in Bali. *International Journal of Hospitality Management*, 8(1), pp. 63–70.

Geertz, H. (1967) Indonesian cultures and communities. In *Indonesia* (ed. R. T. McVey), HRAF Press, New Haven, Conn.

Grant, B. (1964) *Indonesia*, Melbourne University Press, Melbourne.

Hofstede, G. (1980) *Culture's Consequences*, Sage, Beverley Hills, Ca.

Hofstede, G. (1985) The interaction between national and organizational value systems. *Journal of Management Studies*, **22**(4), pp. 347–57.

Lockwood, A. and Guerrier, Y. (1990) Labour shortages in the international hotel industry. *Travel and Tourism Analyst*, No. 6, pp. 17–35.

McTaggart, W. D. (1980) Tourism and tradition in Bali. *World Development*, **8**, pp. 457–66.

Mappisammeng, A. (1988) The Expected Development of Tourism and Needs of Education and Training in Tourism. Paper given at the National Workshop on Tourism Education and Training, Bali, October.

Rodenberg, E. E. (1980) The effects of scale in economic development: tourism in Bali. *Annals of Tourism Research*, **7**, pp. 177–96.

Udayana, U. and Francillon, G. (1975) Tourism in Bali – its economic and socio-cultural impact: three points of view. *International Social Science Journal*, **27**, 721–57.

9 Belgium
Luk van Langenhove
and Els Lowyck

This chapter attempts to place the various issues of human resources in the Belgian tourism industry in the context of the complex history and organization of the Belgian state and tourism in the country as a whole. It is important to consider the history of the political evolution of Belgium. The country consists of a multi-national state, with Flemish-, French- and German-speaking parts. French domination of political and economic life led to the formation of a Flemish movement, dedicated to the recognition of the Flemish language. It is only since 1930 that Flemish has been permitted in schools in Flanders. Today, a complex political structure exists which has consequences for the way in which tourism is supported at government level.

This chapter considers the Belgian tourism product and the ways in which government and non-governmental agencies support its development. Tourism, in Belgium, is dependent on a number of factors, not least culture, natural beauty, climate and the quality of accommodation on offer to the tourist. Although the Belgian tourism product is varied (the coast, the Ardennes, historic cities and other attractions), Belgium is not a major European tourism destination and Belgians have a relatively low level of holiday participation, at home and overseas. Nevertheless, tourism generates an important component of national foreign exchange earnings and employment. Both government and non-government initiatives in tourism are, inevitably, closely linked to the historical and economic development of the Belgian state. Most importantly, the chapter looks at the issues and problems that face the development of human resources and training within Belgian tourism.

Tourism in Belgium

Belgium is a complex state and the issues of tourism and related human resource matters cannot be considered without regard to the political, social and economic history of the country. Moreover, the nature of the tourism product is dependent on a number of factors, some of which are not amenable to control or influence, such as the climate or the main features of the natural environment. The Belgian tourism product is varied within a relatively small geographical area, something characteristic of northern Europe. Climate could be described as a handicap to Belgian tourism, being temperate, rarely very hot or cold, but unpredictable and without any guarantee of sunshine during the summer. However, this is a handicap shared with other northern European destinations, such as the UK, the Netherlands and Denmark, and should not be exaggerated.

Over and above the external factors that are out of the control of the tourism industry and the country as a whole, there are a number of factors which are amenable to influence and which can compensate for negative attributes such as the weather. Examples include the recent phenomenon of 'all-weather park' resorts such as those operated by Center Parcs, which go some way towards making tourism independent of climatic factors. A wide range of recreational activities are contained within a dome-shaped roof and the environment is maintained at an optimum temperature for all-year usage. Overall, Belgium offers a diverse range of tourist attractions, including theme parks, cultural and historic sites, events, folklore, tradition, sporting events, ski-ing and watersports, to name just some. Furthermore, all these are located within easy range of major population concentrations in France, Germany, the Netherlands and the United Kingdom, access from which will be made easier still by the opening of the Channel Tunnel. It is not really surprising that international arrivals are dominated by visitors from other European countries and, in particular, from other European Community countries with common land or sea borders. Indeed, in 1990, some 73% of all international bednights in Belgium were spent by visitors from the four neighbouring countries – France, Germany, the Netherlands and the UK. This dominance represents an increase, from 71% in 1984. Over the same period, a number of other markets have also grown significantly, notably Denmark, Italy, Japan, Spain and Sweden. By contrast, the number of bednights spent by visitors from the United States declined over the same period. The influence of the European Community and its institutions, headquartered in Brussels, cannot be ignored in evaluating these trends.

The quality of Belgian accommodation stock is varied. At the top end of the market, the presence of international hotel chains such as Sheraton, Hilton, Holiday Inn and Accor is significant in the major cities. New and renovated family hotels are also important in the coastal regions, Bruges and Limburg; indeed, the majority of smaller units are family owned and operated and the standard of such facilities is relatively high. Most foreign visitors use hotel accommodation, while domestic tourists are much more likely to utilize camping sites and villas and flats on the coast. These locations vary greatly in quality but, generally, villas and flats are considered expensive in relation to the product they offer. Social tourist centres, often originally sub-sidized through social or cultural organizations, remain important for domestic and Dutch tourists and their standards have risen consider-ably in recent years so that they frequently offer good quality bungalow or chalet accommodation.

That the Belgian tourism industry depends upon Western European visitors, combined with an important domestic market, is of particular note in terms of the demand that this makes on the tourism product. This means that there is likely to be relative homogeneity between the demands of the domestic holiday-maker and those of the visiting, non-business tourist. The business market, with a significant public sector component, associated with European Community matters, has other requirements in terms of accommodation and usage of other facilities. The implications of the Belgian market profile for human resource development, that, on the one hand, there will be demands for high-level technical and communications skills to cater for the international business market while, on the other hand, the holiday market – domestic and international – will be catered for within relatively small, family-orientated businesses, offering relatively limited career opportunities to new entrants who do not have family connections.

Economic importance of tourism in Belgium

The relative economic importance of tourism within the Belgian economy is clearly less than is the case with respect to major holiday destinations such as Greece and Spain. Precise indicators of the importance of tourism to the Belgian economy are not readily available as, for statistical purposes, the industry is not recognized as a separate sector. The overall value of tourism, domestic and international, in relation to the national gross domestic product is relatively small at 2.03%, which exceeds that in France, Germany, Italy, the Netherlands and the United Kingdom but is a long way behind that in Ireland, Portugal and Spain (Euromonitor, 1990). However, the import cost of tourism, that is the expenditure of Belgians in foreign countries, has also grown significantly, reflecting the increasing level of holiday participation by Belgians, particularly overseas. The result of this is that the coverage, that is the proportion of receipts which can be offset against expenditure, has been declining steadily since its rapid rise early in the 1980s.

Tourism not only influences the balance of payments but is a significant source of employment in Belgium, which, in common with most other OECD countries, has become highly dependent upon the service sector as traditional agricultural and manufacturing sectors have declined. This shift is illustrated by figures for 1984, during which year some 21 000 jobs in the manufacturing sector were lost in Belgium while, over the same period, more than 20 000 new service sector positions were created. Tourism and allied services clearly play a role in this transformation, although OECD figures show the significance of this in Belgium is somewhat less than elsewhere (OECD, 1988).

Comparison of the size of the hotel and tourism workforce relative to total employment and that within services, specifically, is a good indicator of the importance of tourism within the economy. On this basis, we can make a distinction between countries that have a heavy involvement in tourism and those where tourism is of rather less significance. In certain European countries where the service sector is of relatively great significance, hotels account for quite a high proportion of service sector employment, for example Luxemburg (9%), Austria (7%), Germany (6%) and Switzerland (4%). Belgium, with 0.7% of its service sector workforce engaged in hotel employment, comes second only to the Netherlands in having the smallest proportion working in this way. When the rather more sketchy data for the tourism sector as a whole are considered, a similar picture emerges, with only 4.1% of the service sector employed in Belgian tourism, compared to 6.2% in the United Kingdom, 9.7% in France, 14.9% in Switzerland and 16.9% in Canada. Thus, Belgium serves as a good illustration of a country where tourism and its attendant economic and employment benefits are of considerable absolute significance but, in relative terms, can be seen to constitute a somewhat minor component when considered alongside other areas of economic activity.

Human resources and training for tourism in Belgium

The human resource environment

In 1987 the OECD estimated total tourism employment, in Belgium, to be 96 930, of whom some 17 000 were employed in a hotel industry of approximately 89 000 beds (OECD, 1988; Euromonitor, 1990). In common with other western European countries, there are a number of trends which are putting increasing pressure on tourism to compete with other sectors of the labour market for a decreasing workforce. These are:

- Demographic trends, which point to a decreasing pool of school leavers coming into the workforce
- Competition from other employment sectors, not withstanding the economic depression of the early 1990s
- Rising expectations of young people and other workers, unwilling to accept traditional tourism industry conditions
- The impact of technology on productivity and job functions
- Demands from other, non-tourism sectors, for the skills traditionally developed within tourism
- The increasing dominance of multi-national companies, forcing change and, in some cases, bankruptcy, upon the smaller tourism businesses

Thus, this review of human resource development within Belgian tourism must be viewed against a backcloth of a changing labour market environment, in which traditional patterns of work in all sectors, and not least within tourism, are changing and developing into new forms and based upon different practices. A further factor and one that cannot be evaluated with any certainty at this stage, is the significance of moves to the right within Belgian politics and the implications this has for the significant immigrant population in the country, many of whom depend on the tourism industry for a livelihood, a dependence that is mutual. It is well recognized, in Belgium, that, as a service industry, tourism is highly dependent upon the human factor. Whatever the attractions of the country and whatever marketing initiatives are put in place to support them, at the end of the day, tourism means dealing with customers. If the quality of service given is poor, then tourists will vote with their feet and will not return, whatever the quality of the physical products.

Critical to the delivery of quality tourism services are well-qualified and highly motivated personnel, selected for the right positions within the industry and enabled to perform to the optimum within that job. This implies that there are two human resource issues at stake. First, there is the question of the availability of well-qualified personnel to fill, in particular, front-line jobs, with direct customer contact. Second, there is a requirement for highly skilled professionals who can carry out the requisite human resource functions, within the tourism industry, specifically to attract, select, train and motivate these front-line employees.

In this section, we will consider the range of educational and training opportunities which exist in Belgium in tourism and focus on the role of government in providing such training facilities. The concentration will be, primarily, on the non-hotel sectors because these are the newly evolving areas within tourism education and training. By contrast, the hotel sector has a well-established tradition of training within Belgium's vocational trade schools and through apprenticeship schemes in the craft areas. Belgian hotel schools, catering for levels from craft through to management, are well known nationally and internationally and their analysis will not contribute significantly to this discussion. This section will be concluded with consideration of some of the problems that face human resource development initiatives, especially in the training area, in Belgium.

Tourism training

The origins of training for tourism, in Belgium, are as recent as the 1960s (Heyvaert, 1984). At that time, a number of vocational schools responded to what was an evident training need within the tourism sector, especially in the travel agency sector. The start was somewhat experimental, with no defined or agreed curricula, no textbooks and, certainly, no trained teachers. The curricula for tourism studies varied from school to school and from year to year. However, after a number of years of trial and error, a more consistent picture emerged and the result has been nationally agreed curricula guidelines and the adoption of relatively consistent educational standards.

Education for tourism in Belgium is organized at different levels with a structure that, basically, mirrors that which was already in place for the hotel sector. Vocational training in tourism is provided by secondary schools, by a final year option after secondary school (a seventh year) and within the higher education system, at the lower level, for three years in non-university institutions. All these institutions offer common curricula, appropriate to the level in question, and approved by the Ministry of Education. The key distinction between tourism education in secondary schools and that offered at a higher level, beyond distinctions in their academic demands, is in the inclusion of traineeships and dissertations within higher education provision.

Tourism curricula can be subdivided into four parts (Heyvaert, 1984). First, there are typical, theoretical and practical studies in tourism, in areas ranging from geography through to ticketing. Second, there is a requirement to complete administrative/business courses, including economics, marketing and accounting. Third, general courses are required in subjects such as history, psychology and law. Finally, in recognition of the international nature of tourism employment opportunities in Belgium and abroad, much attention is paid to languages and all students are required to study four different language options. All these programmes are regulated by a national plan, with some local school autonomy. There are, at present, five schools in both Flanders and Walloon offering three-year, non-university programmes in tourism within the higher education system.

Increasingly, tour operators, airlines and international hotel chains seek to recruit employees who have been educated within the higher education system. In particular demand are potential managers with some tourism sector familiarity. The Free University of Brussels was the innovative institution which introduced tourism education to the university sector, with a programme called Leisure Studies, in 1987. As a response to this growing industry demand, a number of Belgian universities commenced postgraduate programmes in tourism and, at present, four such courses exist. Programmes are strongly influenced, in their design and emphasis, by the department in which they are located, which may be social sciences, economics or psychology.

In addition to these officially recognized programmes, a number of private courses also operate in Belgium. They are not subject to government control with regard to their content or resourcing and their diplomas have no official recognition. These are fee-paying ventures and may be of anything from one month to two years' duration and are, commonly, run by the multi-national tourism companies. Whether these programmes will attain recognition in the wake of European Community moves towards harmonization of vocational qualifications remains to be seen.

In summary, there appear to be adequate education and training opportunities, possibly excessive, within Belgian tourism, both for the hotel and the general tourism sectors. There are, however, a number of difficulties with Belgian tourism, which merit reference by way of conclusion to this chapter.

Issues in human resources within Belgian tourism

The first issue relates to training provision. As mentioned previously, Belgium has a complex, federal state structure and this has repercussions on many aspects of life, including the organization of the educational system. In a report on the current state in tourism training, the National Inspector of Education argued that there was, in fact, over-provision of tourism and hotel schools and that vocational training was far too fragmented and dispersed (Henau, 1989). He went on to argue that the system suffered from 'misorganization with major consequences for the quality of educational programmes' (Henau, 1990). This issue was also addressed by a number of industry associations (Verbruggen-Aelterman, 1989), when they maintained that, because of the number of training initiatives in existence, there was a growing shortage of experienced and trained teachers in tourism. In some cases, existing courses owe their origins to academic enterprise rather than industry demand. The demand, therefore, is for fewer programmes of greater depth and quality.

A second issue is based on the argument that the number of graduating students from tourism programmes, especially in the hotel sector, outstrips the demands of the labour market. According to Henau (1990), one hotel school in Mechelen alone graduates more students than the whole industry can absorb in any one year.

A third issue is related to the seasonal nature of some businesses in Belgian tourism and that 15% of the tourism workforce is employed on a seasonal or casual basis. This problem is not so acute in some other Western European countries, but is prevalent in Ireland and parts of the United Kingdom. This high proportion of seasonal workers has implications for training. Many employees have little or no training within education or companies. It is estimated that 40% of unskilled and semi-skilled workers in Belgian tourism have received no formal training.

A major study of tourism school graduates has identified a significant drop-out rate from the industry once students enter employment, up to 25% (Heyvaert, 1984). While this is not very high by European comparative standards, it remains a matter of considerable concern.

A final issue relates to the human resource needs of small operations within Belgian tourism, often family owned and operated. These businesses, in common with similar concerns in most European countries, do not have a tradition of recruiting trained personnel nor do they have the resources to engage in systematic and formal in-company training in their own right. The impact of technology and, in particular, the CRS, is likely to further disadvantage them, competitively, and their human resource needs require consideration.

In conclusion, therefore, weaknesses within the training system appear to be the main causes for concern with respect to the human resource domain in Belgian tourism.

References

Note: references that appear below are included both in the original and in their English translation to facilitate understanding.

Euromonitor (1990) *The World Hotel Industry: Strategy 2000*, Euromonitor, London.

Henau, E. (1989) *Toerisme-onderwijs, Eindverslag en beleidssuggesties (Tourism education: report and suggestions for policy)*. Unpublished report, December 1989.

Henau, E. (1990) Toerisme onderwijs, We leren om te reizen (Tourism education – we learn to travel). *Trends – Financieel – Economisch Magazine*, 27 December.

Heyvaert, J. (1984) Toerisme onderwijs in Vlaanderen, Een evaluatie van doelstellingen en onderwijsprogramma (Tourism education in Flanders: an evaluation of aims and education programmes). *Persoon en Gemeenscap*, No. 10.

OECD (1988) *Tourism Policy and International Tourism in OECD Countries*, OECD, Paris, p. 17.

Verbruggen-Aelterman, A. (1989) De behoefte aan een navormingscyclus voor leerkrachten toerisme (The need of training for tourism teachers). *ICL – mededelingen*, No. 23–24.

10   Canada
Michael Haywood
and Jim Pickworth

Canada and its tourism industry

As one of the leading industrialized nations in the world, Canada has earned a reputation as a resource-rich country. Its economic prosperity and high standard of living are usually associated with forestry, agriculture, fishing and mining. However, Canada's success as a trading nation relies as much on the export of manufactured goods and a wide variety of services including tourism. In 1990, for example, tourism was Canada's third largest export industry. Expenditures by international visitors exceeded 7.4 billion dollars. As Figure 10.1 reveals, tourism as an export industry generates more foreign exchange than lumber, newsprint or wheat. In fact, tourism in Canada represents a $21.6 million industry or the equivalent of about 4% of Canada's gross domestic product. While Canadians spent a forecasted $14.2 billion on domestic travel and related products and services within their country in 1990, they also have a strong need to travel abroad. Travel payments in 1990 amounted to $12.0 billion, creating a deficit in the travel account of $4.5 billion, an amount that has increased steadily since 1967.

Canada's tourism industry supports numerous sectors of the Canadian economy. Tourism Canada, the federal agency responsible for national tourism policy, marketing and development, suggests that the tourism dollar is distributed 45% to transportation, 21% to food and beverage service, 16% to accommodation, 7% to recreation and entertainment and 11% to a wide variety of other types of businesses. These expenditures generate employment for 632 000 Canadians working in 60 000 core tourism businesses (see Table 10.1)

Human resource situation

Approximately 13 million people out of a total population of just more than 26 million are part of the Canadian labour force. Employment and

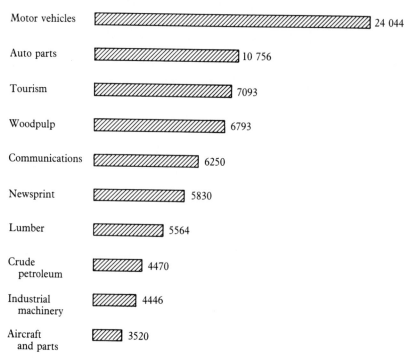

Figure 10.1 *Export earnings by sector, 1989 ($ million). (Source:* Bank of Canada Review, March 1990)

Immigration Canada forecast an annual 1.2% growth in overall employment until the year 2000. This slow growth in labour supply is a function of the nation's demographics. Between 1981 and 1986, Canada's population grew by no more than one million people to 25.3 million. This 4.2% population growth is the lowest intercensal rate since the country's confederation, and will remain low unless there are major changes to the country's immigration policies. As a result, it is estimated that approximately 180 000 persons per year will enter the labour force during the 1990s, as compared to the 'baby boom' years when 200 000 per year were added to the labour force during the 1980s and 300 000 during the 1970s.

During the 1990s Canada's employers will have to adjust to a labour force that will become significantly different. With slower population growth, the share of the labour force made up of younger people, 15–24 years old, will fall from 22% in 1986 to 17% by 2000. In comparison, the percentage of the labour force over 34 years of age will increase from 49% in 1986 to 60% in 2000. The implications are numerous. For

126

example, older Canadians are likely to have less job mobility during economic downturns; those employees likely to be thrown out of work will be older people with families; overall pressures for adjustment, e.g. learning new skills, will demand more adaptability and flexibility from older workers; employers will find it necessary to provide greater opportunities and support to women, native people and visible minorities if they are to participate more fully in the mainstream; and as the Canadian workforce becomes increasingly diverse, hiring, training and many management practices will have to change.

Demographic transitions will reduce the overall labour force to levels below the number of jobs available. Consequently, the ability to attract employees will become an increasingly critical factor particularly for these firms with a large workforce. Changing family structure (single parents, single adults and dual career families) and the increasing need to care for the elderly mean greater pressure on employees, leading to added stress in balancing work and family. Already there is a noticeable increase in provision of child care programmes at work as well as changes in benefit packages to meet the needs of diverse family structures.

Economic, technological and social conditions over the past two decades are culminating in new forms of industrial globalization. The impact on the Canadian labour force will be immense. Unable to compete on the basis of a cheap source of labour, Canadian manufacturers are already discovering that they have little option but to focus on specialized and knowledge-based products. With greater emphasis on utilizing technology to stimulate economic growth through increased productivity, new types of jobs demanding a different and a more sophisticated set of skills will be required. Nowhere is this more evident than in the burgeoning service sector.

Employment and Immigration Canada reports that increasing domination by the service sector has resulted in creating a situation in which for every one person in manufacturing there are four people currently employed in services. In fact approximately 1.25 million net new service jobs were created during the 1980s. These jobs fall into two basic categories: traditional service jobs characterized by low productivity and low pay, and skilled service jobs which are knowledge-based and highly paid. In all service industries, however, there is a drive to incorporate new technologies, often computer-based, and to focus on building competitive advantage through quality/value enhancement. Consequently, there is an increasing demand for more competent employees. To attract these employees, however, employers are realizing the necessity of improving the quality of employment through a wide variety of measures such as greater investment in training and skill upgrading, better salary and benefit packages.

127

Employment and Immigration Canada predict that of all the jobs to be created before the end of the century close to two-thirds will require more than 12 years of education and training, and almost half will require more than 17 years of education and training. However, the educational statistics are gloomy. Almost 60% of the current labour force have no more than secondary school education and 28% of students drop out of secondary school. Even in a developed country like Canada, it has been estimated that 24% of the adult population is illiterate – people who lack the necessary skills to fill out a job application form, read an instructions manual let alone participate in more sophisticated training programmes. Much of this may be attributed to the fact that Canada has a significant native population and a relatively large number of recent immigrants.

Traditionally, the response to change has focused on enhancing either financial, marketing or technological capabilities. While emphasis on these three capabilities will intensify, competitive advantage will ultimately come from inside organizations. It is the people within organizations who make the difference. It is inadequate simply to enact strategies. They must be executed by people who think, make decisions, allocate resources and act to meet customer expectations. The challenge, in short, will be to build a human resource capability.

Building human resource capability in Canada's tourism industry is not an easy task. The industry is comprised of a highly fragmented and diverse array of businesses operating in the lodging, foodservice, transportation, travel trade, recreation, attractions and other related industrial sectors. What follows is a brief explanation of the structure of Canada's hospitality industry. While there are a few large corporations operating in the transport and lodging sectors, most of the 632 000 people employed in the tourism industry work for small independent businesses. For example, in 1988 (the most recent year for available information) less than 2% of the 8900 hotels and motels operating in Canada had 200 guest rooms or more. Of the 14 521 accommodation locations in 1988, 4990 were hotels, 3910 motels, 1557 tourist courts, and cabins, guest houses and tourist homes, 2337 camping grounds and travel trailer parks, and 1727 recreation and vacation camps. Industry receipts were $7573.2 million in 1988 with an estimated payroll in the range of $1790 million. It is estimated that 154 000 employees were working in the accommodation industry in 1989.

Census 1986 data (the most recent available) provide information on the number of males and females in a variety of accommodation jobs. Females made up 64% of the supervisors, 91% of the cleaners, 0% of the bellmen and 39% of the 'other' category. Median age of male supervisors was 47 years, that for females was 43 years. Among those jobs involving some form of cleaning the average age was 36 for females, 28 for males. Census data also show males, whether working as supervisors or cleaners, averaging higher annual incomes than females.

Though not entirely associated with tourism, in the foodservice industry (with restaurant, caterer and tavern receipts amounting to $17.8 billion in 1990) there were 541 000 people employed in 1989. Salaried employees comprised 14% of the workforce, and the remainder were hourly employees. Census data in 1986 provide interesting information on the composition of the foodservice labour force. Of the approximately 622 000 identified (including some food-service employees in the accommodation industry), two-thirds were women with an average age of 27.4 years, whereas the remaining one-third had an average age of 24.4 years. The largest category of employees was comprised of food and beverage servers, which numbered 263 000 and comprised 42% of the workforce.

Comparisons between male and female foodservice workers are quite revealing. There is a pay differential, ranging from 27% less for bartenders and women servers through 21% for women chefs/cooks to 7% less for women food preparers. Approximately 9% of foodservice employees identified themselves as being supervisors, 51% of whom were women. Chefs and cooks accounted for 189 000 employees, of whom 51% were male. Of the 42 000 bartenders, 57% were female. There were 263 people classified as food and beverage servers, and they were predominantly (80%) female. Finally, 47 000 people, 86% of whom were women, were employed in the area of food and beverage preparation. (Note these figures do not correspond with Table 10.1 because not all foodservice employees are considered part of the tourism industry.)

Comparable data for other sectors of the tourism industry have not been presented owing to limitations of space, but it is known that in 1986 approximately 60 900 people were employed in air transport and 145 200 in recreation. A summary of the tourism labour force for 1988 is contained in Table 10.1.

Education and training for tourism

While the specific educational background of the labour force in the tourism industries is not known, the majority of people entering the industry do so with little or no skills training. With the key to high-quality service in the tourism industry being a skilled and professional workforce, it is promising to witness cooperation between provincial and federal governments and industry associations in a number of initiatives, such as the establishment of certification programmes. For

Table 10.1 *Canada's tourism labour force, 1988*

Job category	Number of jobs directly attributable to tourism
Managers and supervisors	72 680
Chef/cook	97 960
Waiter/waitress	151 680
Bartender	21 488
Hotel clerk	6952
Lodging cleaner	17 696
Unskilled	22 120
Travel clerk/agent	15 800
Guide	3160
Travel attendant	4424
Total tourism – specific occupations	413 960
Non-tourism – specific occupations	218 040
Total	632 000

Source: Industry, Science and Technology Canada, Employment and Immigration Canada, Canadian Tourism Research Institute

example, the Tourism Industry Standards and Certification Committee (TISCC) with the support of Industry, Science and Technology Canada–Tourism, and Employment and Immigration Canada has a mandate to:

- Provide a forum for the cooperative development of one set of national occupational standards, established by industry, for tourism industry occupations
- Provide a forum for the cooperative development of nationally recognized, industry-based certification programmes based on national standards
- Provide a forum for the exchange of information on standards and certification to maximize resources and avoid duplication
- Provide a forum for the exchange of information on other human resource activities of member organizations which relate to standards and certification

In response to the lack of competency-based standards in the hospitality/tourism industries, various organizations have recently developed certification programmes. For example, the Canadian Restaurant and Foodservice Association has developed the Certified Foodservice Manager programme; and, since its formation in 1987, the Alberta Tourism Education Council has become a leader in the development of competency-based standards and examinations for occupations in the hospitality industry. Along with other provincial counterparts, such as the Pacific Rim Institute of Tourism, these institutions will continue to act as coordinators and catalysts for the development of tourism education and training. Interest from the industry in these programmes is high, although it is too early to judge their impact.

Many Provincial governments have joined with corporate sponsors to put on training programmes designed to improve service to visitors. The focus of these programmes is to provide smaller firms with a training package that can be used to develop a greater awareness of the importance of customer service. In Ontario, for example, the Ministry of Tourism and Recreation created the Tourism Awareness and Hospitality Training Programme; British Columbia has established the 'SuperHost' programme and Alberta has started Alberta's Best. These programmes will be discussed in more detail later in this chapter.

At a more institutional level, hospitality and tourism education and training in Canada are well established though their history is quite recent. As a provincial responsibility the development of programmes really got under way in the 1960s with the establishment and expansion of the two year post-secondary technical community college system. Prior to this time Ryerson Polytechnic and British Columbia Institute of Technology were the only educational institutions offering courses in this field of study. The first university or degree programme in hospitality management was established at the University of Guelph in 1969. In comparison to the United States, which currently has in excess of 100 two-year programmes and over 150 four-year programmes, hospitality and tourism education does not appear to be as firmly established if you assume that Canada's industry is one-tenth the size of that in the USA. At present there are about 12 700 students per year taking some type of hospitality course whether they be four weeks or four years in duration, or offered at a vocational school or a university. What follows is a brief review of programmes at community colleges, universities and in the area of executive development.

The largest community college in Canada is George Brown College with over 1700 full-time students alone and a faculty in excess of 50. A wide range of courses is offered, including baking and cook apprenticeships, foodservice and bartending, culinary management, hotel front office and reception, and food and beverage management. More than 30 community colleges exist across the country, offering a similar range of courses. There are, however, two exceptions to this pattern. First, L'Institut de Tourisme et Hotelier in Montreal has adopted a European model of education and utilizes a 42 room teaching hotel as part of its facilities. Likewise, the Culinary Institute of Canada in Prince Edward Island has a curriculum that is 80 per cent practical and competency-based.

There are four university level programmes in hospitality and tourism management. In Ontario, Ryerson Polytechnic and the University of Guelph both graduate over 100 students per year. The two most recent programmes, at the University of Calgary and at Mount St Vincent in Nova Scotia, are just beginning to graduate students.

The availability of executive development programmes is somewhat limited. The Canadian Restaurant and Foodservice Association offers a programme of one-day seminars in addition to various short courses provided by community colleges. A part-time certificate programme is offered for practising managers through Ryerson Polytechnic. With respect to senior hospitality executives, the University of Guelph has developed one-week and three-week residential courses. These courses are modelled after the Harvard Business School's Advanced Management Programme and make extensive use of case studies which are all based on the hospitality industry. Those cases, which exceed 80, are now used in many countries.

Issues in the human resource area

The hospitality and tourism industries are people-intensive. Changes in demographics, sectoral shifts in the economy, the structure of occupations and technology are of critical concern if the industries are to remain competitive and continue to grow. The top human resource priorities for 1991 as identified by almost 600 industry executives are noted in Figure 10.2, however, the major issues of concern that are discussed here and make mention of some of these priorities are: labour shortage; recruitment and industry image; employment retention; and productivity and quality – the need for training and technology.

Labour shortage

During the late 1980s, Canada began to experience a chronic labour shortage. In some areas of the country, such as Southern Ontario, the shortage curtailed the expansion plans for foodservice companies. In order to appreciate the underlying dynamics of the labour shortage, it is necessary to focus first on studies identifying future demand for hospitality/tourism employment.

In 1989, the estimated size of the hospitality workforce was 695 000 (not all hospitality workers are deemed to be in the tourism industry) with 541 000 working in the foodservice sector and 154 000 in the

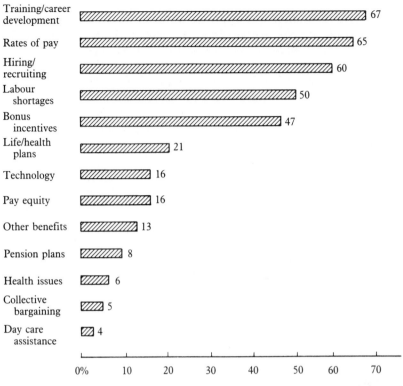

Figure 10.2   *Top human resource priorities for 1991 (number of respondents = 586).* (*Source*: Canadian Tourism Research Institute, 1990, *Compensation Planning Outlook for 1991 – Tourism and Hospitality Industry*, 3rd edn)

lodging sector. It has been estimated by Employment and Immigration Canada that this number could rise to about 935 000 employees by 1995, a 35% increase over the six-year period compared with a projected increase over the same time period for the transportation sector of 4.4% and for the recreation sector of 13.6%. Given that Employment and Immigration Canada forecast an annual 1.2% growth in overall employment for Canada these projected increases in demand for employees seem high. However, it is interesting to note that employment in Ontario grew by 28% during the previous six-year period from 1983 and most of these jobs were in the foodservice service, which had grown at a compound rate of approximately 7.4% per year, as compared to 4.3% for the accommodation sector. Although projections for the early part of the 1990s will be affected by the prevailing economic state of affairs within the country, it is clear that continued strong growth in tourism/hospitality services may be constrained by the availability of workers.

Projected demand for employees includes current vacancies and does not necessarily represent new job creation. A study by Laventhol and Horwath (1989) in Ontario found that the overall job vacancy rate was just over 9.0%. There were 2.3 full-time and 2.3 part-time vacancies in the average accommodation business. Given that more than 75% of the labour force in the hospitality industry is classified as semi-skilled or non-skilled, as would be expected the greatest shortages were in non-skilled positions such as waiting staff, bus-persons, kitchen helpers, bellpersons and chamber maids/boys. In the semi-skilled and skilled job categories, there is a shortage of cooks, host/hostesses and captains. For some jobs, such as reservations, janitors and foodservice managers/supervisors, the shortage is most evident with respect to part-time positions.

Another factor affecting demand for labour is the impact of industry seasonality. One provincial study has shown that employment, not unexpectedly, picks up in March each year and falls off slightly in December, although seasonality varies considerably from one region to another, as may be evidenced by the winter resort market in the West. The traditional sources of seasonal labour are students or young people under the age of 24, and this population segment is declining in size. The proportion of people aged 15–24 entering the labour force is expected to decline from 21.9% in 1986 to 17.1% by 2000. This is a further reason for concern among industry executives.

This pattern of labour shortages began to emerge as early as 1986, when the Canadian Restaurant and Foodservice Association (CFRA) conducted a national survey. Based on the responses of 290 firms, approximately 70% reported shortages of cooks, 61% of kitchen help, 50% of service staff and 41% of supervisory and management positions.

Recruitment and industry image

Recruitment has long since been considered the major human resource issue, particularly during periods of economic growth. As a framework for considering the various dimensions of the problem, the model (Figure 10.3) developed by Nightingale (1990) is useful.

Traditionally, the hospitality industry has depended on teenagers (still in or just leaving school) to fill many of the front-line positions. As previously stated, however, owing to demographic changes this source of labour will diminish throughout the 1990s. Although the hospitality industry will have to rely less on this segment of the labour market, its ability to attract young people should not be under-estimated. A survey by the CRFA established that one in three

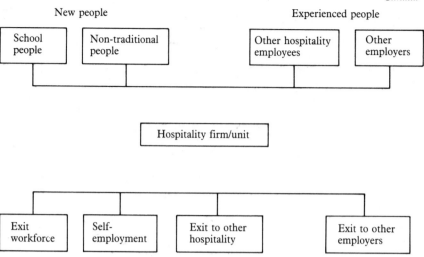

Figure 10.3 *Employment movement model.* (*Source*: Michael Nightingale, 1990, Labour market issues in the hospitality industry. Presentation to AMPHI Policy Advisory Board, Toronto, Ontario)

Canadians has in fact worked in the industry at some point in time. Another traditional source of labour, especially for skilled positions such as chefs, has been immigrants. Immigration rose substantially in the late 1980s, in part as a result of intense lobbying by the CRFA, which demonstrated widespread support among its membership for raising the quotas.

Non-traditional sources of labour include senior citizens, handicapped, and other disadvantaged groups. There is ample anecdotal evidence to indicate these segments of the labour market have responded positively to a well-organized recruitment campaign.

An alternative source of labour is experienced employees who have worked either in other service sectors or in other industries. The case is frequently made that the poor wages and working conditions within the hospitality industry are not conducive to recruitment in these areas. With respect to wages, however, hourly rates have now come to compare favourably to retailing, a major competitor for labour, with a gap of only a few percentage points between the two sectors for salaried positions in particular. Clearly, wages are less of a deterrent to switching sectors than previously; more of a problem in recruiting people is the industry's image. Stressful working conditions, long and unsociable work schedules, low pay, hard work and few benefits are perceived to be the norm. To some extent these perceptions are true, but the realities of jobs and career potentials generally are not fully appreciated. Over the years various industry associations have worked in a piecemeal fashion to enhance the image of the industry but to little avail. The recent labour crunch, however, has forced many of the major firms to become actively involved in improving the image of the industry even though some would seem to be interested in serving their own strategic needs in order to be perceived as an 'employer of choice'.

The process of becoming an 'employer of choice', however, has implications for becoming an 'industry of choice'. One company conducted surveys to determine what motivated, bothered and challenged its employees. Realizing that there would be an increasing diversity of ethnic groups working for the company, the chief executive officer committed, with financial resources, a major language training programme for supervisors and employees. The company embarked on a series of other activities: training programmes, career opportunities and job variety for existing employees; joint-venture internship programmes with high schools and colleges; new work design programmes to give employees feelings of ownership and responsibility for their work areas; and the hiring of retired employees who wanted part-time work. Each divisional manager was given responsibility for setting standards for becoming the 'employer of choice' and these standards were translated into managerial rewards and incentives.

Employee retention

As the recruitment and replacement of workers becomes increasingly difficult, more attention is being paid to employee retention. For example, the Canadian Tourism Research Institute's Compensation Planning Outlook for 1991 discovered that turnover rates for food-service occupations is up to five times the rate reported in other industries. A study commissioned by Employment and Immigration Canada, the Human Resource Study of the Foodservice Industry (Ernst and Young, 1990), indicated that 23% of organizations reported turnover rates in excess of 100% for one or more occupations, and a further 31% had turnover rates of 50–99% for one or more occupations. The cost of turnover was estimated by industry participants to be in the order of $1500 per line employee and $2500 per management employee.

Employee turnover is greatest in the major urban areas where cost of living is highest and a wide variety of job opportunities is available. Consequently, turnover is often associated with wages; however, the explanation for turnover is more complex. First of all the definition of turnover is not clear. For example, should it include full-, part-time and seasonal employees? The hospitality and tourism industries also attract a larger proportion of young employees, many of whom are working part-time and/or are not interested in a permanent position, so job mobility is to be expected. Then there is the question as to what people do when they leave a job. The study of human resource and training needs in the Ontario hospitality industry in 1989 (Laventhol and Horwath, 1989), commissioned by the Ministries of Skills Development, Tourism and Recreation, and colleges and universities, discovered that only 35% of those people who leave their place of employment do so to get out of the industry. A vast amount of turnover represents, therefore, a movement by individuals who want either a more compatible place in which to work, more responsibility, better wages, job variety or even to become self-employed. Experts and focus group interviews revealed that while outsiders characterize the industry as a less-than-ideal place to work, those employed in the industry like the work environment.

Wages are of major concern to all people working in the industry. Among the 16–24 age group it might have been expected that a reduced labour force resulting from a smaller population, combined with rising educational attainment, would increase youth wages in the 1980s. But instead, by 1986 the inflation adjusted average hourly wage of young workers was considerably lower than in the early part of the decade. According to Statistics Canada the average 'real' wage of workers aged 16–24 in 1986 was down 17% from 1981, the hourly wage for 25–34 year olds was also lower, but only by 5% while the average real wage for workers aged 35 and over was up by 6%. This drop in real wages can be attributed to an increase in part-time work since part-time workers are often paid less than full-time workers, industrial restructuring resulting in greater youth employment in consumer services, and a legacy of the 1981–2 recession when unemployment was 22% for 15–24 year old males and 17% for females. During the 1990s this pattern of lower wages and wage differentials between male and female employees is likely to turn around. As Canada's economy restructures and identifies value-added services and products, more intense competition for employees based on wages and benefits will occur. Industry labour costs will have to rise, forcing many employers to find new ways of increasing productivity.

Productivity and quality: the need for training and technology

In a study of the accommodation, food and beverage industry in Canada (Scarfe and Kranz, 1988), it was revealed that the industry suffers from declining and very low rates of productivity. Information from Statistics Canada further indicates that the productivity of the foodservice/accommodation sector declined in real terms over the period 1975–88. In comparison to the Canadian economy, output per hour in 1988 was $7.21 compared to $16.51 for all industries, and 44% of the productivity level for the economy as a whole compared to 60% in 1975. While lower productivity levels are typical of hospitality services because of the need for personalized service, it is only through productivity gains that it will be possible to increase real income levels. Unfortunately, in comparison to the industry in the USA, hospitality/ tourism in Canada is subject to great degrees of seasonal demand, relies more on part-time labour, has high minimum wage levels and contributions to a social service net for employees are larger. Short of laying people off, productivity is difficult to increase. Many firms are discovering, though, that the secret to evaluating, measuring and improving productivity must be based on consideration of service excellence or quality; and quality must be judged from the perspective of the customer's expectations.

Strategic planning documents coming out of provincial and federal ministries of tourism all espouse a commitment to enhancing the visitor experience. However, as the report Human Resource and Training Needs within Ontario's Hospitality Industry (Laventhol and Horwath, 1989) reveals, few employers have established a true 'service culture' in which the visitor experience is really taken seriously. This neglect is partially due to the fact that managers and supervisors have not been given or have not acquired the proper skills to develop a 'service culture'. As a consequence the appropriate recruiting, inter-viewing, selection, training and evaluation skills necessary to encourage and develop employees are lacking. And the effort and expense of training are even considered wasteful due to high employee turnover. It is little wonder that productivity is so low. So how can productivity improvements be made?

During the 1990s the labour intensiveness of the industry will continue to remain high but technical innovation will become an increasingly important ingredient in contributing to productivity and quality. Most organizations expect to see further penetration of computerized systems and information networks, but do not expect that these will displace workers. Rather, employees will have to develop a new range of computer skills in order to manage inventories, make reservations or control costs.

There is an expectation that 'soft' process innovations, such as changes in the organization of the workplace, the decision-making process and the design of jobs, are likely to have a more profound impact on improving productivity and quality than 'hard' technology.

In some leading firms attempts have been made to give employees more responsibility and authority to make decisions; incentive and reward programmes have been designed to reward superior performance; and, management is providing employees with more information on company performance so that they can understand the contributions they make as well as become more familiar with the complex operating environment. It is actions and activities such as these that enhance the 'service culture' of an organization and strengthen employee commitment to a particular company if not the industry. However, implementation of these 'soft' technologies will require a wholesale change in management attitudes towards, and skills in working with, employees. Simply training employees to become more productive is insufficient. Education and training must play a critical role in helping managers and supervisors meet strategic and tactical objectives and maintain a high level of staff competency and vitality as the pace of change quickens and the organization's operating environment becomes more complex.

Initiatives and innovative activities

Tourism Canada, in their first-ever federal policy for the development of Canada's tourism potential, has made an important commitment to the industry:

> With respect to human resource development, the federal government will provide 'best case' scenarios to the tourism industry to demonstrate the value of training. It will disseminate the results of its work on research standards and certification and career awareness. It will improve co-ordination among federal and provincial/territorial policies, programs, and agendas in the area of human resource development. Statistics Canada and Employment and Immigration Canada (EIC) will analyze and evaluate supply/demand data to permit better human resource planning by industry and other levels of government. A Memorandum of Understanding will be drawn up between the federal government and the tourism industry to promote human resource planning and to overcome problems. The needs of the tourism industry will be incorporated into EIC's Labour Force Development Strategy. And the newly formed Department of Multi-culturalism and Citizenship will assist the Canadian tourism industry in providing culturally sensitive services and in managing a multicultural labour force. (*Tourism on the Threshold*, 1990)

Progress on some of these activities has already commenced and various provincial governments are pursuing similar developments. Throughout this chapter reference has been made to a number of

139

studies which focus on improving the industry workforce. The research and effort that went into preparing such documents as the Human Resources Study of the Food Services Industry (Ernst and Young, 1990), and Human Resource and Training Needs within Ontario's Hospitality Industry (Laventhol and Horwath, 1989), is indicative that the human resource problem is finally receiving the attention from government, industry and the academic institutions that is deserved. Other research has also been undertaken. The provinces of Alberta, British Columbia, Saskatchewan, Newfoundland and Labrador, and the Northwest Territories have undertaken studies of their education and training needs for hospitality/tourism.

These studies have resulted primarily in cooperation among federal and provincial governments, and industry associations through the formation of the Tourism Industry Standards and Certification Committee, which, as previously mentioned, was established to develop standards certification of hospitality/tourism occupations. There is potential to certify more than 100 occupations within the industry. To date standards and certification for food and beverage servers, bartenders, foodservice executives, banquet/catering managers, kitchen helpers, events coordinators, maître d', hosts/hostesses, sales representatives, sales and marketing managers, wine stewards, guest services attendants and front desk agents have been completed – a process in which standards and examinations are developed and validated by industry. The development process also involves the production of standards manuals and testing materials.

It is too early to judge the success of this endeavour. Industry appears supportive but the big questions are whether or not individual firms will be willing to pay a premium for certified employees, and whether employees will view certification as a worthwhile endeavour which will yield professional recognition and reward as well as personal satisfaction.

With tourism becoming an increasingly important industry all provinces are attempting to increase public awareness of the value to the economy of providing quality services to every visitor. These tourism awareness programmes essentially have two components – training and public awareness. The training component is designed to provide training in service excellence and hospitality for staff and owners/managers. One-day seminars to employees usually include such topics as: excellence in visitor service, dealing with difficult situations, tourism awareness of the province, hospitality and maintaining a positive attitude. Some provinces also offer a two-day management seminar with additional information on business practices that foster good service – hiring, training, selling and communicating service goals, problem-solving, visitor complaints and encouraging employee performance through positive recognition.

Obviously, these training and public awareness programmes are expensive and little has been done to evaluate their true effectiveness. While they provide a means of making people aware of tourism and the importance of improving service, there is little potential for continuity and reinforcement unless a strong service culture exists within individual organizations. In other words, these programmes may simply heighten the deficiencies of management and a 'care less' attitude which, in turn, could intensify feelings of job dissatisfaction ultimately leading to employee turnover. In all fairness, however, a momentum for training may be under way. Many companies require employees to undertake training on sanitation, alcoholic beverage service in response to legislation or legal responsibilities. A consequence of this activity is that some companies have identified a need for other courses, such as customer service and train-the-trainer, that they believe would be of benefit to their employees.

Many of the leading firms, mainly chains such as Four Seasons, McDonalds and Canadian Pacific Hotels, recognize this problem and indeed are becoming more serious about their responsibilities to create a more appropriate service climate. Four critical elements are in evidence:

1 Shared service mindset. The stellar companies are attempting to create common ways of thinking about goals and the means used to reach these goals.
2 Management and human resource practices. Emphasis is being given to generating competencies within the company through careful employee selection and development. These competencies are then being reinforced through appraisal and rewards, and sustained through improved organizational design and communication.
3 Capacity for change. Increasingly more individuals within firms are being given greater power to make decisions and to influence others. A capacity for change is also evident through a company's ability to diagnose and manage change and to develop the competencies to build more flexible organizational arrangements.
4 Leadership. A strong service culture is being driven by leadership, from individuals with vision at all levels of a company. In other words leadership does not merely exist at the senior levels; leadership exists throughout a company because specific individual competencies are being provided to build leadership across a wide range of activities.

Unfortunately these large chain organizations and a few small, independent firms represent the exception rather than the rule. Industry managers tend to be rewarded more on short-term rather than long-term results; there are few if any measures used in corporations to assess guest satisfaction, to reward it, or to achieve service quality; and job training is largely informal or hit or miss. In other words many businesses may want their workers to be trained but make few provisions to ensure it. In fact companies may be wasting much of the job training they do engage in. For example, a company cannot improve service quality on a property-by-property basis through one-shot training programmes aimed at only a few critical jobs. The whole workforce must be trained and trained on a continuous basis. Training needs to be viewed more as an investment and less as an operating expense.

In a survey of companies carried out by the Canadian Tourism Research Institute in 1991, 50% of responding tourism organizations indicated that they did not have a formal training budget, and of those that did, 65% of the budgets were $5000 or less while another 32% were between $5000 and $50 000. During the period August 1990 to July 1991, however, 60% of the respondents said they planned to provide some type of formal training for their managers and senior staff. The number of respondents indicating provision of training for non-management staff indicated that 56% provided training for front desk clerks and 47–48% provided training for waiting staff, cooks and chambermaids. Certification training accounts for 8% of the training programmes for front desk personnel, 10% for waiting staff and 26% for cooks. The objectives for training in order of priority are to (1) improve productivity, (2) provide orientation, (3) aid in personal development, (4) develop careers, (5) enhance skill requirements and (6) meet regulatory requirements.

Of those companies that engage in training on a regular basis one of the problems is a lack of understanding as to how people actually perform work, acquire skills and learn to solve problems on the job. Only now are trainers realizing that the training of employees has to be supported with physical material and real actions that reflect the social complexity of the workplace. Yet for many jobs there also needs to be a bridge between theoretical learning and actual practice. Leading firms are using simulated workplace and even simulated 'social interactions' in company training classes, as may be evidenced by the increasing usage of interactive videos.

The need for bridging between theory and practice is also required in the colleges and universities that provide education and training for the industry. While tremendous strides have been made to provide a wide variety of educational and training programmes, industry has been quite critical of the educational institutions. Complaints made include the following: an inadequate number of competent instructors; unreasonably high expectations of students about their jobs and careers; insufficient attention to development of people skills; and the low number of graduates who actually stay in the industry. In response, curricula are changing to emphasize people, interpersonal and service skills; some institutions such as the University of Guelph are implementing cooperative education programmes; graduate programmes to train future managers and teachers are being initiated at the Universities of Guelph and Calgary; and community colleges are becoming actively involved in offering the certification courses developed by industry in cooperation with government and industry associations.

A future perspective

Canada's federal and provincial governments recognize that tourism is a vital industry that offers immense opportunities for the future. Despite short-term setbacks, the conditions for continued and extensive growth in international tourism are profound. Expanding world trade, rising real disposable incomes, the ageing of the baby boom generation, and other factors are intensifying consumer demand for business and pleasure travel. At the same time, however, there are forces of change that are making it difficult to achieve competitive advantage. Traveller's demands and needs are changing: changing demographics, time scales, psychographic profiles and overall expectations are challenging existing approaches to tourism development and marketing. Governments around the world are giving a prominent role to tourism in their economic development policies. New strategic alliances between public and private sectors are becoming more common so as to ensure faster response to creating new development initiatives, to encourage a greater degree of commitment among all parties, to ensure higher standards of service, and to foster better research and innovative activity. As Canadian governments continue to place emphasis on protecting and enhancing the country's natural, cultural and man-made resources in an effort to achieve sustainable development, infrastructure will need to be improved and more emphasis will have to be put on education and training to foster the skills necessary to make Canada an internationally competitive tourism destination.

Though attention will be given to improving internationally recognized destination areas such as the Rockies, regional gateways, speciality tourism experiences and themed route-ways, the one area which definitely calls out for continued government–industry partnership is the education and training of Canada's tourism workforce. Since tourism's ultimate goal is a satisfied visitor, the process of achieving quality service will require that tourism organizations go beyond espoused versions of slogans such as 'People are our most important asset'. Tourism awareness and hospitality training programmes such as British Columbia's 'Superhost', Ontario's 'We'll Make You Feel Incredible!', and 'Alberta's Best' are initial steps in the right direction. However, during the 1990s more work will have to be put into determining not only *what* needs to be done but *how* it needs to be done. In terms of human resource development more effort will have to be focused on the process of creating and implementing a human resource strategy than merely on its content.

It is through interactions with tourism's workforce that visitors experience responsiveness, relationships and service quality. Successful tourism firms have found that the biggest single factor in visitor satisfaction and loyalty is the perceived responsiveness of employees. Training employees to be sensitive, supportive and responsive will become a major element in creating and maintaining a positive tourism image. As employees develop good feelings about a company and the tourism industry, they help build positive images and customer loyalty through the building of relationships. In turn these relationships will be fostered through an emphasis on service quality – a strategic weapon that many Canadian tourism organizations might find difficult to implement:

> Organizations concerned with having a competitive edge for the 1980s, 90s and beyond must develop two capacities. The first is the ability to think strategically about service and to build a strong service orientation around and into the vision of their strategic future. The second capacity, which is the more difficult to develop, is the ability to effectively and efficiently manage the design, development, and delivery of service. In our view, the ability to manage the production and delivery of a service differs from the ability to manage the production and delivery of a commodity. (Albrecht and Zemke, 1985)

The ability to achieve service quality among a diverse set of tourism businesses and organizations will be a major challenge. It will require changing methods of managing people, technology, costs, products and services. In other words, it will require pervasive new ways of thinking among all people in the industry.

An example of this new way of thinking about people and their development is contained in an exemplary and comprehensive model for tourism education and training. In the provinces of Alberta and British Columbia:

- Industry and government are working together to develop strategies to meet short-term training needs, while building educational processes to enhance the competence of industry employees over the long term; and
- Educational and training programmes at all levels are being related so as to emphasize career development rather than merely job training (Pollock and Ritchie, 1990).

These strategies are structured around all sectors of the industry, areas of commonality and various levels of occupational activity and skill. Skills, knowledge and competencies are being identified for each occupational level as are the appropriate approaches to programme delivery.

To some extent this strategic approach will help overcome some of the industry's pressing labour-related problems, so long as there is continuity of funding and sustained commitment by all sectors of industry. Anything less could be abortive. However, more attention to workers at the organizational level is critical. After decades of benign neglect and scrimping on human capital, the industry has an obligation to take action. With regard to education and training there is a need to:

- Commit to being a provider of effective, focused solutions for education and training
- Inform stakeholders – employees, stockholders, customers – of the seriousness of the problem
- Develop an action plan, and publicize it
- Create awards for excellence in education and training

As the hospitality/tourism industry enters a new century, other opportunities for action are immense. Canadian firms should attempt to do the following:

- Help hospitality/tourism become the 'industry of job or career choice'
- Focus on becoming 'employers of choice'
- Foster a 'service culture' which allows everyone to excel in the provision of service
- Help workers become literate
- Identify and agree on 'certifiable excellence' in jobs and establish ways in which people can work towards achieving it
- Pay employees fair and equitable wages – equal pay for equal work
- Provide managers and supervisors with the appropriate skills to select, interview, train, develop, motivate and reward employees

(employees who may have diverse cultures, languages and value systems)

- Encourage and support employee training and development programmes
- Find ways to measure service quality and reward for its achievement so that everyone in the Canadian tourism industry can proudly say, 'We absolutely guarantee service.'

References

Albrecht, K. and Zemke, R. (1985) *Service America: doing business in the new economy*, Dow-Jones Irwin, Homewood, Ill. 18.

Canadian Tourism Research Institute (1991) *Compensation Planning Outlook for 1991 – Tourism and Hospitality Industry*. Conference Board of Canada, Ottawa, Ontario.

Ernst and Young, (1990) *Human Resources Study of the Food Service Industry*, Employment and Immigration Canada, Ottawa, Ontario.

Laventhol and Horwath (1989) *Human Resource and Training Needs Within Ontario's Hospitality Industry*, Ontario Ministries of Skills Development, Tourism and Recreation, and Colleges and Universities, Toronto, Ontario

Nightingale, M. (1990) Labour Market Issues in the Hospitality Industry. Presentation made to the Advanced Management Program for the Hospitality Industry Council, Toronto, Ontario.

Pollock, A. and Ritchie, J. R. B. (1990) Integrated strategy for tourism education training. *Annals of Tourism Research*, **17**(4), 568–85.

Scarfe, B. L. and Kranz, M. (1988) *The Market for Hospitality: an Economic Analysis of the Accommodation, Food and Beverage Industry*, The Fraser Institute, Vancouver BC.

Tourism Canada (1990) *Tourism on the Threshold*, Industry, Science and Technology Canada, Ottawa, Ontario.

11 The Caribbean
Michael Conlin

Introduction

Human resource development has increasingly received a tremendous amount of attention in both the public and academic literature. This attention suggests a growing awareness and understanding about the importance of employees and managers in the success of tourism products. This attention comes at a very timely stage in the development of tourism generally because tourism consumers are changing. Consumers are becoming more sophisticated in their tourism product preferences, better informed about tourism product performance, and more aware of the various tourism products available. The result is that they are increasingly becoming more critical of the tourism product and are demanding value and quality to a much greater degree than they did in the past. If a product, be it a specific hotel property, tourist attraction or a regional product such as the Caribbean region, does not offer the value which consumers expect for their expenditure in time and money, they will look elsewhere when the next purchase decision arises.

The increasing interest and concern for human resource development in the tourism industry can be seen as a natural outcome of the increasing maturity of the industry. Like its consumers, the industry is also more sophisticated, better informed, and aware of the competitive situation than was the case in past decades. The industry increasingly realizes that as consumers become more critical, service quality levels become critical to success and that employees are an integral part of the tourism product's success.

A consideration of any tourism product adds support to this notion. The anticipated consumer satisfaction expected by the finest resort facility can quickly become damaging dissatisfaction if the front desk personnel do not meet the consumer's expectations which have been created, in part, by the property's marketing communications programme. The most stunning landscape or interesting attraction may seem like a nightmare in the presence of a rude or unknowledgeable guide, a surly taxi driver or an incompetent operator. And worse, a truly exciting national or regional destination may never achieve the consumer satisfaction anticipated by expensive international promotional campaigns if the consumer's anticipation of a wonderful vacation is trampled at the airport by unfriendly immigration officers and confrontational customs officials. In short, all aspects of the tourism product are affected by the people involved with its delivery. Not just the people in the obvious, direct front-line positions, but all people connected in some way with the tourism product and the experience which the consumer expects from it.

This chapter will examine the issue of human resources within the Caribbean region. It will discuss human resource development in the region and the industry's perspective. Finally, it will identify the various organizations and processes currently in place to respond to the human resource challenge of the 1990s and suggest what these must do in order to ensure that Caribbean tourism will continue to be successful in this decade and beyond.

The Caribbean tourism environment

In discussing Caribbean tourism, it is necessary to keep in mind that there is no universally accepted definition of what the Caribbean is. The Caribbean Hotel Association (CHA) is the premier tourism industry association in the region and it has grappled with this issue for many years. Some of the general principles which it has adopted include considering any country, region or island which is either in the Caribbean Sea or which touches upon it as being part of the Caribbean. Thus, the membership of the CHA includes such obvious island destinations as Jamaica, Barbados and Trinidad but also some not so obvious resort areas such as Cancun and Cozumel. Indeed, the possibility exists that CHA membership may, in the future, include such countries as Panama, Colombia and other Latin American states since Venezuela and Belize already enjoy membership through their Caribbean Sea coastline connection. Table 11.1 lists the CHA membership and is a reasonable statement of what the Caribbean region encompasses.

It is also important to note that the region, no matter how it is defined, includes at least four language groupings. French, Dutch, English and Spanish speaking populations live in the region. In addition to the logistical problems which this multilingual situation sometimes gives rise to, each of the language groupings also embodies historical, cultural and social differences which give rise to a broad

Table 11.1 *Caribbean Hotel Association member countries and regions*

Anguilla	Honduras
Antigua	Jamaica
Aruba	Martinique
Bahamas	Montserrat
Barbados	Puerto Rico
Barbuda	Saba
Belize	St Barthelemy
Bermuda	St Croix
Bonaire	St Eustatius
British Virgin Islands	St John
Cancun	St Kitts/Nevis
Cayman Islands	St Lucia
Cozumel	St Maarten
Curacao	St Martin
Dominica	St Thomas
Dominican Republic	St Vincent and The Grenadines
Grenada	Trinidad and Tobago
Guadaloupe	Turks and Caicos Islands
Haiti	Venezuela

diversity of destination choices but which tend to mitigate against consistent concepts of service and human resource management. For example, Spanish language hospitality training tapes produced at the University of Mexico through the sponsorship of VISA are not accepted fully in other Spanish speaking countries such as Venezuela because they are perceived as being alien to that country's culture.

The geographical dispersion and economic condition of the islands and regions in the area must also be considered when examining human resource development in the Caribbean. The majority of destinations in the region are somewhat isolated from their main markets and are accordingly dependent upon airlines for their tourism survival. With few exceptions, they are characterized by weak economies. Much of their tourism product is comprised of small businesses, locally owned and managed. As a result, they tend to be heavily operations-orientated and bottom-line driven and accordingly insular in their approach to human resource development. They do not appear, as a whole, to have the level of acceptance for the need for human resource development compared with larger destinations. Because of these conditions, destinations do not have the resources or the sophistication necessary adequately to build up a solid national base of skilled tourism workers and managers through education and training.

In addition to these structural complexities, the Caribbean faces a number of industry-specific problems which tend to deprioritize the human resource issue. John Bell, the Executive Vice-President of the

CHA, has said that the region faces a crucial struggle for survival because of the competitive pressures created by the liberalization of Eastern Europe, the embrace of tourism by Cuba, the world-class service offered by the tourism product in the Pacific/Asia region, the exploitation of the Caribbean by cruise ship operators, and the US recession which has contributed to the resurgence of domestic tourism at the expense of the Caribbean (Bell, 1991).

Jean S. Holder, the Secretary General of the Caribbean Tourism Organization (CTO), points also to the problems which the region faces. He states that the region's performance, particularly with respect to its major market, the United States, has deteriorated since 1986 and he further suggests that this cannot be blamed on the current recession completely. US arrivals in the region dropped from 63% of the total in 1986 to 55% in 1990. This corresponds to a drop in the share of US travellers from 29% in 1986 to 23% in 1990. He suggests that these data may result from the umbrella marketing campaigns employed by regional competitors such as Florida, Hawaii, Canada and Mexico which far outstrip the marketing communications activities of the region (Holder, 1992).

In considering this situation, Holder concludes three things. First, based upon CTO market research, the majority of visitors to the Caribbean are satisfied with their experience. Thus, there is nothing fundamentally wrong with the Caribbean tourism product. Second, the majority of complaints involve what are ascribed to poor management, including complaints which are essentially human resource problems. Third, the region suffers from inadequate marketing, particularly in light of the marketing efforts of its competitors. Holder sums up the Caribbean's land-based tourism product's problem this way:

> We have failed to deliver it, pleasantly, courteously and professionally – everytime . . . everytime. (Holder, 1992)

This, then, is the challenge for human resource development in Caribbean tourism in the 1990s. The development of human resources within the industry is critical for the continued success of Caribbean tourism. Caribbean tourism is critical for the future development of the region. Accordingly, it is argued that human resource development within the industry is critical to the region as a whole, not just the industry.

The current human resource development environment

There are two principal areas of human resource development in Caribbean tourism: education and training. Both areas have major problems while at the same time, reasons for hope.

Education

Education's primary focus relating to human resource development for the tourism industry is at the tertiary level. There are several isolated examples of tourism awareness programmes directed at the primary and secondary education levels, such as the programmes found in the US Virgin Islands, and some secondary curricula touch on the subject of tourism. The CTO offers tourism awareness programmes in the region. The Organization of American States (OAS), through its Inter-American Travel Congress' Tourism Plurinational Project, Sub-Project F, also offers tourism awareness programmes designed to raise awareness in entire communities.

The majority of educational contribution to the industry, however, is at the tertiary level. There are approximately 24 schools and programmes within schools which have hospitality and tourism studies as their major concentration. These schools and programmes range widely in their focus, many of them being purely trade schools. A few, such as the University of the West Indies, several programmes found in universities in Puerto Rico, the Dominican Republic and in Latin America, and the diploma programmes at Bermuda College offer degree level education in hospitality and tourism studies. Many of the schools are also active in upgrading their programmes through cooperation with institutions and governments outside the region. The Curacao Hotel Training Centre and the Hotel Escuela de Venezuela in Merida enjoy a relationship with the Den Haag Hotel School in Holland which provides assistance in programme development, faculty strengthening, and can function as an external examining body. The Bahamas Hotel Training College in Nassau enjoys accreditation by the Southern Association of Colleges and Schools.

For the most part, however, the level of development of schools and programmes in the region is poor. John Bell, in discussing the state of the region's schools, states:

Despite the labor intensive nature of the hotel and tourism sector, and the many technical and practical skills involved, those hotel training schools, invariably government-owned, that do exist within the region are horribly underfunded, under-established and in general treated like low grade technical schools for the students who cannot make it into other careers. (Bell, 1991)

This observation says as much for the status of the industry as it does for the schools. The industry suffers from low prestige in much of the world and the Caribbean is no exception.

In a recent study of students at the University of the West Indies Centre for Hotel and Tourism Management in Nassau, Bahamas, several disturbing trends were identified. The study identified student likes and dislikes about the industry at two points in their academic career. The first point was at the beginning of the school's academic year. The second point was at the conclusion of the academic year. The study found that as the students progressed further in their hospitality and tourism studies, their concerns about quality of life issues such as long hours, shift work and the inherent stress of working in the industry increased dramatically. At the first point, 33.3% of those surveyed expressed concerns in this area. However, by the conclusion of their studies, 48.6% were concerned. The other concern which showed significant increase during their studies was the negative view of tourism perceived to be held in the region. At the first point, 7.7% of those surveyed mentioned this as a concern. By the end of the year, 17.1% were concerned. Finally, it is worth noting that whereas 60% of the students were satisfied with their career choice at the beginning of their studies, this proportion had dropped to 42% by the end of the programme. This is particularly troubling since the majority of students, 60%, also identified their internship experience as having had the major impact upon their perceptions of their career choice. The study concludes:

> This finding confirms the critical importance of the student's internship experience for shaping their attitudes and perceptions of their chosen careers and of the industry. It suggests that students' internship experience may have 'opened their eyes' to the reality of the Caribbean hospitality and tourism industry – a reality that may not have met their expectations and hence, the decrease in career satisfaction. (Charles, 1992)

What is required in hospitality and tourism education in the region is institutional strengthening. This is necessary to allow the schools and programmes to command the respect of their institutions and governments in order to access the necessary resources they need to upgrade their physical plants, their programmes, and their faculties. Several organizations active in the region have this express objective.

Council of Caribbean Hospitality Schools (CHOCHS)

CHOCHS was formed in November 1990 through the efforts of the Caribbean Regional Hotel Training Project and the Caribbean Hospitality Training Institute. Originally modelled after the European Association of Hotel School Directors (EUHOFA International), CHOCHS has modified its structure to that of an institutional member body consisting of tertiary programmes and schools of hospitality and tourism studies in colleges, universities and institutions in the region. The organization represents the majority of schools and programmes in the region. Table 11.2 lists the member schools.

Table 11.2 *Council of Caribbean Hospitality Schools*

Albena Lake-Lodge School, Anguilla
Antigua Hotel School
Bahamas Hotel Training College
Barbados Community College
Bermuda College
Caribbean Hospitality Training Institute
College of Arts, Science and Technology, Jamaica
Community College of the Cayman Islands
Curacao Hotel and Training Centre
Grenada National College
HEART Academy, Jamaica
Hotel School of Bonaire
Monserrat Secondary School
Sir Arthur Lewis Community College, St Lucia
Trinidad and Tobago Hotel School
University of the West Indies

Since its inception, CHOCHS has sponsored conferences in Nassau, Grand Cayman and St Lucia. These conferences have provided a forum for faculty and industry representatives to meet and discuss matters of mutual interest and concern. The conferences have also allowed for the sharing of ideas among schools and training institutes through the use of workshops and panel discussion sessions. Given the lack of resources from which the region's schools suffer, these activities are very valuable. The annual CHOCHS conference is often the only time when educators in the region can meet.

CHOCHS enjoys the strong support of the industry through its endorsement by the CHA and the Caribbean Hospitality Training Institute. This endorsement, approved at the 1992 CHA Board of Directors Meeting, is as follows:

High quality programmes of tertiary education and training in hospitality and tourism studies are critical to the success of tourism in the Caribbean. In order to foster the continuing development of high quality programmes, the Caribbean Hotel Association and the Caribbean Hospitality Training Institute recognize the Council of Caribbean Hospitality Schools (CHOCHS) as the representative body for tertiary schools, colleges, universities and institutes of training in the CHA region. This resolution recognizes the function of CHOCHS in developing important initiatives such as regional standards of education and training and the strengthening of its members institutions, programmes, and faculty.

In the sponsoring of its annual conferences, CHOCHS has also enjoyed the strong support of national governments and non-governmental organizations such as tourism boards. In light of this, CHOCHS has also requested the endorsement of the CTO for its activities.

In addition to the annual conferences, which foster cooperation among its member institutions, CHOCHS is actively investigating the concept of a regional programme accreditation scheme. Using the standards of the Accreditation Commission for Programs in Hospitality Administration (ACPHA), the accrediting body which had its genesis in the membership of International CHRIE, the predominantly US hospitality educational organization, CHOCHS is dedicated toward the development and implementation of a regional accreditation scheme. Such a scheme will assist all member institutions in strengthening their programmes and their faculty while recognizing regional differences.

With respect to the aim of a regional programme accreditation scheme, CHOCHS communicates with the Association of Caribbean Tertiary Institutions (ACTI). ACTI, whose members comprise the leadership of the schools in which CHOCHS members reside, is actively examining the concept of regional institutional accreditation. In this way, both organizations are pursuing parallel and complementary paths.

Confederacion Panamericana de Escuelas de Hoteleria y Turismo

The Panamerican Confederation of Hotel and Tourism Schools is the other tertiary educational association which has relevance for the Caribbean region. Whereas the membership of CHOCHS is drawn primarily from the English and Dutch speaking countries and colonies of the traditional Caribbean region, the membership of the Congress is predominantly Spanish speaking and includes those countries which border on the Caribbean Sea and which are eligible for CHA membership.

At the inaugural meeting of the Confederation, I Congresso Panamericano de Escuelas de Hoteleria Y Turismo, held in Mexico City in November 1991, representatives from 40 schools in Argentina, Bahamas, Belize, Bolivia, Brazil, Canada, Chile, Colombia, Costa Rica, Cuba, Dominican Republic, Ecuador, El Salvador, Guatemala, Honduras, Jamaica, Mexico, Nicaragua, Panama, Paraguay, Peru, Puerto Rico, Trinidad and Tobago, the United States, Uruguay and Venezuela met to discuss issues of mutual concern for the hemisphere's hospitality and tourism education and training. At the conclusion of the Congress, 26 hotel and tourism schools from North America, South America, Latin America and the Caribbean approved a set of objectives similar in scope to those which CHOCHS is pursuing (Spivak and Chernish 1992).

Of significance is the absence of any objectives calling for regional accreditation schemes. This may reflect the very wide geographic, political and economic dispersion of its members. In this respect, the Confederation and CHOCHS are quite different.

Training

Training, either by employers or by independent providers, is equally inconsistent in the region and is not necessarily seen as a high priority, again reflecting the characteristics of many of the industry participants as mentioned earlier. John Bell, this time in reference to training, states:

> Many hotels . . . are . . . at fault for not budgeting adequate funds for in-house training and laying the proper foundation for the upward mobility so essential to the professional upgrading of Caribbean tourism. The overall result of these shortcomings is that more people are required to do less work and in the process provide an uncompetitive level of customer service and satisfaction for the region's premier industry. (Bell, 1991)

However, there are credible organizations which are attempting to provide training. The OAS, for example, through the Tourism Plurinational Project, Sub-Project G, offers training in management and marketing for small tourism businesses including five-day seminars on a range of topics. Again, as is the case with education, many efforts tend to be uncoordinated and inconsistent.

The Caribbean Hospitality Training Institute (CHTI)

CHTI is the non-profit training arm of the Caribbean Hotel Association. Formally created in 1980, it drew upon a decade of training initiatives launched through the CHA. CHTI is governed through a Board of Trustees who report to the CHA Board of Directors. CHTI is managed by an Executive Director who is located in Antigua along with a Training Specialist and several administrative support staff.

The Institute offers 33 certificate programmes for the entire tourism industry including the accommodation, food and beverage and ancillary sectors such as taxi drivers, retail employees and government officials such as customs and immigration officers. These programmes can also be customized to suit the particular needs of a client and in this way, the programmes can achieve a fit with regional policies, traditions and practices while maintaining generic core foundations. In an area as diverse as the Caribbean, this is an essential feature of successful training programmes.

CHTI also assists with the placement of industry personnel for whom inter-regional exposure and experience is considered desirable. Much of this work is done in conjunction with the Canadian Training Awards Program (CTAP) and is an example of sound cooperation for the betterment of the industry.

A range of other services are also offered, including consultancies, scholarship management, awards programmes and topic-specific workshops and seminars. Again, many of these activities are done in conjunction with other organizations. For example, the awards programme for the region is sponsored by American Express which also provides sponsorship for workshops, seminars and other training activities.

Notwithstanding its successes, CHTI faces problems in providing training in the region, primarily from international aid agency programmes which provide training for aid recipients without charge. CHTI is aware through its membership that free training is preferable to programmes which have a charge regardless of the quality of the training. This situation underscores the continuing lack of prioritization by the industry for human resource development and its failure to appreciate fully the linkage between education, training and the level of quality service necessary for success. CHTI also faces competition from private consulting firms which offer programmes in the region and from some of the institutes of higher education in the region which offer their own programmes of training in addition to educational programmes.

The Caribbean Regional Hotel Training Project (CRHTP)

The Caribbean Regional Hotel Training Project is a comprehensive human resource development scheme involving government, industry and education. Launched in 1990, the Project is a cooperative effort of the Caribbean Hospitality Training Institute, the Bahamas Hotel Training College and the Government of the Bahamas. Originally conceived by the CHA, funding for the Project in excess of US$6 million, is being provided by the European Community as part of the most recent Lome Convention initiative.

The general aim of the Project is to establish an integrated education and training programme for the Caribbean hospitality industry in all its forms. Specifically the Project aims to:

- Facilitate institutional strengthening of higher education in the hospitality area
- Encourage the development of curriculum
- Incorporate strong private sector involvement
- Provide in-company training
- Create a regional accreditation body
- Create a regional certification body
- Create regional occupational standards
- Create a regional Career Passport scheme
- Foster faculty development
- Facilitate continuing and distance education initiatives

The Project is managed by a Working Group comprising representatives of the European Community, the Bahamian government, CHA, UWI, CHOCHS, CHTI, the Bahamas Hotel Training College and a consulting group which functions as the field coordination body of the Project (Conlin, 1991).

The consulting group is responsible for the operational aspects of the Project which cannot be effectively handled by the other partners. For example, the provision of much of the in-house training is undertaken by trainers who work for the consulting group and in conjunction with CHTI.

In its development stage, the Project calls for Research and Development specifically into areas which are normally thought of as being the purview of either the industry or higher education. These areas include an assessment of the current labour market in the region, the identification of key jobs within the industry, the preparation of regional performance standards, the development of competency testing methods, the development of systems of accreditation and certification, an educational and training needs assessment, the development of curricula, and the establishment of a regional distance education learning scheme (CRHTP, 1991 Implementation Plan).

This research and development is being led by the consulting group with the cooperation of CHOCHS, CHTI and the other members of the Working Group. In this way, the Project involves both the industry and higher education in an integrative activity which addresses many of the problems presently found in both education and training within the region.

The future of human resource development in the Caribbean

Notwithstanding the problems besetting human resource development in the region, there is cause for optimism.

The industry, public sector and educators have recently demonstrated a solid understanding of the need for improvement in human resource development. The CARICOM Summit on Tourism, which was held in Kingston, Jamaica, in February 1992, signalled this new found emphasis on tourism for the region. The proceedings included discussion on human resource development and the Summary of Conclusions contained the following:

> Agreed . . . that Governments would work jointly with the private sector towards the improvement and diversification of the tourism product. Specifically, they would cooperate to address . . . the development and encouragement of programmes of education and public awareness . . . the development of training programmes at higher levels . . . that in respect of human resource development, and availability of skills, Governments would make every effort to up-grade or facilitate the up-grading of their national hotel schools, the Caribbean Hotel (sic) Training Institute (CHTI), the University of West Indies Centre for Hospitality and Tourism Management. To facilitate this, Governments would consider seeking resources from donor sources such as the European Community (EC) or the Inter-American Development Bank (IDB). (CARICOM, 1992)

This is a very significant conclusion. The major problem which the schools face in the region, namely lack of resources, poor physical plants and an absence of faculty development, can be addressed on an international scale which is the only realistic approach. In addition, the conclusion gives public support at the highest level to the importance of hospitality and tourism schools. This can be very valuable as they seek to maximize their access to resources which already exist in their institutions and countries.

The Summit Conclusions also made the following recommendation, to

> encourage the establishment of a Regional Tourism Education Council and National Tourism Education Councils which would have among their functions the coordination of training programmes and the accreditation and articulation of programmes. (CARICOM, 1992)

This level of regional and national integration has proved to be very successful in other parts of the world. It has resulted in a greater understanding of all parties involved in the industry about the importance of education and training. It has helped in reducing duplication of effort and conflicting standards and has resulted in better human resource development generally. In the Caribbean, any of these results would significantly improve the current situation.

The relationship of the various educational and training bodies described above also gives rise for optimism. The same organizations are represented on each other's planning and policy-making boards. Thus, it is possible that further reduction of duplication, wasted effort and expenditure, conflicting standards and sub-standard training and education can be eliminated over time. In addition, the increased communication which is occurring between the various language groupings and sector groupings from education and training promises to raise the profile of education and training generally throughout the region.

The emphasis which all these organizations have on the creation of regional standards, both in training and education, is also promising. The inconsistency of service which is sometimes evident in the region is a problem for the whole region, not just the particular destinations who exhibit inadequate service. The tourism consumer tends to view the region as a relatively singular product and that will become even more the case with the introduction of the Regional Marketing Scheme which resulted from the CARICOM Summit. This regional cooperative marketing scheme will characterize the region as a single product with diverse components. It becomes essential, then, for the level of service quality in all the region to be high and consistent. The need for regional standards has become critical and the activities of CHOCHS, CHTI and CRHTP in this regard give hope that human resource development in the region can and will face the challenges of the 1990s.

References

Bell, J. (1991) Caribbean tourism realities. *World Travel and Tourism Review* (ed. D. E. Hawkins and J. R. B. Ritchie), Vol. 1, CAB International, Wallingford, Oxon, pp. 111–14.

CARICOM (1992) Summit 1992, Summary of Conclusions. Kingston, Jamaica.

Charles, K. R. (1992) Career influences, expectations and perceptions of Caribbean hospitality and tourism students: a Third World perspective. *Hospitality and Tourism Educator*, **4**(3), 9–14.

Conlin, M. W. (1991) Credible higher education in tourism: a Caribbean example: *Proceedings of the Twenty-Second Annual Conference of the Travel and Tourism Research Association*, Long Beach, California, pp. 227–32.

Holder, J. S. (1992) Island tourism and price and value relationship: a global perspective. *Proceedings of the First Island Tourism International Forum*, Bermuda College, Bermuda.

Spivak, S. and Chernish, W. N. (1992) I Congresso Panamericano de Escuelas de Hoteleria Y Turismo. *Annals of Tourism Research* (submitted).

12 Hong Kong
Vincent Heung

Overview

The tourism industry is Hong Kong's third largest earner of foreign
exchange. Total visitor arrivals have been increasing at an average rate
of 10% each year since 1980 but, growth has started to slow down. In
1991, more than six million visitors came to Hong Kong and spent a
total of HK$40 bn (see Tables 12.1, 12.2). Hong Kong remained Asia's
most popular travel destination in 1990, reflecting the high quality and
wide variety of visitor attractions and facilities.

Table 12.1 *Visitor arrivals by region of residence, 1981–91*

	1981	1989	1990	1991
Asia	1 324 661	3 449 836	3 992 835	4 041 350
Australia and Pacific	234 376	311 033	311 725	284 938
Americas	476 343	812 919	807 649	822 394
Europe	409 688	714 756	742 087	794 810
Middle East and Africa	71 089	67 762	73 892	84 778
Not identified	7 093	4 809	4 666	3 811
Total	2 523 250	5 361 170	5 932 854	6 032 081

Source: HKTA

Table 12.2 *Total tourism receipts, 1981–91*

Year	Total receipts HK$m	Annual growth	Receipts from servicemen, air crew members and transit passengers HK$m	Annual growth	Receipts from visitors HK$m	Annual growth
1981	8102.87	+25.2	480.86	+ 2.5	7622.01	+27.0
1989	36 905.24	+10.7	1062.38	+27.7	35 842.86	+10.3
1990	39 251.31	+ 6.4	1273.45	+19.9	37 977.86	+ 6.0
1991	39 606.78	+ 0.9	1306.22	+ 2.6	38 300.56	+ 0.8

Source: HKTA Statistical Review of Tourism

According to the government's Quarterly Report of Employment, Vacancies and Payroll Statistics, 37 618 persons were employed in the hotel sector and boarding houses in September 1991. Further government statistics show that as of September 1991, Hong Kong had a workforce of 2.8 million: 26.5% were engaged in wholesale and retail trades, restaurants and hotels, 9.7% in transport, storage and communications, 8.3% in construction, 8.4% in finance, insurance, real estate and business services, and 26.4% in manufacturing. The unemployment rate was 2.1%.

The tourism industry in Hong Kong has been facing a number of human resource problems in recent years. These problems are caused mainly by an increase in demand for labour due to rapid growth of the industry and a fall in the internal labour supply in the territory due to emigration and other reasons. This chapter examines the labour supply and demand situations in the tourism industry and the resulting problems, analyses the causes, discusses the ways the industry has been handling the problems and concludes with the projection of the future tourism industry in Hong Kong beyond 1997.

Labour problems

The labour issue has always been a major concern in the service industries in Hong Kong. Tourism is no exception, particularly in the hotel sector which has been trying to attract and maintain its labour force due to rapid expansion in recent years.

The demand for labour in Hong Kong is not confined to the tourism industry. As the Hong Kong economy maintained an average rate of 7% growth from 1986 to 1991 (see Figure 12.1), other industries have created employment opportunities for the working population. Over the same period, the unemployment rate has been kept at about 2%. The labour market has been generally tight. Labour shortages were reported in many sectors and industries of the economy. Hong Kong has already changed from a manufacturing-orientated economy to a service-orientated economy with its main manufacturing plants positioned in Southern China. Government sources indicate that in 1981, 41% of the working population were engaged in the manufacturing industry but by 1991 this was down to 28%. Competition for labour has become a daily activity for many companies.

Labour supply in the tourism industry

The picture looks gloomy in the human resource area of the tourism industry. In addition to the general labour shortage problem, there are

162

further problems of the 'brain drain' of qualified personnel within the industry; high labour turnover; rising payroll costs; problems relating to training; and the attitude of youngsters. The rapid expansion of the industry makes these problems more acute.

The 'brain drain'

In view of the political uncertainty after June 1997 when Britain hands over the sovereignty of Hong Kong to China, many people are leaving the territory to settle in other countries. Table 12.3 shows that in 1987 there were about 30 000 emigrants; within three years this figure rose to 62 000 (an increase of over 100%) according to government statistics, with similar numbers emigrating in 1991 and 1992. Most of these emigrants were young professionals and executives (Table 12.4).

Although there are no official figures on the effects of the 'brain drain' on the tourism and hotel industries, it is certain that there would be a significant impact on more experienced and qualified staff. The effect is also noticeable with respect to educational institutions offering hotel and tourism management courses; there has been a marked increase in the number of students leaving during their studies because of emigration with their families. Furthermore, as the tourism industry in China develops, its draws away experienced personnel from Hong Kong.

For the tourism industry, it has lost some of the key personnel who

Table 12.3 *Emigration statistics, 1987–1992*

1987	30 000
1988	45 800
1989	42 000
1990	62 000
1991	60 000
1992	60 000*

* Estimated figure
Source: Government statistics

Table 12.4 *Characteristics of emigrants, 1991*

	% of all emigrants	% of total pop.
Age 25–44	47	37
University degree	17	4.6
Professionals/executives	35	11

Source: Government statistics

are fairly difficult to replace, while, from the point of view of the training institutions, the loss of students means less supply of graduates for the industry.

Labour turnover

The Hong Kong Hotels Association's Survey reveals that in 1991 more than half of the workforce in the hotel industry changed jobs or resigned. This was slightly better than the 56.88% recorded in 1990 but it remained one of the highest among all industries in Hong Kong and Asia. Other hotel markets in Asia, including China, Taiwan and Japan were also affected by high labour turnover, but their situation was not as severe as in Hong Kong.

According to some industry experts there were several major reasons for the high turnover rate. First, a significant increase in the number of hotels in recent years, which provides opportunities for promotion or increase in salary. Second, the labour market in Hong Kong remains tight with a very low unemployment rate. Third, a large number of new entrants to tourism, especially those recruited from other industries, were relatively likely to leave during the first few months of employment. Fourth, in a highly materialistic society such as Hong Kong, people do change job even for a small increase in benefits package.

Rising payroll costs

The problem of labour shortage in Hong Kong coupled with high inflation in recent years has increased salaries and wages in all sectors of the economy. A survey by the Institute of Personnel Management on personnel practices in the Hong Kong workforce revealed that the highest increase in salary in the private sector was in 1989 at 17.3%, based on performance when the inflation rate stood at 10.1%. The inflation rate remained at over two digits up to the end of 1991.

In the hotel sector, the payroll and related expenses as a proportion of total costs rose from 19% in 1988 to 26.9% in 1991 according to the Hong Kong Tourist Association's *Hong Kong Hotel Industry Report* (1989, 1992). However, a comparison of total pay rises with other industries indicates that the increases in salary were the lowest, at 11.7%. This could mean the remuneration factors alone may not be sufficient to attract the required workforce to the hotel industry.

Labour shortage

Labour shortage problems first came to the fore in 1986 when Hong Kong's economy recovered from the downturn periods of 1982 to 1986. In that year, gross domestic product (GDP) grew 11.2% in real terms. This was followed by a growth rate of 13.6% in 1987 making labour shortage one of the most worrying problems facing Hong Kong's growing economy. (Figure 12.1 shows the growth of GDP from 1986 to 1991).

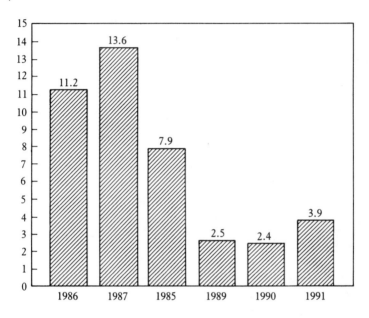

Figure 12.1   *Percentage growth in GDP, 1986–91.* (*Source:* Government statistics)

The unemployment rate was maintained below 2% from 1987 to 1990 and just above 2% in 1991. As the economy enjoyed boom, however, a decrease in the labour force took place because of the changes in immigration policy and the 'brain drain' problem. The shortage of labour affects all economic sectors in Hong Kong: from the financial services in the Central District to the manufacturing units of the New Territories. As a consequence, labour costs have increased considerably and labour turnover has become a major problem for all sectors, not least those businesses involved with tourism.

Growth in demand for labour in the tourism industry

The Hong Kong tourist industry has enjoyed a steady growth of 10% per year over the ten years to 1991 with the largest growth in 1988, when the growth rate was 24%. The total number of visitor arrivals from 1982 to 1991 is shown in Table 12.5. The only year with a negative growth rate was 1989 which was down by 4% over 1988. The fall in number of visitors was mainly caused by the Tienanmen Square incident in Beijing in June 1989.

Table 12.5 *Visitor arrivals, 1982–91*

Year	Total	% growth
1982	2 592 000	2.7
1983	2 754 000	6.3
1984	3 151 672	14.4
1985	3 370 308	6.9
1986	3 733 347	10.8
1987	4 501 889	20.6
1988	5 589 292	24.2
1989	5 361 170	−4.1
1990	5 932 854	10.7
1991	6 032 081	1.7

Source: HKTA (1991a) *Statistics Review of Tourism in Hong Kong*

The growth of the industry in recent years can be attributed to several causes:

1 A weak Hong Kong dollar. As the Hong Kong dollar exchange rate is tied to the US dollar, the currency has been weak since 1986. The continued depreciation of the US dollar has a significant impact on the local tourist trade. The industry has become more price competitive and more visitors have been attracted to Hong Kong.
2 China's 'open door' policy. To many visitors, Hong Kong is a gateway to China. The ease of access and the convenient location makes Hong Kong 'a city where west meets east'. In 1986, over 50% of the foreign visitors to China passed through Hong Kong and they represented 52% of the total visitor arrivals. In 1988, the Taiwanese government lifted bans on Taiwanese nationals visiting Hong Kong. The relaxation of the rule has brought many Taiwanese visitors to Hong Kong.
3 The conference and exhibition market. With the completion of the Hong Kong convention and exhibition centre in Wanchai, the growth in this market has been rapid.

In response to the increase in number of visitors, the supply of hotel

Table 12.6 *Number of hotels and rooms, 1982–95*

Year end	No. of hotels		No. of rooms
Actual*			
1982	47		17 415
1983	48		17 570
1984	50		18 031
1985	51		18 180
1986	57		20 230
1987	56		21 022
1988	65		22 882
1989	69		27 031
1990	75		28 146
1991	82		31 163
Estimate			
1992	93		35 324
1993	94	÷ 1 of 2 extension projects	35 623
1994	94	÷ 2 of 2 extension projects	35 779
1995	95		36 474

* Figures confined to HKTA member hotels only.

rooms has increased from 17 415 in 1982 to 31 163 in 1991 or from 47 hotels to 82 hotels (Table 12.6). The major growth was in the period from 1986 to 1991 (over 70%) (HKTA, 1991b).

In 1991, the number of hotel employees stood at 36 077 compared to 21 447 in 1982, an increase of almost 70% in ten years (Table 12.7). The average reported job vacancies in the hotel industry grew from 496 in 1986 to over 2200 in 1991. For the period 1989–91, the vacancies remained at above 2200 for the year, a 6.5% shortage on average (Table 12.8) (Census and Statistics Department, Hong Kong, 1991).

Table 12.7 *Number of hotel employees by category, 1982–91*

Year end	High tariff A hotels	High tariff B hotels	Medium tariff hotels	Hostels/ guest houses	All categories
1982	7095	12 188	1726	438	21 447
1983	7225	12 038	1733	413	21 409
1984	7274	12 111	1619	464	21 468
1985	7389	12 311	1564	603	21 867
1986	8097	13 507	1706	728	24 038
1987	8945	13 548	2671	520	25 684
1988	10 546	15 238	2921	486	29 191
1989	14 494	14 272	3367	496	32 629
1990	14 732	14 645	3925	527	33 829
1991	15 475	14 295	5578	729	36 077

Source: HKTA

Table 12.8 *Reported vacancies in hotel and boarding houses from 1986 to 1991*

1986	496
1987	829
1988	1910
1989	2450
1990	2224
1991	2279

Source: Hong Kong Annual Digest of Statistics, 1986–91

Response of the industry

The manufacturing sector has already taken major steps to cope with the labour shortage problem in Hong Kong by moving manufacturing activities across the border to Southern China where abundant supply of labour is available and wages are much lower. Furthermore, they can also employ more efficient, high technology methods of production such as the utilization of automated and computerized equipment. Unlike its manufacturing counterpart, the service sector, including tourism and hotels, has the problem of fixed location and much of the work cannot simply be replaced by machines.

Facing a number of major problems in the human resource area, the Hong Kong hotel and tourist industry has responded in different ways. These measures can be categorized under three main headings: retention strategies, recruitment strategies and productivity and efficiency strategies.

Retention strategies

Improvement of remuneration packages

While employers are reluctant to raise salaries and wages, arguing that it would fuel inflation, there is evidence that some hotel employers have faced this issue in a creative manner. In 1989, Mandarin Oriental Hotel Group, which owns the Mandarin and Excelsior hotels in Hong Kong, launched a $10m profit-sharing scheme for 1700 of its 1900 employees. The incentive package includes offering the employees free shares in the group, increased annual bonuses and home mortgage subsidies. The Hong Kong Hilton spent $20m on four-month bonuses, overseas training programmes and incentives such as helicopter rides for model employees. The Peninsula substantially increased salaries and wages for the group employees.

These measures were geared up for increased competition for

labour, especially the need to retain staff at a time when the unemployment rate is below 2% and more new hotels are in the development stage.

Better opportunities for advancement

The 'brain drain' and rapid growth of tourism in China has led to the emigration of many experienced hotel personnel, particularly at the middle level. This has created promotional opportunities for less experienced staff. In addition, it is a general practice in the industry to adopt a policy of promotion from within. Therefore, a newcomer would have greater and faster opportunities to be promoted than was the case before. This chain effect has been evident in a tourism industry facing shrinkage in the labour market. Some hoteliers have changed their attitude in the hiring of staff: instead of hiring experienced supervisory staff which is rather difficult, they have tended to hire junior staff with the right attitude, personality and, above all, potential for development, and provided them with the necessary opportunity for training. The former general manager of the Peninsula Hotel, Mr Eric Waldburger explained the advantages of hiring waiters instead of captains with three to five years' experience and training them to be captains: this not only beats the labour shortage problem, but also helps to build up loyalty for the hotel and for top management. He argued that people who are given the opportunity to take on a more senior job would work much harder. Some hotels, for example the Peninsula, have gone so far as to create new positions in order to promote their experienced workers in danger of being 'poached' by other hotels.

Training and development

In view of the manpower shortage in the Hong Kong tourism industry, training has become more important in order to maintain high-quality service and to retain staff. Many businesses have invested heavily in and put significant stress on staff training. Examples include the Hilton Hotel, which spent about $2m on training staff at all levels in 1988. In line with company policy, training programmes are reviewed annually to ensure they help staff to reach their full potential. The range of on-the-job training and continuous development programmes allow Hilton staff to assume greater responsibilities and to maintain job satisfaction. The two Holiday Inns, Golden Mile and Harbour View, have devised a staff training and retraining programme which has helped to retain their employees. They have developed the pro-gramme over three years and it was probably the most comprehensive in the industry in 1990, covering 38 job-related courses. The group claim to have the best hotel training centre in Hong Kong for the provision of in-house training. Regal Hotels International also place great emphasis on training. Some of the training courses were tailor-made by Constellation College of Hospitality in Toronto. In a move aimed at retaining staff, the Furama Kempinski Hotel Group has put in place a staff exchange programme where local employees have an opportunity to work in other Kempinski hotels world wide.

Outside of the hotel sector, the Hong Kong-based airline Cathay Pacific has an international reputation for the approaches they adopt in the training and development of staff at all levels. It is the airline's policy to recruit staff on a regional basis, reflecting the variety of Asian destinations that they serve, and this cultural and educational diversity provides a further challenge to their training.

Recruitment strategies

Careers exhibitions and talks

Large-scale recruitment campaigns, mainly to attract new hands, have been launched by major hotels in Hong Kong. Examples of such initiatives include those by Regal Hotels International and New World Hotels Group, both of which offered jobs from rank-and-file to junior management levels. The Regal Group promised a corporate training programme for all newly recruited staff and New World sought to attract people for all its properties including those in China. Career Days were arranged so as to give potential recruits first-hand know-ledge about the hotel work. The candidates were given the chance to enquire about job and career opportunities directly from the hotel's existing staff and executives.

Hotel employee training scheme

In October 1988, a new training scheme for hotel staff in Hong Kong was started with a view to easing the industry's labour shortage. The Hong Kong Hotel Association (HKHA), which represents almost all major hotels in Hong Kong, organized the scheme in the hope of attracting school leavers who fail to get places in the five hotel and catering institutions. About 5000 applicants are turned away from these colleges each year. The scheme aims to produce up to 500 workers for all sectors of the industry each year. They serve an apprenticeship in one of the 28 hotels and receive training in food and beverage, front and back office duties and housekeeping. At the end of the two-year course it is intended that the trainees will be offered a job, generally by the training hotel.

Importation of skilled labour

As the labour shortage problem persists, tourism managers have urged the government to relax its quota on importing skilled workers from overseas. The Executive Director of the Federation of Hong Kong Hotel Owners, Mr Michael Li, stated that the Federation's target was to employ English-speakers from the Philippines and Thailand who had received at least two years' hospitality training and three years' hotel work experience. Although the government approved more than 200 skilled workers for the supervisory or management level of the hotel industry in 1990, Mr Li said this was hardly adequate to ease the shortage, which was mostly at rank and file level. Traditional overseas recruitment has been at executive level from countries in Europe, North America, Australasia and Japan and generally linked to the needs of the major tourism companies. While there has been some growth in the employment of local management at senior levels, the tendency towards expatriate executive recruitment has had a negative effect on the career prospects of local personnel.

In January 1992, when government extended the labour importation scheme, the hotel and catering industry was at the top of the list registered for importation of foreign workers. The industry placed 3706 applications out of a total of 9400 vacancies which had been declared by various industries seeking workers from abroad.

More graduates from the education sector

In cooperation with the industry, the education sector has taken on

Table 12.9 *Supply of graduates from hotel courses in education/training institutions to the hotel industry, 1989/90*

	Full-time	Part-time
Degree	50	–
Higher diploma	80	114
Technician	118	524
Craft	129	220
Operative	1403	2982
	1850	3840

Output of five training institutions: Hong Kong Polytechnic; Haking Wong Technical Institute; Caritas; Kwon Tong Vocational Training Centre; Hotel Industry Training Centre.
Source: Vocational Training Council (1990)

171

more students in recent years. There were five major local hotel training institutions in 1989 producing over 5000 graduates a year (Vocational Training Council, 1990) (Table 12.9). With the addition of the Institute of Hotel Management of the Hong Kong Baptist College in 1990, the output is now well over 5500 graduates a year. Institutions include a number of technical facilities, catering for craft and supervisory programmes, while the main management programmes operate through the Hong Kong's Polytechnic, which offers courses in hotel management and tourism at undergraduate and postgraduate levels.

Productivity and efficiency strategies

Rising labour costs, high labour turnover and scarcity of labour have driven tourism managers to think critically about productivity and efficiency. Various suggestions have been put forward which include reduction in staff-to-room ratio, introduction of more labour-saving equipment and procedures, introduction of computerized productivity systems and more flexible use of staff. Not all these proposals were agreed by hoteliers, particularly the contraction of the staff-to-room ratio. 'Hong Kong's international reputation has been built on the standards of our facilities and service, if we lower them, we will be asking for serious trouble. Neighbouring countries like Singapore, Malaysia, the Philippines and Thailand will be quick to capitalize on our lack of initiative,' said Mr James Smith, chairman of the Hong Kong Hotels Association in 1989. Mr Phil Stephenson, group director of personnel for the Shangri-la said, in 1990, 'We are not talking cutting staff here, what we are saying is that there are ways of having fewer people and improved productivity'. The industry's staff-to-room ratio has been held steady at 1.2, one of the highest ratios in the developed world.

Despite these reservations, the tourism industry has taken positive steps to employ more casual staff, to introduce job rotation and enrichment, and with respect to the installation and updating of computerized systems. Early in 1989, the industry drew up contingency plans to operate their hotels with fewer employees and more part-time staff. One such example was the Park Lane Hotel. According to Mr Kenneth Mullins, senior vice-president at Park Lane Hotels International, the policy of the hotels regarding the use of casual staff has been adjusted. He saw casual labour taking on a growing role in the hotel service sector. 'We are encouraging our employees to work on their day off for extra pay, and we also encourage a cross-over of skills. A houseman can become a waiter, and staff from other hotels may choose to work for us on specific days,' he said.

The idea of a five-day working week policy was brought about by Marriott when it opened the Hong Kong Marriott in 1989. All staff at the hotel work 9½ hours a day and 48 hours per week which is roughly equal to the standard six-day week adopted by other hotels. While members of the Hong Kong Hotel Association criticized Marriott's move, claiming that it would only aggravate the labour shortage problem because hotels would have to hire more staff, Marriott argued that it helped to alleviate the problem because the freed labour could take up casual work on their sixth days. There were 4000 applications for the 1100 vacancies when the hotel was opened. According to Mr Kent Maury, director of marketing at the Marriott, the five-day week scheme has turned out to be very successful.

Finally, the installation and updating of computerized systems is widespread in many Hong Kong hotels and other tourism businesses, especially in the travel sector, and acts as an important contributor to enhanced productivity.

Conclusions

The labour issue remains one of the biggest problems facing the tourism and hotel industries in Hong Kong. With a flourishing economy and a shrinkage in the workforce, labour shortages are to be found in all industries. China's 'open door' policy, the weak Hong Kong dollar and the increasing importance of Hong Kong as an international city for conference and other activities have helped to boost tourism. Indeed, it is one of Hong Kong's biggest growth industries. On the other hand, political uncertainty regarding Hong Kong after 1997 has created waves of migration which lead to a decrease in the workforce. As a result of these, a gap has been formed between the supply side and demand side for labour, making demand far exceed supply. The consequences are that labour costs have been pushed up, turnover rate has increased and competition for labour has become fierce.

Finding a solution has not been easy and the industry has focused its efforts on retention, recruitment and productivity. These include improvement in benefits packages, offering more promotion opportunities, investment in training and development of staff, promotion of school leavers, enhancement of education and training institutions, importation of skilled labour, employment of more casual labour, better scheduling and updating of computerized productivity systems.

In the short run, these measures seem to have relieved aspects of the problems to a large extent. However, long-term strategies are also required as the problems will, inevitably, continue to affect Hong Kong's tourism industry in the foreseeable future.

Future prospects

Hong Kong's hotel and tourism industry is optimistic about the future, although it may not enjoy the same rate of growth as in the 1980s. The hotel occupancy forecast shows a steady growth to 1996 (HKTA, 1991) (Figure 12.2). The downturn between 1988 and 1992 was attributed to the political turmoil in China, the Gulf War, the recession in the West and a significant increase in room supply. Despite all these, the average hotel occupancy still compared favourably with the rest of the world.

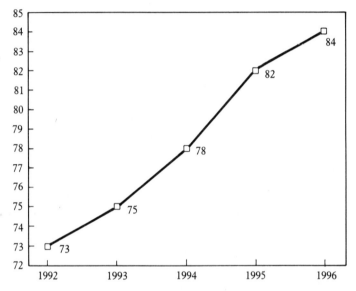

Figure 12.2 *Hotel occupancy forecast, 1992–6 (%). (Source: HKTA)*

There are quite a number of positive signs lying ahead. As China has reiterated its 'open door' policy and politically becomes more stable, the local tourism industry in Hong Kong is likely to benefit as it is considered by many to be a gateway to China. China is also active in promoting its tourism industry, 1992 being China travel year. Despite economic uncertainty in the West, long-haul travel to the Far East is expected to grow further. The growth in Asian economies will create traffic both inside and outside the region and therefore growth in the medium-tariff category is expected to continue. The supply of hotel rooms is estimated to grow at a slow pace, adding about 380 rooms each year up to 1995 (HKTA, 1991b).

From a longer term and post-1997 perspective, the picture still looks promising. The new airport at Chek Lap Kok will remove capacity constraints needed for the growth. The possibility of China as the host country for the Summer Olympic Games in year 2000 will be of further value and Hong Kong may have a chance to stage some part of the Games. Ten million visitors and HK$130 bn to HK$140 bn from tourism receipts are projected annually by 2000 according to the Hong Kong Tourist Association (Sullivan, 1992).

However, there are some uncertainties which merit mention. First, whether in the near future Taiwan would have direct routes to China, which would affect the Taiwanese market. Taiwanese represented more than 21% of all the visitor arrivals in Hong Kong in 1991. The Hong Kong government may in the future introduce a sales tax which would also have an impact on tourists to Hong Kong. One of the main reasons many come to Hong Kong is because it is a laissez-faire, duty-free port.

In the human resource area the problems are likely to continue, although there is some evidence that some are reducing in significance. According to the latest available unemployment figure, in the first quarter of 1992, the level is put at 2.4%, the highest in five years. This will probably help to ease the labour shortage in the short term. Another initiative worthy of mention is that tourism studies will be introduced in secondary schools in 1993 as an examination subject. This is likely to help in attracting youngsters at an earlier school age. On the other hand, emigration, rising labour costs, labour turnover and competition for labour continue to present problems to the industry.

In the final analysis, the tourism industry in Hong Kong, as elsewhere, is inextricably dependent on the local and international economy and the political environment in which the country operates. The human resource issues in tourism are likely to remain near the top of the Hong Kong agenda so long as the overall economy continues to remain buoyant and provided the political situation remains stable. What happens after 1997 is not easy to predict. What is certain is that the political outcome of the re-integration of Hong Kong into China will have significant impact on the performance of the tourism industry and on how human resource concerns are tackled.

References

Census and Statistics Department, Hong Kong (1991) *Hong Kong Annual Digest of Statistics 1986–1991*, Government Printer, Hong Kong.

HKTA (Hong Kong Tourist Association) (1989, 1992) *Hong Kong Hotel Industry Report*, HKTA, Hong Kong.

HKTA (Hong Kong Tourist Association) (1991a) *Statistical Review of Tourism in Hong Kong*, HKTA, Hong Kong.

HKTA (Hong Kong Tourist Association) (1991b) *Hotel Supply Situation No. 1 1992*, HKTA, Hong Kong.

Sullivan, Eugene C. (1992) Outlook optimistic for Hong Kong tourism. Tourism News (HKTA), April–June.

Vocational Training Council (1990) *1989 Manpower Survey Report on the Hotel Industry*, Hotel Catering and Tourism Training Board, Hong Kong.

13 India
Sudhir Andrews

Introduction

India is a country of rich diversity in every aspect of its geography, history, culture, religions, economy and society in general. It is also a country of absolute contradictions, of charm and incalculable frustrations, of richness and abject poverty, of natural and historic beauty and industrial pollution, of power and fragility so that any introductory pan over the tourism environment in India can only touch upon, and never do justice to, this complexity. This problem affects, by extension, the manpower and training environment for tourism, the main focus of this chapter.

India, as a tourist destination, has a great potential that has, by no means, been fully developed or attained and is, currently, under threat from a combination of domestic and international factors. The origins of Indian tourism, from an international viewpoint and on any significant scale, are relatively recent. While India as a place to visit for the business, cultural and adventure visitor has a reasonably long tradition, entry into the world tourism market as anything like a major player dates from as recently as the 1970s. Even in this short timespan the performance of the industry has been chequered and has been significantly affected by a number of key factors.

(1) Perceptions of specialist and limited markets, notably of a cultural, exotic nature, have hampered the evolution of alternative markets. The range of opportunity and potential diversity of India's tourism product has only been recently appreciated and development, to date, is limited.

(2) India has suffered from general barriers to long-haul tourism and has only overcome this in tandem or, indeed, following in the footsteps of other major Asian destinations, such as Thailand.

(3) There has been a transition in the Indian economy from major food and commodity shortages to sufficiency and export status in

many of these areas. The widely held perception of India as a country of famine has taken time to counterbalance and, even today, the apparent and evident poverty of both urban and rural populations can be difficult to reconcile with mass, high-consumption tourism.

(4) Under-developed infrastructure has also affected tourism's growth, with many facilities unable to cope with domestic demand, let alone the additional pressures of extensive tourism. At the local level, this problem has inhibited the development of new facilities for tourism, because of the priority need to meet domestic demand. At a regional and national level, the most acute manifestation of this problem, and one that has immediate and direct impact on the tourist, has been with respect to domestic transportation, particularly under-capacity on airlines and the railway system, which has hindered tourist traffic. Alternatives, such as road transport, have been inhibited by a poor network of trunk routes.

(5) A further difficulty, with respect to tourism development, has been created by what the Economist Intelligence Unit described, in 1986, as 'an overly bureaucratic administration and lack of tax and investment incentives', not exclusively, but with major impact, in tourism. Until relatively recently, there appears to have been less than wholehearted commitment, by government, to the development of tourism, with priority accorded to other areas of industrial and economic growth. While tourism has featured in official planning since the 1956 Second Five Year Plan, the level of investment and prominence given to this area were low. In terms of bureaucracy, the strangle-hold approach of 'red tape' with respect both to the actions of public servants involved with tourism and the initiatives within the private sector has been recognized as a major barrier and inhibitor of growth, within Indian tourism, over the past decades.

(6) Protectionist policies in the field of aviation, which are designed to protect the State carrier, Air India, have also contributed to restricting access to India for large numbers, especially through charter services. However, as a result of the adoption of the National Tourism Policy (NTP) in 1988, there is some evidence of moves towards change. Ahmed points to fairly rapid change as an immediate consequence of the NTP. Both Air India and Indian Airlines have been partially privatized and the number of holiday charter flights increased from 24 in 1986 to 170 in 1990 (Ahmed, 1991).

(7) There have been conflicting national, regional and local objectives within the development of tourism, focusing, in part, on the relative priority of international as opposed to domestic tourism growth. There is a significant voice, within Indian tourism, for emphasizing low-cost, domestically orientated development at the expense of international-standard facilities. The benefits of this

approach, in terms of reducing culture clash, are also stressed. India is a very good example of a country where the consumer use overlap between the international and domestic tourist is minimal and, thus, facilities for each have developed in an independent manner.

(8) India has suffered from sporadic civil disturbance, which has also inhibited the growth of international tourism and this continues to have both a national and a more regionalized affect. Tourism, as a business, is highly volatile in its response to perceived problems and events, as well as to the geographical ignorance of many travellers, and thus dramatic fluctuations in visitor numbers can occur over relatively short time-spans. The assassinations of Mrs Indira Gandhi in 1984, and Rajiv Gandhi in 1991, had immediate effects on international arrivals, as did the Gulf crisis and subsequent war in 1990/91. Localized difficulties in the Punjab and regional problems in Sri Lanka and Afghanistan also impact on Indian tourism performance. It is fair to add, however, that media coverage of India does tend to give prominence to negative news items in a way that does not do the country justice and the consequent effects on tourism cannot be underestimated.

These difficulties and tensions, within Indian tourism, have by no means all been resolved and are likely to feature on the agenda of the country's tourism development agencies, public and private sector, for the foreseeable future. Ahmed is, probably, justified when he describes Indian tourism as 'a victim of mismanagement' (Ahmed, 1991) as this dimension cannot be ignored when analysing the problems associated with the industry's growth. At the same time, India has made significant strides, particularly in terms of economic and regulatory control, in order to support the development of tourism as a major industry and the result has been significant domestic and international investment in facilities and infrastructure, during the 1980s, and the consequent ability to offer the Indian and international tourist competitive and attractive vacation experiences in all major destination areas.

The economy

Economically, India has a strong element of duality. It is one of the ten most industrialized countries in the world, with a high level of indigenous technological achievement which extends into such fields as nuclear energy, satellite communications and armaments, and yet three-quarters of the population owe their livelihood to agriculture (which accounts for 40% of the GDP), the majority of which is still at subsistence level and dependent on the annual monsoon.

Since independence in 1947 India's economic development has been guided by a central planning process, key in which has been the five year plan cycle, commencing in 1951. Early plans focused on correcting disequilibrium in the economy, caused by war, partition and the effects of colonial control, with priority on agriculture and power. Subsequent plans have sought to develop the heavy industrial capacity of the country, while, at the same time, securing agricultural independence. The combination of social objectives, including employment, with economic necessities, both domestic and in relation to foreign exchange concerns, has placed considerable strains on the planning process and on the economy as a consequence. Strong protectionism and control policies were hallmarks of the economy for the three post-independence decades and have only recently been relaxed. This acted as a barrier to foreign investment in many industries, including tourism. The seventh five year plan (1985–9) gave priority to food, work and productivity within all sectors of the economy, the eighth plan (1990–5) proposals took up these themes and focused on elevation of the population from poverty, employment generation, food security, greater use of technology, self-reliance and the expansion of exports. In this context, tourism was given significant recognition for possibly the first time.

India's non-subsistence economy has developed very rapidly over the past two decades, with the result that the bulk of food demands and consumer goods are home-produced. Industrial manufactured output has grown in parallel to agricultural progress. However, a consequence of this rapid growth and of the increased affluence of the urban, middle class population is a critical balance of payments deficit, inflation and erratic growth patterns in the economy. The traditional heavy industrial base of the country, while not stagnating, is primarily expanding through technology and production enhancement, rather than through an expanding workforce. High technology and service sector industries, by contrast, account for the vast majority of new employment opportunities created within the past ten years. This trend, combined with increasing economic liberalism and a climate encouraging both domestic and foreign investment, promises a major and sustained restructuring of the non-agricultural economy. Given a domestic and international climate conducive to its development, tourism could be a major beneficiary of this scenario, if other factors work in its favour.

Despite the fact that tourism has only recently achieved a significant place in India's development plans, its contribution to foreign exchange earnings and domestic employment is already very significant. In the decade up to 1990, tourism was, in fact, the largest single net earner of foreign exchange in the Indian economy; at 2.2 bn Rupees in 1989, it was ahead of ready-made garments, engineering goods, leather and gems and jewellery as the major foreign exchange earner (Mahesh, 1990). Furthermore, the industry's economic impact goes beyond the earning of exchange and employment. It makes relatively low demands on the import budget; it features what might be termed 'backward integration' to enhance rural development through de-centralization of the economy and the development of non-industrial growth centres; it provides an economic means for the protection of archaeological monuments and the environment; and it promotes rural and village industries and crafts (Mahesh, 1990).

Administratively, the geographical diversity of India is translated into 25 States and seven Union Territories. The relationship between centre and periphery is politically and culturally complex and the States assert considerable autonomy and self-government in many aspects of domestic economic, social and cultural policy. Thus, while central government may determine macro-economic policies, includ-ing those relating to tourism, local administrations also retain and exercise considerable control as to how (or, indeed, if) such policy is translated at a regional or local level.

National tourism policy

Five key objectives for Indian tourism are articulated by the Ministry of Tourism and merit restatement here. They aim to develop tourism so that:

1 It becomes a unifying force nationally and internationally fostering better understanding through travel.
2 It helps to preserve, retain and enrich the Indian world-view and lifestyle, cultural expressions and heritage in all its manifestations. The prosperity that tourism brings must cause accretion and strength rather than damage to social and cultural values and depletion of natural resources. In tourism, India must present itself on its own terms – not as an echo or imitation of other countries, other cultures and other lifestyles.
3 It brings socio-economic benefits to the community and the State in terms of employment opportunities, income generation, revenue generation for the States, foreign exchange earnings and, in general, causes human-habitat improvement.
4 It gives a direction and opportunity to the youth of the country both through international and domestic tourism to understand the aspirations and viewpoints of others and thus to bring about a greater national integration and cohesion.

5 It also offers opportunities to the youth of the country not only for employment but also for taking up activities of nation-building character like sports, adventure and the like. Thus as a programme for the moulding of the youth of the country, tourism is of inestimable value.

India's tourism product

Tourism product can be considered in terms of the attractions which bring the tourist to India (natural, historic/cultural and man-made) and the facilities that the tourist utilizes in support of that visit, including accommodation, international and domestic transportation. These will be considered separately.

Attractions

With such diverse geography, history, culture and economy, it is hardly surprising that the Indian tourism product is likewise varied and features a combination of natural, culturo-historic and more recent man-made tourism products. While major tourism centres are clearly identifiable, along with their evident attraction products, it is true to say that all regions have the potential to offer the domestic or international tourist a range of products, reflecting one or more of the above categories and the dispersement of tourists to a variety of 'undiscovered' Indian locations offers one of the main strategies through which the country can achieve its tourism potential.

In terms of natural tourism products, India has a wide range of attractions to offer, from mountain experiences in the Himalayas and other ranges, to tropical adventure environments, rivers, deserts and world-standard beaches. The range of flora and fauna that India has to offer, reflects the variety in the natural environment of the country. Likewise, archaeological, historic and cultural locations of considerable interest are to be found throughout India: the Taj Mahal and the Red Fort are of international repute and have been developed to appropriate standards. However, there are a large number of other locations and attractions which currently receive insignificant tourist interest, due to limited marketing, poor access and infrastructure or sensitivity regarding their development. Physical attractions of a cultural or historic nature are complemented by rich traditions in paintings and sculpture, frequently linked to religious themes, literature, music, dance, crafts and cuisine, all of which already or potentially stand as tourism product attractions in their own right.

Table 13.1 *Distribution of graded hotel rooms, 1988*

Grade	%
Five-star deluxe	18.76
Five-star	19.40
Four-star	10.54
Three-star	21.93
Two-star	22.14
One-star	7.23

More recent contributions to the tourism product environment include the hill stations, a legacy of British colonialism; national and regional fairs and events, co-ordinated through central or state government agencies; sports locations, notably linked to the natural environment such as ski-ing, water sports (sea and river), and safari adventures; and international conference facilities.

Facilities and transportation

Accommodation

It is fair to say that one of the main barriers to achieving the full potential of Indian tourism has been a lack of an adequate and appropriately located hotel and other accommodation stock. Currently, some half of the nation's hotel room stock is located in the four major cities of Bombay, Calcutta, Delhi and Madras; state capitals and smaller business centres are largely underprovided in terms of reasonable standard hotels. Non-hotel stock, currently providing, largely, for the domestic market, is also of varied quality and is unevenly dispersed.

India has some of the finest luxury hotels in the world, both city and resort-based, and the quality and level of service are equal, if not superior, to that in competitor countries. However, these hotels cater for a primarily premium market and there have been long-standing gaps in appropriate facilities at other levels. This balance is shown in the distribution of Indian graded hotel rooms in 1988 (Table 13.1).

Transport

International tourists arrive in India, predominantly, by air; close to 90% use this mode of transport and the only major alternatives (land and sea) are used, almost exclusively, by visitors from neighbouring countries. Tourism cannot be seen, exclusively, in international terms, however, as domestic access, on a regional or State basis, is also very important.

India's development since independence has, understandably, focused primarily on infrastructural development to the benefit of domestic needs and much of this has been at a fairly fundamental level. This is as true in the case of transportation, as it is in areas such as power and other utilities. The consequence of these priorities has been that the internal travel requirements of tourists, especially those of international origin, have not been accorded primacy in the development of road, rail or air links. All these systems have suffered from significant undercapacity and over-utilization.

International tourism – key markets

Current government policies seek to increase international tourist arrivals from the 1990 level of approximately 1.8 million to in excess of 2.5 million by the late 1990s. A key plank, within this objective, is market diversification in order to attract growth from the major emerging markets within Asia and Europe. Excluding Bangladesh and Pakistan, Western Europe remains the major source of international tourist arrivals, followed by North America and other Asian regions. In percentage terms, the regional market breakdown is as shown in Table 13.2 for 1990. Within this regional breakdown, the main source markets are the United Kingdom, the United States, Sri Lanka, Germany, France, Japan and Italy.

Table 13.2 *Regional breakdown of international tourist arrivals, 1990*

Region	% of arrivals
Africa	4.5
N America	14.8
S America	0.7
E Asia	5.2
S Asia*	11.2
S E Asia	6.2
W Asia	10.5
Australasia	3.6
E Europe	4.0
W Europe	39.3
	100.0

Excludes Bangladesh and Pakistan

The manpower environment in India

Recent estimates put the population of India at in excess of 800 million, with a sustained rapid rate of growth. This population is, pre-dominantly, rural with only 24% living in urban locations, a proportion that is gradually increasing. The level of illiteracy is high; 36% of the population are deemed to be functionally literate. That said, India has a highly educated and well-trained minority population which, in absolute number terms, exceeds that of most developed countries. The breakdown of employment in India indicates the significance of rural life (Table 13.3). Tourism, it will be noted, is not a defined employment category in India. To all intents and purposes, an economic analysis of manpower, in India, can disregard much of the agricultural sector (with the exception of the modern, production units in the Punjab, in some of the export crop plantations and in limited other locations) as its subsistence emphasis offers little scope for either short-term development or the redeployment of labour into other sectors of the economy.

Table 13.3 *Employment in India by sector, 1990*

Sector	%
Subsistence farming	43
Agricultural labouring	26
Other agriculture	2
Mining and Quarrying	0.5
Manufacturing	9
Construction	1
Trade and commerce	6
Transport and communications	2.5
Other categories	10
	100

The manpower situation, within agriculture, is relatively static, not withstanding a certain urban drift. In other sectors, however, clear trends are discernible, chief of which is the growing significance of the service or non-manufacturing sector to the Indian economy. In this India is not unique, although this trend is one that is normally associated with developed rather than developing economies. It is a picture that is most clearly represented through analysis of new employment openings; Mahesh (1990) suggests that in excess of 70% of new jobs created annually are in the service sector as against 7% in manufacturing and this is a trend likely to be maintained and accelerated during the 1990s. It is arguable that this picture represents, to a certain degree, the settling of an imbalance within the Indian

185

economy, caused by government priorities during the 1950s, 60s and 70s. However, it is a trend that is of major importance to tourism and its growth and manpower requirements.

In absolute terms, labour is plentiful in India. In terms of requisite skills, the situation is very different, given the high level of illiteracy and increasing competition for an educated and trained labour pool that is growing at a slower rate than demands upon it. Growth in the service sector puts particular strains upon certain areas of skills demand, especially those requiring language, communications and 'people' capabilities. These are precisely those skills required by the modern tourism industry and, therefore, tourism finds itself in growing competition for a finite pool of trained personnel, with other new and emerging service industries. Furthermore, education and training provision has only responded, in part, to these changes in labour and skills demands.

Employment in tourism

The tourism industry in India, as in most countries, is a complex amalgam of small and large businesses, fragmented into a large number of sectors and catering for a diversity of markets. It is also an industry that impacts, indirectly, upon a variety of other primary and manufacturing sectors. Thus, to undertake a valid analysis of the industry and to describe the extent of employment within it presents certain difficulties. Official and reliable information sources are limited.

In 1986, the Economist Intelligence Unit estimated that total direct and indirect employment in tourism was about 4.5 million, of which 1.5 million were the direct employment figures and the balance indirectly created jobs in areas such as building, transportation, handicrafts, furnishings and furniture (EIU, 1986). This, in itself, constitutes a 50% growth over 1975 estimates. However, these estimates must be treated with some caution. Mahesh (1990) estimated total direct employment in tourism at 822 000 as significantly lower than the EIU figure and indeed, rather less than that of the National Council of Applied Economic Research (NCAER) in 1975. Mahesh's figure, in turn, is an extrapolation from base statistics dated 1981 and thus open to some debate. Clearly, some problems with establishing base employment figures do exist, caused, in part, by the extent to which businesses in allied fields and providing for a primarily domestic market (food, budget accommodation etc.) are taken into account. Mahesh projects growth, in employment, to reach approximately 1.3 million by 1995 (Mahesh, 1990), with the dominant sectors, for employment, being accommodation and food (41%), transport (36%) and retail (16%).

An important consideration, in reviewing the manpower situation in Indian tourism, is traditional family antipathy to work within the hospitality sector which, to some religious and cultural groups, had and still retains images of servitude and menial, demeaning employment. A lingering consequence of this tradition is to be found in the large number of Catholic Goans who still work in the hotel industry, recruited when other religious groups would not accept employment in this sector. This perception, combined with the desire to protect girls from undesirable contact with 'outsiders' or foreigners, has acted as a barrier to the industry in its attempts to recruit quality and well-educated school leavers. This situation has, to a significant extent, been overcome in some urban areas but continues to pose some difficulties to employment in new, rurally located tourism projects.

A further manpower challenge that already faces tourism and is likely to increase, relates to the overall, national competition for skilled and educated labour, especially in the service sectors. As in other countries, training received within colleges and within tourism businesses is highly marketable within other, allied service industries, which may offer more attractive conditions and working environments. Thus, increasing attrition of skilled personnel to other positions both within India and overseas seems a likely trend.

Education and training for tourism

Education and training for tourism in India have relatively early origins, commencing in the mid-1950s in Bombay with United Nations funding support. In this sense, the system commenced with considerable advantages over that in comparable developing tourism economies in that the main growth of tourism in the country was paralleled, from its early days, by investment, albeit limited, in basic training. By 1962, four regional institutes were established in Bombay, Calcutta, Delhi and Madras but, to a certain extent, their tourism focus was submerged by priorities in the field of food and nutrition. Indeed, from 1962, the institutes were placed under the Ministry of Agriculture Department of Food and considerable emphasis was placed on their educational and training role in the field of nutrition and food education linked to international aid and the 'freedom from hunger' programme. While this focus is, in retrospect, wholly understandable in the context of India's development and the priorities of the time, it also constitutes a major lost opportunity from the tourism perspective because the potential to provide trained support for the fledgling tourism industry, especially accommodation and food sectors, was undoubtedly lost at this time, and never fully regained. The four regional institutes, along with 12 foodcraft centres that had evolved during the 1970s, were transferred to the Ministry of Tourism as late as 1982 but have retained their 'nutrition' tag alongside hotel management and their courses still reflect this balance.

Under the Ministry of Tourism, some significant development has taken place. Nine of the foodcraft institutes have been upgraded to management status, but with varying quality and a further group of lower-level centres have been established. As a consequence, current provision for the accommodation sector runs at:

- Thirteen Institutes of Hotel Management, Catering Technology and Applied Nutrition, graduating some 2400 sub-diploma and diploma students per year
- Thirteen Foodcraft Institutes with a capacity to train about 2500 students at sub-diploma level each year

In addition, private sector institutions, under the auspices of major tourism companies and the Tourism Development Corporation, provide for the training of a limited number of craft, supervisory and management trainees each year. The main focus of craft training, however, is within the industry itself, through apprenticeship schemes ranging from six months to two years in duration and of somewhat varied quality and consistency. No external recognition, through certification, or link up to college-based programmes, is provided by this training route.

A major development in support of accommodation and food sector training was the establishment of the National Council for Hotel Management and Technology in 1983, representative of industry, educational and Ministry interests and co-ordinated through a Ministry secretariat. This body coordinates the levels and standards of training within all Foodcraft and Management Institutes and certifies graduates of approved programmes. Recruitment is also coordinated on a national basis. Of particular note, under the National Council, has been the establishment of more advanced management courses in Bombay and Delhi (the Postgraduate Diploma) and the certified Teacher Training Certificate, run by the Bombay Institute, for all 26 establishments, and, in its conception and potential, undoubtedly a highlight development within the system.

The National Council has not extended its brief beyond that of accommodation and food, with the result that developments for other sectors have been largely uncoordinated and independent. The Indian Institute of Tourism and Travel Management was established in 1986, as a nodal agency for coordinating education and training for the travel and tourism sectors through other academic institutions, nation-wide. Currently, graduate output is limited but it is planned to attain a level of 850 per annum by 2000 through five centres and a range of courses varying from six months to two years.

Manpower issues in Indian tourism

India has a comparatively well-developed education and training support system for tourism and one that can form the nucleus in meeting the prime manpower challenge that faces the industry, both the public and private sector, over the next ten years, that of a shortage of appropriately trained and skilled manpower at all levels. The system requires considerable overhaul, development and investment in order to meet existing requirements of the industry, let alone those projected into the future.

Currently, the system suffers from major weaknesses in both qualitative and quantitative terms. These can be identified as including the following:

- The combined supply of trained manpower, for the accommodation and food sectors, is woefully inadequate to meet existing, let alone projected needs. Thus graduates are monopolized by prestige deluxe and five-star companies and the impact of the state's investment in tourism makes little impression on those businesses trading at a somewhat lower standard or aimed at alternative and domestic markets. The impact of depression in the tourism industry during the early 1990s (as a consequence of the Gulf War, domestic instability and international recession) was to reduce recruitment by the major hotel companies. As a consequence, graduates have been forced to seek employment with other, less prestigious employers, possibly to the benefit of industry standards as a whole.
- The very limited training available for the travel and tourism sector is a further major weakness and must inhibit the professionalism and standards in this sector. Projected developments, here, are unlikely to keep pace with demand.
- Education and training for the accommodation and food sectors are to craft and diploma level, with little or no provision to graduate status and beyond. This situation is compounded by the tendency of the industry to place graduates of these courses, even at diploma level, in posts at relatively junior, operational and even normal entry level. Thus the contribution of the present system is, primarily, to supervisory and junior management posts in the industry and

limited benefits accrue to general management needs. These are frequently met through alternative recruitment of non-specialist degree or postgraduate management or business qualification holders, who receive their hotel or tourism training within their employing companies.

- Training, at apprenticeship level, through the Statutory Apprenticeship Act, is totally inadequate to meet current or projected demand.
- The quality of training facilities, within Foodcraft and Management Institutes, is mixed and not always adequate as a preparation for work in major international establishments.
- The existing teacher training programme is a major innovation. However, in terms of its capacity and duration/depth, it cannot meet the expanding needs of the tourism education and training system. As a consequence, many faculty are insufficiently trained and have limited and inadequate experience of professional responsibility in the industry.
- There is no recognition of the tourism industry or its training needs through the country's vocational education system.
- Facility for rapid expansion of training provision for tourism to meet new demand is not evident within existing structures or institutions.

The National Committee for Tourism (Mahesh, 1990) adopted an action plan which, if implemented, would go some way towards meeting the above concerns. This plan included the following provisions:

- The capacity and number of institutions, both at the craft and diploma level, should be increased.
- The intake of apprentices, under the Statutory Apprentice-ship Act, should be increased and the travel trade should also be brought withir the ambit of the Act.
- The quality of the training programmes and that of teaching faculty should be improved; the former by restructuring the programmes and the latter by lateral induction of suitable staff and by 'retraining the trainers'.
- Training of first level staff, such as stewards and bellboys, should be organized on a modular basis.
- Universities should be encouraged to introduce tourism-linked courses.
- The Indian Institute of Tourism and Travel Management should be effectively established in order that it can perform its full function.
- There should be an integration of programmes between industry and academia.

India represents an excellent example of a manpower environment where numbers are plentiful but where skills are in shortage. In addition, the competition for skills, within a growing service and high technology economy, is increasing in precisely those competency areas from which tourism draws much of its skills requirements. Furthermore, facilities and infrastructure for education and training, within tourism, while innovative and far-sighted at the time of their inception some 25 years ago, have not kept pace with the development or demands of a maturing tourism industry with the consequence that the supply of trained manpower is well short of current and, more so, projected requirements. Fairly radical and innovative strategies will be required to overcome this deficiency combined with the political will to retain tourism as a priority development area.

References

Ahmed, Zafar (1991) Indian tourism: a victim of mismanagement. *Cornell HRA Quarterly*, October.

Economist Intelligence Unit (EIU) (1986) India National Report No. 113. *International Tourism Reports*, No. 2, EIU.

Mahesh, V. S. (1990) Human resource development in the tourism sector. In *Report of the National Committee for Tourism*, Ministry for Tourism, New Delhi.

14   Kenya
M. K. Sio

Kenya – the country

Geography and climate

Kenya is a land of contrasts, described by many as displaying all that is beautiful in Africa. This colourful and exciting country, situated on the east coast of Africa, straddles the equator which divides it into two approximately equal halves. In a little more than 582 600 sq km (approximately 224 900 sq ml) a great variety of climatic conditions are to be encountered, ranging from the semi-desert sun of the northern parts of the country to the snow of Mt Kenya. The topography ranges in altitude from sea level to 5199 m (17 058 ft). The vegetation likewise offers much variety, ranging from arid and semi-arid scrubland, rolling savannah, damp moorland of the highlands to thick mountain forests.

Kenya's climate is amongst the most agreeable in the world. It is generally warm and relatively dry throughout the year, with mean temperatures varying according to the altitude above sea level, with two distinct rainy seasons March to May (long rains), and October to November (short rains), when it is generally wet throughout the country. The rains are characterized by heavy downpours, mostly in the afternoons, with high probability of thunderstorms in the lake region.

At the coast day time temperatures average 24–29°C with high humidity, though it is cooler at night. At Nairobi (1676 m) the climate is very pleasant, with warm sunny days giving way to cool nights. Here and at higher altitudes, during the months of June and July, temperatures often get chilly, but hardly falling below 13°C.

Population

Kenya's multi-racial population is estimated at 23.4 million, and projected to top 34.8 million by the year 2000. According to available data (1979 census) the racial breakdown of Kenya's population is: Africans (Blacks) 98.3%; Asians 1.1%; Europeans 0.4% and Arabs 0.2%. More than 50 different languages are spoken in Kenya, with Kiswahili as the national language and English the official language. Kenya has found wealth in this ethnic diversity and is reputed to be one of the most economically and politically stable countries on the African Continent.

The economy

Kenya's economy has developed satisfactorily since independence in 1963, with a much broader range of products than many other African countries. The Kenyan economy has, however, traditionally had a heavy reliance on agricultural exports, notably coffee and tea, a factor which is seen by many, including the World Bank and the International Monetary Fund as its greatest weakness. This reliance is seen as precarious, as these commodities are prone to price fluctuations in the world market, and production is subject to unpredictable climatic conditions. For this reason the Kenyan government is laying a lot of emphasis on diversification for a more broadly based economy, particularly in the area of export orientated manufacturing.

Tourism in the economy

An ILO sponsored study on employment generation in the hotel catering and tourism sector in 1987 forecast that tourism was most likely to become the country's most profitable export as well as its largest employer in the coming years. Indeed, developments in this sector during the 1980s saw it emerge as the country's top foreign exchange earner, overtaking both coffee and tea by 1988 (Figure 14.1).

The ILO study identified the following breakdown in tourism expenditure/earnings within the country: accommodation, meals and drinks, 60.0%; transport and tours, 22.0%; shopping, 13.0%; entertainment and other, 5.0%. In terms of employment, tourism generated 9.0% of total wage employment in the country at the time of the study. Using the 3.0 multiplier, commonly used in the industry, tourism generates up to 17% of employment in the whole of the private sector, 57% in the agricultural sector, and more than 86% in the manufacturing sector.

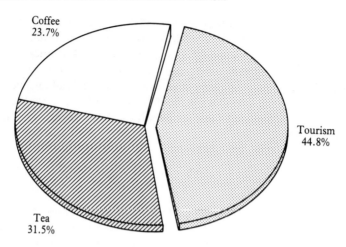

Figure 14.1 *Major foreign exchange earners (K£m), 1988. (Source*: Tourism Market Report, 1987/8)

The market

The leading industrial countries of Western Europe continue to be Kenya's most important tourist generating areas. By continent of residence, figures available for 1988 show visitors to Kenya as follows: Europe, 63.2% of the market share; Africa, 22.2%; North America, 10.4%; Asia, 2.4%; others, 1.8%.

In its fifth development plan (1989–93), the Kenya government projected an increase of 70% in the number of tourists visiting Kenya. Over the same period, earnings from tourism were projected to rise by 79%, from K£349m, to K£623m (Table 14.1).

Human resources and demographics

Kenya is not particularly well endowed with natural resources such as mineral deposits, nor with capital and technology. As such, the country's potential for sustained socio-economic growth lies in the abundance and vitality of its human resources, to provide the creative genius and impetus for development. However, with a population growth rate of 3.2% per annum, one of the highest in the world, the successful management of the human resources poses a considerable challenge. Some of the problems facing the country in this regard include:

• A rapidly growing dependent population which diverts much of the

Table 14.1 *Tourism in the Kenyan economy: projected number of tourists and foreign exchange earnings*

	1988	1989	1990	1991	1992	1993
Total of tourists	735 000	808 000	889 000	978 000	1 076 000	1 183 000
Bednights:						
Residents	1 131 000	1 216 000	1 336 000	1 467 000	1 615 000	1 705 000
Non-residents	272 000	294 000	323 000	349 000	357 000	378 000
Foreigners	3 930 000	4 145 000	4 331 000	4 534 000	4 759 000	5 062 000
Total	5 333 000	5 655 000	5 990 000	6 350 000	6 731 000	7 145 000
Foreign exchange earnings (£Km)	326	375	431	472	543	623

Source: Development Plan 1988–93

country's resources to consumption, thereby leaving less for saving and investment.
- A rising number of unemployed in the urban areas, coupled with widespread under-employment in the rural areas.
- Shortages of persons with a wide range of critically important skills, constituting a major constraint in achieving planned goals.

From the human resources point of view, the Kenyan population, estimated at 23 513 000 as at 1989, is structured as follows:

	%
Children (0–14)	50.3
Pre-school (0–5)	23.5
Primary school age (6–13)	24.3
Secondary school age (14–17)	9.6
Females of reproductive age (14–49)	21.3
Productive age (15–64)	47.6
Old age (65 and above)	2.1
Potential labour force	38.9

Employment

According to the government's fifth development plan (1989–93), the potential labour force is defined as members of the population who are economically active, i.e. those between 15 and 64 years of age, either working or searching for work. The plan expected the workforce to grow from 8.6 million in 1988 to 10.6 million by 1993.

Education

To meet the manpower needs of the country, the Kenyan government lays much emphasis on the development of educational and training infrastructure in the country. According to the development plan, the fiscal budgetary allocation for the development of human resources is about 40%. The combined private as well as public sector spending on education amounts to between 10 and 15% of the GDP.

Human resources in tourism

An insight into the human resource situation in tourism is perhaps best provided by the ILO study (1987). The results of the study, which focuses mainly on the hotels and restaurants sector, are as follows.

Employees by sex

The industry is dominated by males, constituting 91.7% of the labour force. This result is indeed in agreement with the finding of a survey carried out in 1985 by Kenya Utalii College, the leading hotel and tourism training institution in Kenya. The college is run by the state under the auspices of the Ministry of Tourism and Wildlife. The study aimed to determine the employment opportunities for the college's female graduates. In view of the fact that females represent more than half of the potential labour force and that Kenya has a rising population of single-parent households headed by females. This state of affairs constitutes an undesirable imbalance that still requires urgent attention in the 1990s.

Nationality

The study reveals that 99.4% of employees in hotels and restaurants are Kenya citizens. While this result reflects the level of success achieved in the Kenyanization of the industry, a closer look at this state of affairs in terms of skill level indicates that more effort is still required to place the running of the industry completely in the hands of Kenyans. In this respect, an analysis of the 0.6% of non-citizens reveals the following picture:

	%
Managers	10.0
Department heads	4.4
Supervisors	1.1

Skilled workers (basic level)	0.3
Unskilled and trainees	0.1

Much success in the area of Kenyanization may be attributed to the existence of Kenya Utalii College, which has won much acclaim for its role in the supply of qualified manpower to the industry.

Education level

The ILO study (1987) indicated that the majority of the employees in the industry were of relatively low education level. A survey which covered 17 198 employees gave the following results:

	%
Primary school	38.3
Secondary ('O' level)	28.1
Secondary ('A' level)	1.6
College	0.9
University	0.4
Others	3.7
Nil	27.0

These results are indicative of what remains to be done in terms of uplifting the quality of manpower in the industry. The results are also consistent with the views previously held by many that jobs in the industry were for those who could not make it elsewhere. This image problem coupled with poor remuneration and working conditions made careers in the industry attractive to only those with basic education. This in turn further reinforced the negative image about careers in the industry. However, post-1987 trends, particularly the demand for hotel and tourism courses at Kenya's colleges indicate that this image problem is now a thing of the past and that careers in the industry are as attractive to talented young school leavers as in other sectors. This change in the attitudes of young people towards careers in the industry will enable the industry to select and recruit employees of higher calibre than previously.

Other trends in the education system in the country will also have some additional impact. Given the large number of university enrolments from 1988 onwards viewed against the slow rate of employment generation within the economy, the picture is likely to change quite rapidly in the next few years, with many university graduates seeking employment within the industry.

Proposed strategies for manpower training and development for the industry

To ensure that the industry will be on a better footing in terms of competition with other sectors for high calibre manpower for the future, the following policies and strategies were adopted at a recent national tourism seminar.

● **Introduction of tourism studies in the primary and secondary school curricula**. Since tourism is a relatively new phenomenon in Kenya, there is a need to promote greater public awareness and appreciation of its value, and to develop a 'tourism culture' within the populace. This will go a long way in improving the image of the industry, and in making the Kenyan people even more hospitable to tourists than at present. Figure 14.2 and Table 14.2 illustrate the concept of tourism manpower training and development infrastructure.

Figure 14.2 *Proposed global policy for manpower training and development for the tourist industry*

● **Increased volume of training.** As existing colleges currently cannot satisfy the demand for qualified employees in quantitative terms, it is proposed that the volume of training should be intensified through:

● Expansion of the training facilities at existing colleges

Table 14.2 *Proposed future tourism manpower training and development infrastructure*

Type of training	Infrastructural provisions required
Conceptual skills	Universities Institutions of higher learning Training centres etc.
Management, marketing and conservation	Universities Colleges Technical institutes
Craftsmanship	Junior colleges Institutes of technology Polytechnics etc.
Public awareness and appreciation for tourism	Secondary schools Technical schools Primary schools Adult literacy programmes The mass media etc.

- Establishing subsidiary institutions, preferably at the Kenya coast, which is the hub of the country's tourist industry
- Intensifying refresher courses and seminars for industry employees
- Introducing hotel and tourism training programmes initially at provincial institutes of technology, and eventually at district institutes and polytechnics

The intensification of these training activities, apart from responding to the supply gap, will also go a long way in meeting the manpower needs of small scale establishments catering primarily for domestic tourists.

- **Diversification of training.** The establishment of tourism training programmes in other institutes will create demand for trainers to run those programmes. It has been suggested that diversification of training at Kenya's colleges should therefore address this need and plan for the production of the necessary personnel.

- **Training in tourism research.** In order to keep abreast of, and respond effectively to technological changes and to facilitate the adoption of technological developments by the industry, it has been suggested that research becomes part of training and manpower development. To this end, it has been suggested research capability should be developed at Kenya's tourism training institutions.

- **Higher level professional training.** It is proposed that Kenya Utalii College, being the only institution of its kind at present in Kenya, should be upgraded to be able to provide an even higher level of professional training leading to the award of higher level qualifications such as degrees. This will provide the country with the necessary conceptual skills needed at higher levels of responsibilities in both the public as well as private sectors in the industry. To this end, the college is already pursuing an intensive manpower development programme for its academic staff.

• **Involvement of the industry in training activities.** It has been suggested that the industry should be intimately involved in the training activities of the colleges. This is because the industry is the best barometer of training needs, and is the ultimate market for the manpower produced.

Conclusion

Tourism, according to a forecast by the ILO, will be the world's largest industry of the twenty-first century. It will likewise be the most important in terms of trade (foreign exchange earnings). In Kenya, the industry is already emerging as the most important earner of foreign exchange. Its efficient management and development for the long-term benefit of the country are therefore of crucial importance, and hence the need for careful planning for an adequate supply of qualified manpower, both in quantitative and qualitative terms.

References

International Labour Office (ILO) (1987) *Employment Generation in the Hotel, Catering and Tourism Sector*. Terminal Report, ILO, Geneva.
Kenya Utalii College (1985) Survey of Employment Opportunities for Kenya Utalii College Female Graduates. Unpublished.

15 Republic of Ireland
Mary Ena Walsh

This chapter looks at the development of tourism in Ireland in the context of the country's cultural and economic background. Tourism in the 1990s is a major growth sector in Ireland but the decade also sees the effects of the decreasing birth rate. This is a phenomenon that commenced later in Ireland than in other countries, but will have no less serious results.

For a country with a population of less than 4 million the realistic expectation of 5 million tourists per annum by the mid-1990s will create demands in terms of personnel, skills and infrastructure. In addition the potentially detrimental environmental effects need to be guarded against. However, it appears that Ireland is planning for this influx not only by developing the tourist product but also by enlarging and diversifying the training and educational provision for those employed and to be employed in tourism.

Background to the country and its tourism industry

Geography

Ireland is an island located on the north-west of Europe. The island lies on the continental shelf, separated from Britain by the Irish Sea. Within the 84 121 sq km of the island (politically divided into the southern Republic and the north-eastern corner which is part of the UK), there are many mountains, which form a barrier along the coast, long sandy beaches and the inevitable 'Many Shades of Green'.

Even though the island is only 450 km long, the scenery and attractions change frequently. The east coast, with the capital, Dublin, is home to many monuments, stately houses and gardens. Added to this are the attractions of a modern city with extensive shopping facilities, entertainment and activities. Moving southwards along the coast to the south-east, one finds a long coastline with many sandy beaches, long rivers such as the Barrow and Nore, and medieval cities and towns such as Kilkenny. Ireland's second city, Cork is located in the south of the country. The popular Cork–Kerry tourist area is bordered by the Atlantic ocean, and has the country's highest peak, Carrantouhill (1040m). The glacier lakes of this region are among the most famous in Europe, situated in this picturesque Ring of Kerry. The west coast is characterized by granite mountains and a ragged Atlantic coastline as well as the scenic tourist areas of the Burren and Connemara. Further north, the counties of Donegal, Sligo and Leitrim, provide steep mountains and deep valleys with dramatic peninsulae. Moving inland, to the flatter midlands, there is an area characterized by two distinct features, the Shannon Basin, with over 200 km of navigable water, and the lakelands of Cavan, world renowned for angling.

Ireland is one of the least densely populated countries in Europe. The population median age in Ireland, while rising, is younger than the EC average. Almost 40% of the population is under the age of 20. However, present demographic trends and projections show that there is now a declining birth rate.

Economy

Ireland has always been considered an agricultural country, with agriculture one of the main sources of employment. Since the 1950s, a significant change has occurred. In 1949, 42.9% of the labour force was engaged in agriculture, by 1968 it was 29.4%, by 1986 there had been a further 40% decline, leaving just under 16% employed in agriculture. Concurrent with this has been the growth of industrial employment, which has increased from 21.5% to 28.7% of total employment. However, the services sector now accounts for 55% of all employment which is almost twice its 1949 level.

Since joining the Community, with the UK and Denmark in 1973, both income and consumption, while continuing to grow, have done so at a slower rate than the Community average. Ireland now has the second highest unemployment rate in the Community. The country's main exports continue to be agriculture-related products, particularly meat, meat preparations and dairy products. The chief growth area has been computer equipment from businesses mainly owned by foreign multi-nationals. Tourism is now one of the top earners of foreign currency for Ireland, second only to computer equipment.

Tourism product – natural, cultural, fabricated

The tourism product

Traditionally Irish tourism accepted a product-orientated approach in which the natural attractions of the country have been marketed. Sites such as the passage graves at Newgrange, the ports on the Aran Islands and the round towers strategically placed around the country were left in their raw state. Increasingly in the late 1980s a more fabricated product was created. People's needs were catered for, most noticeably through the growth in interpretive, heritage and leisure centres. A desire to provide 'something to do' has superseded the dependence of Irish tourism on unspoilt countryside. The predicted boom in leisure facilities is beginning to happen. The Tourist Board, Bord Failte, has targeted this as part of its development plan.

The idea of 'The Green Island' is being encouraged with programmes for Irish peatlands, wetlands and nature reserves. The relatively unpolluted environment is mirrored in the development of walking, golfing, angling, equestrian sports, canoeing, sailing and cruising holidays.

Irish culture has much to offer the tourist. Traditional music is very much alive and performed in many venues throughout the country, while Irish theatres and plays are among the best in the world. Irish crafts are internationally renowned, from Waterford crystal to the smallest traditional basket makers. Craftspeople are to be found throughout the country, working in a wide range of materials such as wood, leather, batik, pottery and precious metals.

Since its inception, tourism in Ireland has been characterized by the friendliness of the people. It has been commented on by travellers to Ireland down the years, and more recently the *National Geographic* has portrayed people with an easy friendliness, accompanied by wonderful photography, the combination of which makes a forceful bid for visitors.

Tourism within the economy

Tourism is one of Ireland's oldest established industries and today is a major source of employment and of foreign revenue. Organized touring in Ireland began early in the nineteenth century. By 1845 the Bianconi network of coaches was averaging 4000 miles a day and opening many new areas to a new travelling public. Coaching inns were introduced to accommodate these travellers. The invention of the steam engine had far reaching effects on the hotel industry. The railways enabled still more people to travel. Seaside holidays became popular and the growth of the seaside resort, as we know it today, with its holiday hotels, began. Day trips also became very popular.

In the early days almost all visitors came from Britain. It was 1895 before the first package tour from the United States arrived in Killarney and Glengarriff. The first official tourist office was founded in the 1920s but, as with most modern tourism centres, the industry really grew over the last 30 years from 1960. Tourism is one of the most important sectors of the Irish economy. Tourist revenue in 1990 (domestic and foreign) amounted to IR£1551m or about 7% of gross national product. Figure 15.1 shows foreign exchange earnings from tourism from 1985 to 1990. In terms of exports this amounts to about 7% of revenue gained from abroad in the period, second only to computer equipment. Most recent estimates suggest that tourism supported in the region of 75 000 job equivalents in 1989, 50 000 of which are supported by foreign revenue. These figures do not include jobs supported by the recycling of taxes.

A significant proportion of foreign tourism spending within Ireland goes to the Exchequer via various taxes and charges. Unlike many sectors of the economy, the import requirement for tourism is extremely low. Nearly all inputs to the tourism sector come from within Ireland.

The government has recognized the importance of tourism and its growth potential. In 1988, one of the most serious government initiatives for the industry was introduced, this laid out targets to be achieved by 1992 in an expansion programme using EC structural fund money. This involved the doubling of tourism numbers to 4.2 million from 2.1 million, and an increase in spending by IR£500m, thus creating 25 000 jobs.

The nature of tourism often means it is based in less central and less developed areas of a country, which thus helps redistribute income and employment to poorer regions that are otherwise unattractive to industries or economic investment. This makes tourism an obvious area for investment by peripheral countries of the European Community, of which Ireland is one.

Markets: trends and projections

The market for Irish tourism is broadly based. Ireland has a worldwide ethnic market of people of Irish descent living in countries which are considered important 'out-bound tourism markets' such as Britain, the USA, Canada and Australia. On top of this the type of holiday which is provided in Ireland appeals to many in the EC who regard Ireland as

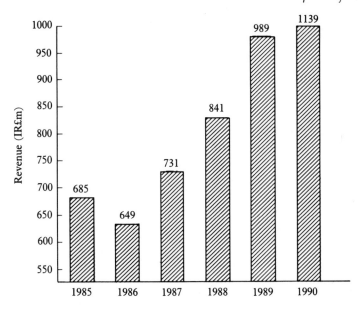

Figure 15.1   *Foreign exchange tourism earnings, 1985–90*

having a clean and fresh environment which is an important factor in their choice of Ireland as a holiday destination. Since 1986 there has been a steady increase in people visiting Ireland (Figure 15.2) and in the revenue gained from these visits (1881 million people/£436.5m in 1986 to 3096/£795.8m in 1990).

There were increases in all the main areas of tourism during the latter half of the 1980s. One of the biggest growth areas in the country has been educational tourism, students visiting Ireland for the summer to learn English or as part of their studies. The forecasts for Irish tourism from 1988 onwards and the launch of the government development plan for the industry saw large projected increases for the country: general holiday-makers to be increased by 120%; specialist holidays, 182%; visiting relatives, 59%; business visitors, 53%. This entailed 4.6 million visitors to Ireland in 1993 as compared to 2.425 million in 1988. Expenditure from foreign visitors alone was expected to increase to £1020m in 1992, while 25 000 new jobs were expected to be created by 1992.

Human resources situation

Despite the high levels of economic growth in Ireland between 1960 and 1973 there was almost no increase in the total number of people at

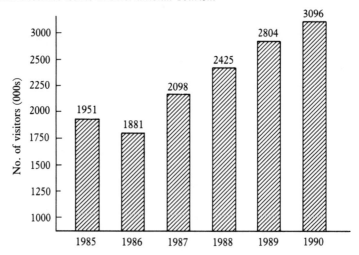

Figure 15.2   *Overseas tourist numbers, 1985–90*

work in the country. Growing services and manufacturing employment have partially made up for the decline in agricultural employment. In the first five years of EC membership, employment grew by 5%. Due to population trends in the 1970s, this did not lead to a decline in unemployment, which increased by 50% from 66 000 to 100 000. In the 13 years of EC membership between 1973 and 1986 total employment grew by 1.5% while agriculture and industry both declined (−41.6% and −7.6% respectively), while services saw a large increase (22.5%). Throughout the late 1980s and early 1990 the level of unemployment stabilized at between 17% and 18% of the labour force. This has led to the growth of considerable outward migration since 1986, exact figures for which are not available. Estimates range from between 20 000 and 50 000 per annum since the last census. Apparent declining numbers in receipt of unemployment benefit may be due to the fact that many are leaving the country. However, with the recent slowdown of the UK economy and tougher USA immigration laws, fewer people have been leaving for these traditional destinations for migrant Irish workers. Irish young people who are well educated and good workers have been able to obtain employment relatively easily in other countries, particularly in the tourism sector, while ironically tourism in Ireland is greatly understaffed in many areas.

Demographic situation

Population figures are based on the initial results of the 1991 census. Throughout the 1980s the traditional picture of the Irish population has changed. For the first time the rate of natural population increase is in decline, the numbers in the younger age groups are dropping, and the average age of the population is getting consistently older. The traditional rural based population is changing also, now 58% of the population is urban based.

Along with outward migration (mostly among the 15–29 age group), conservatively estimated to be the same as the natural increase, Ireland, after experiencing 25 years of rising population since 1961, is now experiencing the opposite. There has been a steady decrease in the birth rate since 1981 and the population is expected to continue to fall until well into the next century.

Human resources in tourism

Because of the broad area covered by tourism, it is very hard to ascertain the exact number of people directly employed in the industry, a problem compounded by the seasonality of the business. In the hotel and catering sector of the industry it is easier to quantify the numbers of people employed. In a 1988 CERT survey, it was found that 58 000 people were employed in hotels, guesthouses and restaurants. About 75% of employment in such establishments is directly related to tourism. Staff turnover is less than 10%.

CERT carried out a survey on employment and training in the tourism and leisure sectors in 1990. These reports provide valuable information to those involved with this industry. These showed that about 14 500 people are employed in the non-food and accommodation sectors of tourism and 2400 in leisure centres. When one adds in the travel sector and the large number of indirect and induced jobs, it is clear that tourism is a significant source of employment. The diversification and development of new tourism products generate ancillary occupations in the sector and often promote the creation of small and medium-sized enterprises requiring low investment costs.

Status of tourism as employment

In the economy in general, tourism is responsible for 7.5% of the non-agricultural workforce and 11% of those employed in the service sector. By its nature tourism is highly labour-intensive, relying to a great extent on personal service and face-to-face contact. In economic terms it is probably the sector least vulnerable to substitution of capital for labour. Additionally much tourist based employment is in otherwise economically under-developed areas, particularly the south-west, west and north-west.

The fact that tourism has its own training organization underlines the importance of the industry. In 1990 CERT placed all of its college graduates in employment and overall training was provided for 9400. In 1993 CERT, through college courses, courses for the unemployed, external courses and courses in industry, hopes to be training 12 130 people, a 10% cumulative increase on its 1988 figures.

Education and training for tourism

Until relatively recently education and training for the tourism industry in Ireland were centred around the hotel and restaurant sectors. Dublin College of Catering, founded in 1941, was the first college to provide courses and it continues to train both management and craft students. Shannon College of Hotel Management founded in 1952 trains management students.

In 1963, CERT, the Council for Education, Recruitment and Training for the hotel and catering industry, was founded. It is a state sponsored agency, governed by a council representative of employers, trade unions and educational organizations and government departments. CERT's brief was extended in 1975 to include tourism and it is now known as CERT – the State Tourism Training Agency. Initially CERT operated courses mainly in seasonal hotels, but with the advent of the regional technical colleges in 1970 and the provision, through CERT's intervention, of schools of hotel, catering and tourism studies in many of these colleges, provision transferred to these institutions. Most of its craft students follow National Craft Curricula and Certification Board courses.

Training and education have become formalized within the tertiary educational system. In addition to Dublin College of Catering, the Hotel, Catering and Training School in Killybegs and six regional technical colleges, courses are now provided in four centres run directly by CERT in order to provide additional trainee places to those provided by the educational authorities. Trainees in these centres follow exactly the same course as do those in the colleges.

In 1979 CERT initiated its first formal training programme for tour guides. This is a part-time course from September to March and comprises classroom sessions, guest lecturers and visits, national tours and tour simulation. It is now mandatory to have passed the CERT examination before being formally recognized as a tour guide by the tourist board, Bord Failte Eireann (BFE). In the 1980s a very small number of college courses in tourism began to emerge, mainly in the areas of tourism reception and tourism administration.

In 1982 CERT established the National Craft Curricula and Certification Board (NCCCB) as the Irish national certifying body for the hotel, catering and tourism industry. The board is appointed by the council of CERT, is representative of the social partners and the educationalists and operates under the auspices of CERT and the Department of Education. The NCCCB, through its committees, undertakes research of industry and educational needs, design of training courses and implementation of assessment procedures. The certificates awarded by it to trainees are recognized throughout the industry in Ireland and in all EC countries. There are three NCCCB tourism (as distinct from hotel and catering) programmes in operation and these are dealt with in more detail in the following section.

Some of the third level institutions now offer tourism as an option on business or language courses, but there is as yet no degree course in tourism. However, in 1990 a postgraduate degree in Irish Heritage Management was launched in University College Cork. Within the second level educational system there is a range of vocational preparation and training programmes (VPTP) that relate to tourism and additional courses in the tourism and leisure areas have been available from 1991.

In addition to formal college and school programmes, CERT run in-service training courses for those in the industry. These courses are conducted internally and externally and cover a broad spectrum of tourism activities. A 'Start Your Own Tourism Business' course has also been developed and is run in modular form over six months.

Ireland has now become involved in the exciting and innovative arena of serious tourism educational development. Tourism is a uniquely multi-faceted industry and it is clear that it is important to have a definitive approach to the education and training required to optimize the opportunities it presents, while minimizing the detrimental effects to national culture and natural heritage. Existing tourism educators are only too well aware of its diverse and complex nature. As an academic discipline, while it is emerging it is also fragmented. This fragmentation indicates the diverse nature of tourism and compounds the problem of gaining recognition for the importance of tourism education.

Historically, tourism development has been thought to involve rather narrow or limited functions. While this may be so in the case of individual operations or businesses (hotels, airlines, rental firms), tourism education cannot and should not respond to these needs alone. A professional must be prepared with the knowledge and skills to understand the totality of the field, the inter-relationships involved and the impacts on people and economics. The fact that tourism directly or indirectly touches the lives of so many, increases the

209

responsibility of those involved in tourism education. The primary aim of a professional tourism education programme should be to enable the students to meet the changing needs of the industry while continuing to pursue the traditional principles of learning and research.

Tourism suffers in the public perception by not being a unified entity and the generation of academic studies would help to raise the public perception as well as to raise and maintain the academic status of tourism. This would give society the planners and providers it will require in the not so distant era – 'beyond 2000'. It is important that all tourism programmes be respected by the providers and by the industry as high-calibre courses, professionally developed and taught. The courses should provide well-educated, broadly based individuals who can work to a high level of professionalism in such a wide-reaching and significant industry. It must never be forgotten that tourism is an increasingly competitive service industry which requires high-calibre personnel. Those individuals who work in it will require a broad education within a relevant context which can assist them to meet the needs of a complex work environment while developing and practising the management principles appropriate to the service sector.

Whether tourism has become the world's major industry already, and Somerset Waters (author of the annual *Travel Industry World Yearbook*) says it reached that status in 1985, or whether it will wait until 2000 to do so, it is clear the tourist of 2000, due to changing demographics, will be older, better educated, more affluent and less encumbered with dependants. These tourists will be more demanding, less brand-loyal, and certainly less willing to tolerate shoddy service and exorbitant prices. Future success is likely to belong to those who have been educated to understand that service is of paramount importance in both the tourism industry and in tourism marketing.

Initiatives to overcome human resources issues

National initiatives

The establishment of CERT, nearly 30 years ago, was a far sighted national initiative by government. CERT initiates, plans and develops new courses and course structures as a result of research carried out nationally to identify industry needs and changing trends. The results of this research provide the starting point for the development of curricula and the resultant courses are piloted and then offered to the prospective employees in a range of centres nationally. CERT is uniquely placed to identify national trends and to plan for them on a short-, medium- and long-term basis. The ability to respond rapidly and professionally to industry needs and government initiatives has always been a hallmark of CERT's product.

The present funding of tourism-related courses for unemployed people permits such courses to be run in areas of tourism potential. These CERT-run courses are very often in areas of high unemployment, thus these courses provide employment for those without jobs and at the same time provide people with a training for a growing and labour-intensive industry. This may be seen as part of the government's aim to give priority to tourism in its efforts to tackle unemployment (White Paper on Tourism Policy, 1985).

Initiatives with education and training

The introduction by CERT in 1979 of a preliminary course in Hotel, Catering and Tourism Studies, was innovative in being an introduction to basic tourism-related skills for students of average ability and also, perhaps more importantly, it adopted 'an integrated approach to the teaching of practical skills, hospitality and tourism theory, cultural studies and functional literacy, numeracy and communications' (Baum and Walsh, 1988). This course was the forerunner of the present Vocational Preparation and Training Programmes (VPTP) and indeed in 1985 the course was revised to run under the VPT guidelines at level two. Those who complete these courses have opportunities for direct employment as well as entry to NCCCB Courses. Due to the demand for these and similar programmes, some tourism-related courses were developed at VPT level, designed to meet local employment needs and to respond to the local environment.

As a result of research in the 1980s, the need was identified for personnel trained in a range of skills – 'multi-skilled', to operate in a range of departments within the one establishment. This reflected the fact that most Irish tourism businesses are relatively small and are family run. To meet this need the Hospitality Skills programme was developed – the steps in its development have been well documented elsewhere (Baum, 1987). Briefly, the course gives young people basic skills, experience and knowledge which have application through the hospitality industry. An interdisciplinary approach is used for the teaching of this course, utilizing the concept of customers' needs and hospitality as the strand common to all the technical areas of work. This course is offered in regional technical colleges and CERT centres. Research carried out in 1989 showed that 79% of the participants were working in jobs involving multi-skilling and that employers found that

211

those who had attended this course displayed confidence, a positive attitude to work and an ability to relate well to customers and colleagues.

In the late 1980s a number of full-time advanced level and supervisory programmes were developed, in order to provide a career ladder within the craft areas – these programmes are Supervision of Food and Beverage Services, Supervision of Bar Operations, Supervision of Accommodation Services. All these combine advanced practical skills with the leadership and operational skills required to adjust more easily and effectively to the new managerial role of the supervisor. From 1990 participants on these programmes have also had a four-week intensive French language programme.

In 1990 two new tourism programmes commenced in one of the regional technical colleges. One of the courses is for school leavers. It aims to develop young tourism professionals who have a keen understanding of tourism and have the customer service skills needed to start a career within the industry. In addition to in-depth tourism studies, the programme focuses on customer relations, sales techniques and language ability. As part of the training, trainees will be placed on work experience within the tourism industry to give them an opportunity to apply their skills in a real life situation. Work experience will take place at the end of the college phase of the course and will form part of the on-going assessment for certification.

The second programme is an Advanced Certificate in Tourism Studies and has been designed for people already working or involved in the tourism industry. It allows them to take advantage of the winter period to further develop their professional skills, to enhance their knowledge of the tourism industry in Ireland and to gain a formal qualification.

Particular target groups include:

- Proprietors of tourism businesses
- Tourism supervisors who wish to upgrade their supervisory skills.
- Tourism workers who wish to diversify in a new area of the tourism industry

In addition, CERT has developed an adult education programme, using a range of teaching methodologies, for those employed in tourist information offices and visitor attractions. This Customer and Information Skills Certificate Programme commenced in 1990 and was developed to meet the job requirements of tourism advisers and to provide the skills, knowledge and attitude required for a high standard of job performance. The primary areas of interpersonal skills, technical knowledge and knowledge of the Irish culture are integrated throughout the programme. Considerable emphasis is placed on interpersonal skills and the application of knowledge in a way that anticipates and satisfies the customers' needs. The main tourism agencies in Ireland cooperated in this development programme.

Many schools are now beginning to provide programmes for school leavers that relate to the tourist industry. As mentioned earlier, a number of VPT level two programmes were piloted in 1991 by CERT and the educational providers. These include:

- Rural and agri-tourism. This programme will aim to provide a basic knowledge of agriculture, relevant to tourism, for school leavers, particularly for those who live in areas where agri-tourism is a significant part of the local economy.
- Tourism and leisure. This programme will aim to provide school leavers with a basic knowledge of leisure and possible leisure pursuits and leisure centre activities as related to the tourism industry. It will complement some other leisure-related programmes at the same level.
- Tourism and travel. This programme will relate to very specific aspects of the tourism industry and should prepare students for a wide range of occupations.

Trainees on all programmes will have the option of taking up employment or of continuing to tertiary education on completion of these programmes.

Industry initiatives

While the training agencies and educational providers are doing as much as possible to provide a range of training courses that are attractive to the school leaver and that meet the needs of the tourism industry, it is important that the young person sees tourism as a worthwhile and rewarding career. As we have seen, the industry is expanding and at the same time the number of school leavers is declining.

At present the hotel and restaurant sectors of tourism are those most seriously in need of additional personnel. In the spring of 1990 the Irish Hotels Federation (IHF) mounted a job shop in London to show those working in London and elsewhere in the UK the opportunities available in Ireland. For the past two years the IHF have also run open days at hotels throughout the country to give young people information on the range of jobs and training available in the sector.

Women who wish to return to work are, as yet, a relatively untapped source of personnel in the tourism industry in Ireland. Inadequate childcare facilities militate against their doing so and the hours to be worked are not always convenient for those with family commitments. However, if industry approached the matter with a degree of goodwill, innovation and flexibility as well as lateral thinking, it might well prove possible to rearrange some of the workload to suit the hours that this cohort of the workforce would find convenient while yet maintaining adequate staff levels to ensure satisfied customers and an efficient operation. In 1990, CERT commenced short Return to Work programmes in Dublin and Cork.

Conclusions and projections for the future

Over IR£300m was spent between 1990 and 1992 in developing Ireland as a quality tourism destination offering the tourist a wide range of leisure activities. Forty per cent of Irish hotels now offer leisure facilities and the number of heritage centres, activity centres and managed historical sites has mushroomed. At the same time there has been a record investment in training the tourism workforce and in raising overall standards of product and service.

Irish tourism offers a lifetime career in a fast growing industry. Recent growth has been quite phenomenal, at twice the world average rate, and over 700 new tourism and catering businesses have come into existence since 1984. The traditional employment profile of the industry is changing as it grows and adapts to new market demands. All-weather facilities, special packages and the encouragement of incentive tours have extended the tourism season considerably.

The tourism industry in Ireland, as well as internationally, has expanded over the past decade and the peak of this expansion does yet not appear to have been reached. The diversity in travellers' motivation has spurred a diversification of the tourism industry. Plans are in hand for the increase and development of new products in all sectors of the industry. It is important that those involved in the design of the tourism product take measures to ensure that the potentially negative aspects of tourism on both the environment and culture are minimized. This requires both education and foresight if those very aspects of Irish life that attract the tourists are not to be eroded by them to the detriment of tourism, the economy and most important of all, the Irish people.

The demand for quality suits the Irish tourist market which neither sells itself as a cheap nor as a sunshine destination (though recent summers have tended to belie the stereotypical view of Irish weather). In order to achieve and maintain this quality standard it is essential to have a well-educated and well-trained workforce. The range of occupations within that work-force is enormous and growing; as well as the traditional culinary, service and accommodation personnel, there are tour guides, interpreters of heritage and historical sites, airline, other carrier and car hire personnel, visitor attraction personnel, entertainers, coach drivers, Bureaux de Change personnel, traditional craftspeople (weavers, thatchers, woodcarvers and many others), organizers of outdoor pursuits and leisure activities, both indoor and outdoor, active and passive, information personnel – this list is by no means exhaustive and no mention has been made of support services and indirect and induced employments. To attempt to meet these staffing requirements the educators and trainers need to be flexible and innovative and to be blessed with a considerable degree of foresight.

For its part, the tourism industry must constantly promotes and projects itself as a rewarding and caring source of employment to those about to enter the workforce. Competition for employees must and can be addressed just as competition for tourists has and is being successfully addressed.

Training and education in and for tourism have advanced rapidly and new training courses in private as well as in state educational establishments are proliferating. Those involved in tourism education must ensure that this rapid expansion is not at the cost of quality and professionalism and that the courses are geared to meet realistic present and future needs.

Bibliography

Baum, T. (1987) Introducing educational innovation in hospitality studies: a case study in practical curriculum change. *International Journal of Hospitality Management*, **6**(2), 97–102.

Baum, T. and Walsh, M. E. (1988) Developing tourism/education in the Republic of Ireland. Paper presented at 'Teaching Tourism into the 1990s', University of Surrey, 1988.

Bord Failte Eireann (1987) *Trade Information Manual*, BFE, Dublin.

Bord Failte Eireann (1989a) *Developing for Growth. A Framework Development Plan for Irish Tourism*, BFE, Dublin.

Bord Failte Eireann (1989b) *Tourism in the Irish Economy*, BFE, Dublin.

Bord Failte Eireann (1990) *Tourist Facts 1989*, BFE, Dublin.

Central Statistics Office (1987) Census Figures. CSO, Dublin.

Central Statistics Office (1990) Monthly Figures, May. CSO, Dublin.

CERT (1985) (1989) *Manpower Study of the Hotel and Catering Industry* (11 vols), CERT, Dublin.

CERT (1987) *Scope of Tourism Industry in Ireland*, CERT, Dublin.

CERT (1989) *Review of the Hospitality Crafts Course and of Multi-skills in the Hotel and Catering Industry*, CERT, Dublin.

CERT (1989) (1990) *Annual Report*, CERT, Dublin.

CERT (1991) *Profile of Employment in the Tourism Industry in Ireland – Non-Food and Accommodation Sectors*, CERT, Dublin.

CERT (1991) *Profile of Employment in Leisure Centres in Ireland*, CERT, Dublin.

Commission of the European Communities (1988) *Eurostat Demographic Statistics*, European Commission, Luxemburg.

Brian de Breffny (ed.) (1977) *The Irish World*, Thames and Hudson, London.

Davy Kelleher McCarthy (1989) *Ireland's Changing Population Structure – with Forecasts of Population and Labour Force to 2011*, Davy Kelleher McCarthy Ltd, Dublin.

Department of Tourism and Transport (1989) *Operational Programme for Tourism 1989–1995*, DTT, Dublin.

Dully, Martin (1990) Adopting a visitor oriented approach (interview with Martin Dully, Chairman Bord Failte). *Irish Times*, 14 May.

ILO (1989) *Productivity and Training in the Hotel, Catering and Tourism Industry*, International Labour Office, Geneva.

National Economic and Social Council (1989) Ireland in the European Community: Performance, Prospects and Strategy. NESC report No. 88, August 1989.

Nugent, James (1990) Tourism offers lifetime career (interview with James Nugent, Chairman CERT). *Irish Times*, 17 August.

Walsh, M. E. (1989) Making the most of HR in tourism. Paper presented at 'Making the Most of Tourism Resources' Conference, Tourism Society/University of Ulster, 1989.

White Paper on Tourism Policy (1985) Dublin, Stationery Office.

16 United Kingdom
Tom Baum

Introduction

The United Kingdom, consisting of England, Scotland, Wales and Northern Ireland, is characterized by diversity in terms of its geography, history and culture and this variation is one of the most significant features and strengths within the country's tourism product and its attractions for visitors. Well-known tourism destinations and locations come readily to mind when thinking about the industry in Great Britain and Northern Ireland. These include urban historic and cultural locations such as London, Oxford, Stratford-upon-Avon, Bath, Londonderry and Edinburgh; countryside attractions, large and small, such as the Highlands of Scotland, the Cotswolds, Snowdonia National Park or the Giant's Causeway Coast in Northern Ireland; the growing interest in locations representing Britain's industrial heritage such as Bradford, Liverpool, Glasgow and Ironbridge; and, lastly, traditional (but changing) coastal resorts such as Blackpool, Bournemouth, Brighton, Skegness, Ayr, Portrush and Llandudno. However, while these and similar locations remain the focus of United Kingdom tourism, a feature of recent tourism policy, at local and national level, has been attempts at dispersement of tourists to a wider range of localities and to encourage visitors outside of the main summer season. The former objective has been singularly unsuccessful as a means of persuading overseas visitors to visit locations other than London (in fact, since 1979, the situation has steadily declined and London's dominance has increased by a number of percentage points) but the policy has succeeded in spreading visits more widely between non-London locations. The latter aspect of the policy has been relatively successful, with a strong trend towards visits during off peak and shoulder periods. The result of these initiatives is that the notion of tourism as 'an industry of every parish' is coming close to reality. Thus, tourism impinges on all areas of the country, prosperous and depressed, with the facility to spread its economic benefits (as well as its problems and difficulties) very widely.

Tourism has also proved its temporary 'quick fix' capabilities for areas and regions of particular depression; the United Kingdom has exploited this through, for example, the series of major Garden Festivals in Liverpool, Stoke on Trent, Glasgow, Gateshead and Ebbw Vale. While the sustained benefit of these events is open to dispute, immediate economic and employment impacts are evident and appear to link to longer-term tourism growth. Glasgow, for example, has now attained considerable status as a visitor destination. Conversely, of course, tourism in the United Kingdom, as elsewhere, is highly vulnerable to the negative effects of terrorism, environmental pollution or the weather, which impact on localities with dramatic, immediate consequences for the economy and local employment. The dramatic downturn in international tourism arising out of the Gulf War of 1991 is a good example of this.

This chapter considers the structure, value and performance of United Kingdom tourism and places major emphasis on how these impact on the full range of human resource issues within the industry.

Structure of the tourism industry in the United Kingdom

The tourism industry in the United Kingdom, as in any other country, features a disparate amalgam of sectors carrying out very different business activities but with a common purpose of meeting business and service objectives through satisfying domestic and overseas tourist needs. Businesses are, primarily, in the private domain, although public sector involvement cannot be ignored. Some of these businesses are wholly or for the most part involved in tourism while the balance have a partial involvement which is still of major significance to the operation of the industry (Parsons, 1987). The actual number of companies involved in UK tourism is not known but a very conservative estimate of those primarily involved with tourism is well in excess of 50 000. To the diverse commercial sectors should be added a wide spectrum of public sector and support operations, predominantly involved in tourism-related activity.

The number of businesses involved at a partial level is estimated, again fairly conservatively, at 150 000 within the private sector and this figure does not appear to include the major retail area, to which very significant benefit accrues from tourist expenditure (Parsons, 1987).

The UK tourism economy and markets

The tourist industry, in the United Kingdom, is a major and expanding generator of wealth and employment. Statistics for 1991 provide an estimate of £171 968 million turnover. This represents over 4% of the total UK gross domestic product. In 1990, over 40% of these earnings represented foreign exchange income, estimated at some £7800 million (BTA, 1991), which means that tourism compares favourably, in terms of both turnover and foreign exchange earnings, with major industrial/ manufacturing and other service sectors. Indeed, tourism's earnings overseas constitute 28% of the country's service export earnings (more than the City of London) or 4.6% of the country's total export earnings. In terms of employment, the significance of tourism is of equal if not greater impact; this will be covered at a later stage in the chapter.

Overseas visitors totalled some 18.0 million in 1991 (BTA, 1991), representing an increase of 1.4 million over 1988 (+9%) and of 4.7 million over the figure for 1980. The overall increase in overseas visitors was dominated by strong Western European growth of some 10% (to 10.6 million), but all originating markets saw significant increases. The expenditure corollary of this growth indicates a total foreign exchange income of some £7800 million in 1991. These increases are greater, by some 3% and 5% respectively, than the cost of living rises/inflation rates over the corresponding periods.

The major overseas markets, in terms of expenditure, for UK tourism are the USA (21%), followed by the Middle East (7%), France and Germany (6%) and the Irish Republic (5%). In terms of visitor numbers, the top five countries are the USA, France, Germany, the Irish Republic and the Netherlands. These top five have remained the same for over a decade and account for more than 50% of total overseas visitors. Japan, although only eleventh in the rank order by numbers, is a rapidly growing market. Visitors come to the United Kingdom for a variety of reasons, the predominant motive (but one that is declining in significance) is that of holiday-making. Business and VFR (visiting friends and relatives) motives are also of considerable significance and increased their share proportionately during the 1980s.

Domestic tourism in the United Kingdom is a major contributor both to the performance and character of the industry as the pattern and spread of this sector of the business is rather different from that of overseas visitors, although there are areas of similarity. Spending by UK residents accounts for nearly 60% of total tourism revenues, for approximately £10 470 million in 1991 (English Tourist Board, 1992). A considerably higher proportion (60%) of domestic trips are primarily for holiday purposes than is the case with visits from overseas (42%), followed by VFR and business which lag somewhat behind.

219

The regional breakdown of domestic tourist bednights for English Tourist Board regions and those areas under the jurisdiction of the Northern Ireland, the Scottish and the Wales Tourist Boards respectively, shows a major difference from the overseas pattern. The West Country of England has been, over the past decade, and remains the dominant region in terms of domestic tourism within the United Kingdom. Scotland and Wales account for the next highest returns, followed by a cluster of seven English regions, ahead of London. Northern Ireland, with its particular problems and access factors, brings up the rear. This contrasts with London's dominance (41%) of overseas tourist bednights and the relative poverty of Scotland (7%) and Wales (3%). Data collection weaknesses mean that it is difficult to report the impact of overseas visitors to Northern Ireland, although significant business is generated within the Irish Republic and through joint marketing initiatives with Bord Failte, the Irish Tourist Board. Thus, it is clear that market demands, character and spending power vary significantly within the different tourist destinations of the United Kingdom. This, in turn, has consequences for the human resource arena.

Employment in United Kingdom tourism

Tourism is a major and growing employer in the United Kingdom and, although the basis for various estimates of the actual numbers may be open to debate, the overall human resource scenario and the employment challenges that face all sectors of the industry attract consensus and agreement. Official 1992 statistics (BTA, 1992) put the total employment figure at 1.5 million to include those who provide direct service for overseas and domestic tourists. Looked at from a sector-specific viewpoint and one that sprawls over both tourism- and non-tourism-related activity, the hotel and catering industry is estimated to employ some 2.4 million persons in full- and part-time capacities, out of a total labour force of approximately 25 million (Battersby, 1990). The dominant employment sectors are, not unexpectedly, the accommodation and food-related areas although growth was evident during the 1980s within all the major categories outlined above. Projections suggested sustained growth within all sectors of the industry in the early 1990s – creation of new positions within hotels and catering was estimated to reach about 1000 per week. Projections of subsectoral growth for the period 1987–93 were more uneven, however, ranging from a high of 34% with respect to restaurants to a low of 13% for pubs.

Variations in the geographical impact of tourism employment are of particular significance. All regions witnessed employment growth within hotels and catering in the ten years to 1987 and continuation of this trend was projected up to 1993, with the possible exception of the North, for which data are contradictory (Baty, 1990). Despite the impact of the recession, during the early 1990s, employment demand in some sectors of the industry, continued to remain strong (Afiya, 1992). The actual employment distribution reflects the spread of business, with the South East (including London) offering the lion's share of positions, followed, at considerable distance, by the South West, the North West and Scotland.

The nature of tourism businesses varies considerably between regions of the United Kingdom and this impacts directly on the employment environment. There is a very clear pattern of 'centre to periphery' in terms of the size and structure of tourism businesses, the commercial and product focus and the nature of the markets for which they cater. This, only in part, represents urban–rural issues. Tourism businesses in the more remote western and northern parts of the United Kingdom are, characteristically, small in size and number of employees, seasonal in operation and frequently family owned and managed. Thus, the relationship of these businesses to the labour market is totally different from that of the large hotel, attraction or tour operator in the metropolitan areas. Likewise, the skills demand they place on local education and training providers is very different from the larger companies and their ability and facility to invest in in-company training, for example, are very limited. This environment should give a strong regional focus to manpower policies for tourism in the United Kingdom, particularly from the point of view of educational and training provision. In practice, the flexibility and sensitivity of local and regional providers varies greatly from area to area. The case of Wales provides a good illustration of the manpower and employment issues within one major UK region.

Wales – a case study

Wales represents a very good example of peripheral United Kingdom tourism. The predominant visitor market is domestic (this includes day trips) and, in actual visits, the approximately 12 million trips made by domestic visitors represent over 90% of all tourists coming to Wales (Wales Tourist Board, 1988). The expenditure ratio is not quite so extreme but, none the less, domestic tourism accounts for over 80% of the total income to the industry in Wales. The region accounts for 8–9% of domestic tourist trips and 10–12% of bednights within the United Kingdom as a whole. By contrast, overseas tourism accounts for 4% of visits, 3% of bednights and 2% of the total expenditure of visitors to the UK.

Wales offers a relatively traditional and, it could be argued, underdeveloped tourism product, possibly because of its predominant domestic market orientation. It could also be argued that the product profile is a major cause of the market balance. The country is, geographically, mainly rural, with industrial and urban concentration in the south-east and north-east. Holiday locations tend to be the small, coastal, largely old fashioned resorts along the north, west and south-west coast, complemented by limited inland attractions and urban, historic cities such as Cardiff. The distribution of tourism in Wales is very uneven and contrasts strongly with population patterns. This is reflected in the distribution of accommodation; 65% of recorded bedspaces are in the counties of Gwynedd and Dyfed which, in turn, account for just 20% of the total population of Wales. This has important ramifications for employment.

The business structure of Welsh tourism reflects its market orientation, with a preponderance of small operations, trading on a highly seasonal basis. Up to 80% of the accommodation stock in Wales is of the non-serviced type, frequently permanent caravans and other self- catering sites. This proportion is much higher than for the United Kingdom as a whole. Wales has no major 'magnet' attraction and this means that the promotion of the tourism product, by the Wales Tourist Board and the local authorities, is largely of a general destination rather than of specific products. Tourism accounts for more than 9% of all employment in Wales, or over 80 000 full-time equivalent jobs. Taking seasonality (a very important consideration in Welsh tourism) and part-time work into account means that the actual number employed directly in tourism exceeds this figure by a significant amount. Tourism employment in Wales represents some 6% of tourism employment in the United Kingdom, compared with the Welsh share of some 4% of total UK employment (Medlik, 1989). This gives graphic illustration to the significance of tourism to peripheral areas within the United Kingdom.

Medlik, in his analysis of the impact of tourism on the economy in Wales, identifies five key characteristics of tourism employment which have particular impact in the region and these transfer, with little adjustment, to the majority of 'periphery' areas in the United Kingdom (Scotland, Northern Ireland, the Lake District, the South-West) as well as elsewhere in northern Europe (the west of Ireland, the Atlantic seaboard of Norway, Normandy etc.). These characteristics are:

• Tourism employment in Wales is *broadly based*, extending over a diversity of business sectors and involving variety in both direct and indirect employment. To this can be added the aforementioned

222

point regarding business size, and the lack of diversification in many operations. Thus, employment dependency on tourism is also very high.

- Tourism employment features a high level of self-employment and, also, family employment. While, generally, the industry has witnessed increasing concentration, a feature of the marginal tourism areas and, thus, of Wales, is that this trend has been slower to impact. Within self- and family employment, the impact, on employment, of business cycles, whether growth or decline, is not so immediate or significant.
- Women have, traditionally, played a major part in staffing tourism businesses, especially within the family and seasonal tourism environment of a region such as Wales. Traditional employment sources (agricultural and industrial) have also been in considerable decline in Wales, with the result that female labour in the tourism industry has taken on added significance as the major bread winner in many households. However, the proportionate importance of women within the Welsh labour force is less than that within the UK as a whole.
- Part-time employment is another characteristic of tourism-related sectors and, in Wales, it features considerably more strongly in, for example hotel/catering and leisure/recreation than it does in the United Kingdom as a whole, indicating, once again, the more marginal and small business features of the industry in Wales.
- Seasonality, as has been said, is a significant feature within Welsh tourism, although its impact is actually quite difficult to monitor and is not felt evenly throughout the region. The industrial and commercial centres certainly do not experience the same pattern of visitors as seaside resorts in Mid and North Wales. However, employment statistics show considerable variation between low periods early in the year and summer high points; more so than for the UK as a whole (Medlik, 1989).

Human resource issues, in Welsh tourism, mirror many of those that feature in the UK in general and which will be covered later in this chapter. Skills shortages within the hotel and catering sector of one Welsh county, for example, are critical with respect to jobs such as chefs/cooks, waiting staff, barpersons, counterhands/assistants and catering supervisors (Hotel and Catering Training Board, 1990). Welsh needs, in terms of educational provision, appear to focus on the desirability of providing more locally sensitive and responsive pro-grammes. The vehicle for this, should, according to the Welsh Joint Education Committee Report, focus on Wales-wide structures for the coordination, development and resourcing of tourism education in

Wales, integrating the contributions of a number of agencies and public departments (Welsh Joint Education Committee, 1990).

Demographic and labour market trends

The key issue facing United Kingdom tourism in terms of demographic and labour market trends centres on the decreasing number of young people available to a growing industry during the 1990s. Between 1990 and 1995, there will be a decline of 20% or 1.2 million in the number of 16–24-year-olds, the prime recruitment cohort for the country's tourism industry in terms of both its qualified entrants and its lesser skilled and temporary workforce. The decline with respect to the 16–19-year-old school leaver group will be even more pronounced, at 25%. At the same time, pressures are increasing for young people to remain in school longer in order to bring the United Kingdom into line with other countries in the European Community and other developed economies, thus further restricting the pool of relatively unskilled labour, upon which the tourism industry has traditionally depended. However, paradoxically, changes in funding arrangements for higher education are likely to mean that more and more students will seek to work their way through college, following the American tradition, and this should increase the availability of part-time employees to tourism businesses. The labour shortages in the United Kingdom impact in different ways on various vocational areas and skills levels. Key current shortages, which are likely to persist, are in the semi-skilled and skilled craft designations in all sectors.

These demographic changes will have further impact as a result of uneven economic growth and development within the United Kingdom, in particular competition for labour within all industry sectors in the South-East of England will continue to 'suck' young people away from other regions of the country, many of which have significantly tourism-dependent economic and employment structures. This pressure on labour to migrate from the periphery to the centre and its particular impact on tourism has a parallel within the European context where additional competition will increasingly come from major European locations. Demographic issues pertain, with equal force, in most northern European countries and, as a result, marginal UK locations may see their potential tourism workforce drawn towards 'magnet' centres such as Paris (especially with its new international attractions), Frankfurt and Amsterdam. The very relevant parallel experience of the Irish tourism industry (with respect to both the Republic and Northern Ireland) and the skills drain to Britain, Germany and Belgium exemplify how this process can operate. Moves towards common European qualifications within the tourism industry will clearly contribute to, and facilitate, this tendency.

The corollary of a declining youth population is an increasing average age within the country as a whole. Thus, the number in the age range 25–60 will increase by 2 million between 1990 and 1995. Likewise, the proportion of the population over the retirement age will increase during the 1990s, due to both falling birthrate and improved health care factors. This has evident implications for tourism markets and product provision. These trends also have considerable significance for labour recruitment and the need for the tourism industry in the United Kingdom actively to consider facilitating the assimilation of 'non-traditional' recruits into the workforce, especially women returners, older workers and members of ethnic minorities (Worsfold and Jameson, 1991). This will involve consideration of a wide variety of alternative work-related structures and initiatives, including changes to rosters, provision of special support facilities, revision of training strategies, more attractive part-time and job-share models and the development of new perceptions of the tourism industry as a 'good place to work'.

Education and training for tourism in the United Kingdom

The origins of education and training for the tourism industry in the United Kingdom lie, very clearly, within provision for the food and accommodation sector, at secondary, further, higher and in-company levels. Home economics or domestic science as a school subject and hotel and catering studies within technical/vocational education are the mainstream starting points for much of the educational and training provision for all sectors within tourism.

These origins resulted in the evolution of fairly consistent national provision of full-time and part-time/apprenticeship education and training for hotel and catering studies at craft, supervisory and management levels, with a wide-reaching network of provision within colleges of further education, colleges of higher education, polytechnics and, increasingly, universities. Specialist, monotechnic provision of the type common in the Netherlands and Switzerland, for example, was and remains unusual in the United Kingdom. Indeed, the trend has been towards institutional amalgamation, so that the few existing specialist colleges have, often, been subsumed by larger neighbours. Examples, from Northern Ireland, saw Newry Hotel and Catering College become a department within the local further education college (albeit with new facilities and increased resources) and Garnaville College merged with what has evolved to be the University of Ulster. An independent paradox, however, remains in the Portrush Hotel and Catering College. The same picture is true elsewhere in the United Kingdom.

The needs of other sectors of the tourism industry, however, have been met through far more patchy provision. Indeed, it is only in the past decade that the educational and training requirements of the broader tourism and travel industry have been considered on a national and comprehensive basis. Early initiatives, for example by the Universities of Strathclyde and Surrey, were the first of their kind to address tourism as an academic and vocational field independent from hotels and catering, although, interestingly and possibly to their detriment, both grew out of existing hotel school structures and environments. At the more technical end of educational and training provision, the specialist needs of, for example, travel agencies, were met through the focused provision of training initiated by the Association of British Travel Agents (ABTA) in colleges and independent training agencies, leading to, for example, International Air Transport Association (IATA) ticketing qualifications. The consequence of developments up to the late 1980s was that education and training provision for some tourism industry sectors was relatively comprehensive and sophisticated, if a little traditional and inflexible, while, for other sectors (arts and heritage, for example), formal provision through public institutions and agencies was much more limited. Likewise, private sector provision, primarily in-company, shows wide variation in scope, sophistication and impact, with almost inevitable correlation with company size and industry sector.

Yet, despite a long-established tradition of education and training for the tourism industry in the United Kingdom, the impact of this training is very patchy. A most telling (and alarming) statistic about a major sector within the industry is that 94% of all staff in hotel and catering occupations have no formal training or qualifications; thus, more than 2 200 000 full- and part-time employees in hotels, restaurants, pubs, cafes, fast food and institutional catering outlets (Battersby, 1990), have never benefited from college or formal in-company based training, leading to recognized certification, despite apparent widespread availability of courses and training schemes. There is little evidence that the situation is significantly different within many other sectors, notably small businesses in the leisure, attractions, heritage, retail and transport areas; however, major companies such as airlines and tour operators provide good examples of a contrary picture.

Responsibility for the coordination, provision and funding of education and training for tourism is largely a public sector concern in the United Kingdom. Central or local government funded institutions provide capital and recurrent costs for almost all programmes within further and higher education at craft, supervisory and management level. Exceptions exist in the shape of the independent University of Buckingham, specialist culinary schools and UK campuses of American colleges.

In addition, alternative private sector models are a likely development in the 1990s. A number of hotel and other tourism-related companies already operate their own in-company training schools, generally focusing on short or specific skills courses but increasingly moving towards more formalized and certified courses and qualifications. This exists, in part, through tourism-related companies which act as managing agents under the Youth Training (YT) scheme, providing both technical and related educational components within one- and two-year courses. At management level, private sector initiatives such as Forte's Academy are moving towards more extended and formal provision. Collectively, there is evidence, in the United Kingdom, that local or sector-specific employers are collaborating in the development of alternatives to public sector education and training.

There were considerable changes in the coordination and management of non-college-based education and training for tourism during the 1980s. The approach that operated up to the mid 1980s featured the industrial training model, whereby government-sponsored agencies managed and provided training for the major industry sectors (sectorally limited in impact within tourism) through the operation of a training levy on payroll. The main training board, within the tourism industry was, probably, the Hotel and Catering Industry Training Board (HCITB), which offered a range of skills and supervisory external and in-company courses at low cost or cost-recovery rates to industry. The industrial training boards, in the UK, lost their statutory base in the 1980s; some were disbanded and others privatized. Thus, the HCITB now trades as a private consultancy, the Hotel and Training Company (HCTC), albeit while maintaining significant public funding for specifically contracted work.

In contrast to the release from local authority within higher education, the funding and provision of training within all sectors is currently moving from the central and national Training Agency to locally managed Training and Enterprise Councils (TECs) in England and Wales and Local Enterprise Councils (LECs) in Scotland which are given direction and managed by appointed representatives of local industry. Membership of TECs is multi-sectoral but there is early evidence of domination and, possible over-representation of

227

manufacturing interests. Thus, the interests of tourism may be in danger of being muted in some areas. Particular focus of TEC initiatives is on partnership funding with local industry, designed to put in place new and innovative training initiatives in support of business growth and development. It is premature to anticipate the impact of these initiatives on tourism.

A further major programme, which is designed to impact on education and training for all industries and has significance for tourism within the UK, is the institution of National Vocational Qualifications (NVQ) at various levels from pre-craft to junior management. These qualifications will establish equivalence between various modes and locations (college and/or industry) of provision and link the certification of various institutions and bodies. NVQ will provide a very ready access to parallel moves towards European equivalence and thus contribute to labour mobility, both inward to the UK and outwards from the country. Potentially, one of the main benefits of NVQ will be its contribution to the recognition of education and training within those sectors of the tourism industry for which formal public provision is limited or non-existent. Thus, in-company programmes in, for example, major attractions or heritage locations, will attract nationally and internationally 'tradable' qualifications to participants (Messenger, 1991). The country's main certification bodies, at craft and supervisory level, including City and Guilds, the Scottish Technical and Vocational Education Council (SCOTVEC) and the Business and Technician Education Council (BTEC), have responded to the challenge of NVQ, within tourism, through major changes in the nature of courses which they certify. Notable developments include moves to flexible and open learning, work-based certification and the encouragement of technology-based training systems. In addition, the role of industry in some sectors has increased as the driving force for change, notably in travel facilitation and transportation, where the impact of technology has been particularly significant.

Education towards the attainment of management qualifications within the tourism industry has been strongly influenced by the general vocational trend, in the UK, towards graduate and, indeed, postgraduate status. As already indicated, the lead sector was, undoubtedly, hotels and catering and there are now well in excess of twenty institutions offering programmes to degree level, increasingly with honours. Some of these programmes are available as 'top-up' courses to candidates who have completed Higher National Diploma (HND) qualifications. Postgraduate courses, at diploma or masters level, are also expanding in availability, in order to:

• Give postgraduate standing to existing hotel and catering graduates

- Give formal recognition, at postgraduate level, to experienced industry personnel holding professional or sub-degree qualifications or
- Provide 'conversion' opportunities to graduates of non-hospitality disciplines.

At the same time, sub-degree qualification alternatives in hotel and catering studies are also available, especially for those working in the industry, through the Hotel, Catering and Institutional Management Association (HCIMA) and through a new distance learning initiative, sponsored by HCTC and BTEC.

Specific provision, to graduate and postgraduate level, for other sectors is rather more patchy. Generic degree and masters courses in tourism are increasingly available, with varying emphases, including local/national government administration of tourism, international tourism and tourism in the European context (in association with institutions in countries such as Germany, France and the Netherlands). However, the vocational thrust of these courses is rather more limited. There is some evidence of increasing 'fine tuning' of programmes towards selected sector or industry needs. The University of Bournemouth's degree in Heritage and Conservation Tourism is an example of this. An altogether different thrust, at this level, is represented by the participation of personnel from major tourism-related businesses in MBA programmes, both of a general and company-specific nature, such as that run by the University of Lancaster for British Airways. The picture, however, is one of some confusion and lack of coordination or leadership from either the industry or from educational providers at the higher education level.

Key human resource issues and responses in UK tourism

This chapter has identified some of the key human resource issues facing United Kingdom tourism, and some of the responses to them. Many of these are not unique to the UK and space has precluded consideration of all of them in this chapter. It is useful to summarize these prior to considering further responses that are required from government and the private sector if tourist needs are to be met over the coming decade.

- A diverse nation, consisting of four countries and many regions with all the benefits and problems that such heterogeneity

229

generates for business, management, employment and skills demand.

- Demography, in particular the declining youth workforce.
- An increasingly educated and skilled workforce, reducing the potential pool for front-line, labour-intensive industry functions.
- Continued de-skilling and increased productivity demands.
- Mixed perceptions of the industry as an employer, with the result that potential entrants are reluctant to consider tourism vocations as career options.
- Limited realization, in the industry, of potential, alternative labour sources (older workers, returners to work, overseas workers etc.) and the measures that may be required to attract such workers.
- Competitive labour market pressures from other regions within the UK and from other countries within the European Community and further afield.
- Lack of professionalism and structured career opportunities within many sectors.
- The small and family business structure of the majority of tourism ventures.
- Uncompetitive pay and conditions within many businesses, especially within the food and accommodation sectors.
- The impact of moves towards private sector, market-led control of 'traditional' government functions in the fields of development, marketing, education and training within tourism.
- Apparent deficiencies in national planning of manpower requirements, education and training for tourism, what some commentators describe as a significantly undertrained workforce within this and related service industries.
- Possible neglect, by default, of the needs of smaller, geographically and economically peripheral tourism businesses in the provision of appropriate courses and training opportunities.
- Wide variation in the quality and extent of educational and training provision for different tourism sectors.
- The relatively high 'drop-out' rate from the industry, by graduates of tourism disciplines.
- Moves to question the cost-effectiveness of traditional models of vocational education and training in terms of returns and benefits to the industry and the economy.
- Lack of sustained investment in training within many tourism businesses.
- Consequent high levels of labour turnover and problems of staff retention within major sectors.
- High reliance on part-time, casual and seasonal labour.
- Limited appreciation of the role and management of technology

within the tourism environment and its potential to contribute to enhanced productivity and service without necessarily adversely impacting on product quality.

• Lastly, and perhaps most tellingly, the already quoted statistic that 94% of employees in one major tourism sector (and probably a significant proportion in others too) are not formally trained.

The above issues provide a demanding agenda for the UK tourism industry as well as for public authorities. Responses have already been considered – the growing range of educational provision, the introduction of NVQ, and the potential of the TECs and LECs all represent good examples. There are many others at a local level. However, the consequences of these issues cannot be addressed purely as local concerns. Therefore, what will be required is the collective will on behalf of all industry sectors, education and training providers and public sector authorities really to address these issues in a planned and coherent manner. As things stand at present, such will is not clearly in evidence.

As with any major tourism industry, that in the United Kingdom is highly people-dependent. It faces some problems which are common to the industries of many other countries as well as others which reflect local history, culture and traditions as well as the country's economic/social fabric. For a country which featured in many of the earliest ventures in modern tourism and tourism education, the quality of planning, development and provision could be deemed mediocre, at best, with fragmentation, duplication, poor anticipation of major trends and changes and overall lack of leadership and direction from either the public or private sector associated with the industry. It is as if the conceptual realization that tourism in the United Kingdom is facing complex human resource crises, which show no sign of diminishing, is wholly accepted. The problem lies in this collective lack of will actually to do anything about it. This situation will be maintained at the peril of the UK tourism industry.

References

Afiya, A. (1992) Industry 'will need two million extra staff'. *Caterer and Hotelkeeper*, 15 October 1992.

Battersby, David (1990) Lifting the barriers: employment and training in tourism and leisure. *Insights* (The English Tourist Board).

Baty, Brian (1990) Tourism and the tourism industry. *Employment Gazette*, September 1990.

British Tourist Authority (1991) UK Visitor Forecasts to 1995. *Travel Industry Monitor*, no. 20.

British Tourist Authority (1992) United Kingdom Indicators. *World Travel and Tourism Review*, vol. 2 (ed. D. Hawkins and J. R. B. Ritchie) CABI, Wallingford, Oxon.

English Tourist Board (1992) Tourism by UK Residents in 1991. *Insights*, September 1992.

Hotel and Catering Training Board (HCTB) (1990) *Skills Shortages in Gwent*, London: HCTB.

Medlik, S. (1989) *Tourism Employment in Wales*, Wales Tourist Board, Cardiff.

Messenger, Sally (1991) Towards a system of national vocational qualifications for the hospitality industry. *Planning for Uncertainty in Hospitality Markets*, Richard Teare (ed.) Proceedings of the Third International Journal of Contemporary Hospitality Management Conference, Bournemouth.

Parsons, David (1987) Tourism and leisure jobs: a statistical review. *The Services Industries Journal*, **3/7**, 365–78.

Shaw, Gareth, Greenwood, Justin and Williams, Allan (1991) The United Kingdom: market responses and public policy. In *Tourism and Economic Development: Western European Experiences* (ed. Allan Williams and Gareth Shaw) 2nd edn, Belhaven, London.

Welsh Joint Education Committee (WJEC) (1990) *Tourism Education at Further and Higher Levels in Wales*, WJEC, Cardiff.

Wales Tourist Board (WTB) (1988) *Tourism in Wales: Developing the Potential*, WTB, Cardiff.

Worsfold, P. and Jameson, S. (1991) Human resource management: a response to change in the 1990s. In *Strategic Hospitality Management* (ed. Richard Teare and Andrew Boer), Cassell, London.

Part Three
Conclusion

17 Creating an integrated human resource environment for tourism
Tom Baum

Introduction

The preceding chapters of this book have considered various aspects of what has been described as the 'macro' human resource environment within the tourism industry world wide. Part One, through chapters 1–6, considers these matters in a relatively general sense, reviewing the global issues in this field, how they can be approached through effective human resource planning and development, and, finally, the importance of quality, valid and reliable information to the management of human resources within tourism. Part Two considers these and a host of other, related issues through the eyes of authors based in key tourism countries or regions across the major continents. These case studies attempt to provide links between the wider tourism environment, consisting of products, markets, economics, socio-cultural and ecological impacts, and the human resource considerations in those countries. How the human resource issues are approached in each of the countries, in other words, the local response, is a central feature of these chapters and one from which many practitioners and students can learn.

It is clear, from these preceding chapters, that there is no single panacea or universal response to the diversity of human resource issues that face the tourism industry world wide. Countries and, indeed, localities construct strategies to cater for their own local needs that are derived from a complex amalgam of influences, notably

- The nature of the tourism industry in question, its structure, products and markets.
- Social and cultural perceptions of tourism as an industry and as an employer.
- The labour market in the locality in question, especially demographic trends, levels of unemployment and competition for skilled labour.

- Existing human resource provision as a product of an ad hoc developmental history.
- The education system and its traditions.
- Government policy and priorities, with respect to tourism, manpower and educational issues.
- Diverse and, frequently, uncoordinated management of the implementation of human resource policies and priorities in tourism by a number of public and private sector agencies.

This chapter is concerned with extracting the seminal components from the preceding contributions and presenting them as part of a comprehensive, integrated and cohesive plan for the development and management of human resources within tourism. Mahesh's contribution to this objective, in Chapter 3, provides a very useful starting point in that he considers some of the main features within the human resource planning process, both from the micro company level and from the macro national perspective. Mahesh's approach is highly pragmatic and designed to illustrate responses to real situations at both levels. In this sense, therefore, his proposals for action, at a national level, are drawn directly out of the specific analysis of skills and skills shortages, which the human resource projections, for the period in question, generated. Many of the recommendations which he considers have validity within the conceptual framework that will be developed here, alongside those from the case studies.

The approach that is considered here, leading to the development of an integrated framework for the management of human resource environment within tourism, is highly dependent on the quality and validity of the information which is fed into it. Two approaches to the preparation of such information, in relation to employment and training needs, are considerd in Part One, in Chapters 5 and 6 by Baum and Fletcher, respectively. Clearly, the wealth of information required for this exercise means that a diversity of other sources and field methodologies will be required in addition to the approaches which are considered in detail here. It is beyond the scope of this chapter to consider them but that is not intended to underestimate the significance of their role.

The plan is intended to integrate the main features of the two ends of the HRPD process, as described by Mahesh, and to constitute a 'blueprint', drawn from the good practice that exists in a variety of countries, both within our case studies and elsewhere. As such, some aspects of the plan will prove more suitable for practical implementation by some localities, countries or regions than others and some may require modification.

This 'blueprint' is prepared at a time when international tourism is facing conflicting tensions with respect to the process of product 'homogenization' and it is not the intention, here, to argue the merits of uniformity for its own sake within human resource management in tourism. The history of tourism, since it has moved on to a mass market scale, mirrors much that has occurred in other social domains, with one of the dominant trends being that of changes from diversity to uniformity while, at the same time, exposing local communities to a range of new, and not always desirable, influences. These processes have been influenced by a number of important factors, which include:

- Mass immigration and the migration of populations, creating new cultural, artistic and culinary environments while at the same time establishing global expectations with regard to some products and standards.
- The almost universal marketing and availability of mass produced consumer products, notably in food and drink but also relevant in the tourism product area ('Take me to the Hilton').
- The demands of the growing international travel market, on the one hand exposed to new experiences but also creating needs which modify what is available locally, for example the 'international hotel version' of a local culinary specialty.
- The growth of transnational hotel and restaurant companies, offering standard international accommodation and food fare throughout the world.
- The influence of the international media in creating common expectations and demands from both the travelling and indigenous population.

As a result of this homogenization process within the international tourism product, there is no doubt that there has been considerable convergence in the demands that the industry makes of its human resources and this is clearly reflected in the common ground that is evident between the case studies. At the same time, there is evidence that changes may be expected in tourism and that these will include significant shifts in consumer preferences. Kurent describes these in some detail:

> The once-dominant middle market of 'Happy Mediums' will also continue to decline during the 1990s under the impact of consumer sophistication. Demand will continue to grow for more individualized, high quality vacations and services geared to widely varying consumer desires. As Alvin Toffler described in *The Third Wave*, post modern life will turn from 'mass' production of all kinds to customization whereby technologies make possible more tailored products to meet individual tastes. In the case of

tourism it will be a further fragmentation of the market to accommodate customization of individual tastes for travel experiences. (Kurent, 1991)

These apparently contradictory images of homogenization and customization need not be as uncomfortable together as may, at first, be thought. The benefits of common administrative, reservations, energy and information systems are apparent and their interface with the customer provides a quality enhancement that will be welcomed by most tourists. Likewise, the application of similar quality criteria in the area of service and hygiene, for example, will also benefit tourists wherever they travel. However, demands for customization will result in increased prominence for the tourism product that is both unique and authentic to the locality or country in question.

The implications for human resource management in tourism of, on the one hand, trends towards uniformity and, on the other, demands for product customization and authenticity, are that this area requires the capacity to respond to and cater for what appear to be two divergent demands. The keys to this duality are flexibility and responsiveness, both within the overall human resource management system and its structures and at the level of the individual. Olsen, Crawford-Welch and Tse, in my view, encapsulate this requirement when they talk about the need to educate (as opposed to train) the tourism workforce at management level, but what they have to say applies, equally, to other positions.

> Management culture in the hospitality industry is rooted in the 'how-to' side of the business, as opposed to the behavioural side. Traditionally, hospitality managers have been very task oriented and have practised reactive, as opposed to proactive, management styles. If hospitality management is truly to come of age, we need to pay increasing attention to developing a more behaviourally oriented manager . . . As the hospitality industry becomes more and more global in focus, we need to devote increasing attention and resources to educating (not training) individuals to be aware of, and adapt to, the multicultural nature of the industry. (Olsen et al., 1991)

The conceptual framework developed in this chapter is intended to be one that can respond to the diversity of, at times, contradictory demands which the tourist of the future will place upon tourism employees at all levels as well as on the whole host population.

Developing the conceptual framework

A constant theme, within the chapters of this book, has been the variety of influences that impact on the planning, management and development of human resources within the tourism industry world wide. These influences are complex and do not interact with the tourism environment in the same way in different countries and regions. Their origins can be found in factors such as:

- The nature of current and projected tourism products and markets, and how these influence the human resource requirements of the locality or country.
- National or local culture, religion or history and the impact this has on employment in sectors of the tourism industry.
- Contemporary perceptions of tourism and tourists, as presented by the media and official agencies, particularly in relation to employment.
- The traditions, orientations and priorities within national educational systems, both within vocational and academic areas.
- The role of higher educational institutions, especially universities, in tourism-related education, research and development.
- The position of tourism sector requirements, within national industrial training provision.
- The labour market environment, especially competition for labour and skills and policy priorities with respect to new job generation.
- The demographics of the labour market.
- The cultural and ethnic mix of the workforce and the impact of immigration, emigration and transnational labour mobility.
- Government (local and national) tourism policies and the emphasis, within these, that is accorded to employment creation and skills development.
- Incentives and support for investment, by both the public and private sector, in human resource development, generally and within tourism.
- The role of national and local tourism promotion and development agencies in the human resource field.

The conceptual framework for the integrated development of human resources in tourism which is considered in this chapter is designed to reflect the need for flexibility and responsiveness in the face of diversity such as that exemplified above. It is intended to bring together and link the key features of this diversity into a unit that is

- Comprehensive, in that it includes all sectors of the tourism industry; all relevant aspects of human resource development; all levels of training and development; and reflects the demands of local cultures, traditions and tourism markets

- Integrated, in that all components, in the model, have clear and identifiable links to other elements and contribute to, or are beneficiaries of, other parts of the model
- Cohesive, in that the total model, the overall outcome of the process, has a logic and applicability in its own right, almost independent of its individual parts.

The value of the approach described below is, primarily, as an aid to policy formulation and the establishment of national, regional or local priorities with respect to human resource concerns in tourism. Where this approach differs from that practised in most tourism environments is in its breadth. The approach is designed to incorporate as many as possible of the diverse influences and considerations which affect the development and management of an effective human resource policy in tourism. It is non-evaluatory in the sense that the implementing agencies will not receive clear judgements as to the relative importance of the components. However, it provides a practical framework through which such judgements can be made.

The framework, therefore, will be developed on the basis of five main divisions. These are, by no means, mutually exclusive and definite cross-divisional links exist between all of them. They do have a certain sequential logic but the order is not intended to imply priority of importance. The divisions are:

- **A** The tourism environment
- **B** Tourism and the labour market
- **C** Tourism in the community
- **D** Tourism and education
- **E** Human resource development in the tourism industry

Each division contains a number of key elements or considerations which should be evaluated by those responsible for policy formulation and the identification of priorities. They may be deemed significant factors within the human resource environment or they may be considered to be beyond its scope. Other considerations may also be of importance and may be added to the framework. At the end of the process, however, responsible agencies and practitioners alike will have the information and, consequently, the basis for the development of a relevant human resource planning and development structure within the requisite tourism industry.

The components of the conceptual framework are summarized in Figure 17.1.

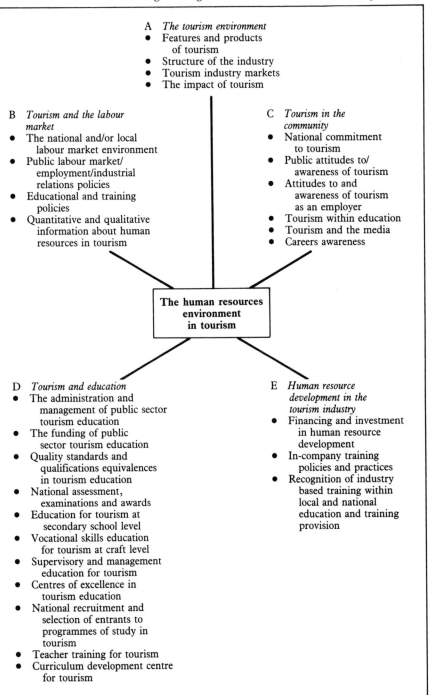

A *The tourism environment*
- Features and products of tourism
- Structure of the industry
- Tourism industry markets
- The impact of tourism

B *Tourism and the labour market*
- The national and/or local labour market environment
- Public labour market/ employment/industrial relations policies
- Educational and training policies
- Quantitative and qualitative information about human resources in tourism

C *Tourism in the community*
- National commitment to tourism
- Public attitudes to/ awareness of tourism
- Attitudes to and awareness of tourism as an employer
- Tourism within education
- Tourism and the media
- Careers awareness

The human resources environment in tourism

D *Tourism and education*
- The administration and management of public sector tourism education
- The funding of public sector tourism education
- Quality standards and qualifications equivalences in tourism education
- National assessment, examinations and awards
- Education for tourism at secondary school level
- Vocational skills education for tourism at craft level
- Supervisory and management education for tourism
- Centres of excellence in tourism education
- National recruitment and selection of entrants to programmes of study in tourism
- Teacher training for tourism
- Curriculum development centre for tourism

E *Human resource development in the tourism industry*
- Financing and investment in human resource development
- In-company training policies and practices
- Recognition of industry based training within local and national education and training provision

Figure 17.1 *An integrated human resource development model for tourism*

A   The tourism environment

This starting division covers the broad tourism environment, within which human resource issues require consideration. Tourism, in this context, may relate to both or either the national or local industry and includes both the domestic and international markets. Inputs, to this division, include:

- **A1   Features and products of tourism**
  Consideration of the main features of the tourism industry, why visitors come to the locality or country and the origins of the industry, including:

  – the main attractions, natural and man-made
  – location
  – accessibility
  – historical development

- **A2   Structure of the industry**
  Review of the main tourism industry sectors and their organization, including:

  – the relative importance of the various sectors
  – business size and organization
  – ownership and management – family, local, chain, multi-national etc.

- **A3   Tourism industry markets**
  Consideration of the main tourist originating markets for the locality country, including:

  – domestic tourists
  – international tourists
  – expenditure and activity profile
  – price/value issues
  – quality issues
  – responsibility for and organization of tourism marketing

- **A4   The impact of tourism**
  Consideration of how tourism impacts upon the locality or country, with particular reference to employment and human resource factors, including:

  – economic impact
  – employment impact, direct, indirect and induced (see B below)
  – cultural and social impact
  – environmental impact

- **A5   Other related considerations**

B   Tourism and the labour market

This division covers the relatively wide scope of the interface between the tourism industry and the general labour market, in particular how the human resource requirements and priorities of tourism relate to those of other industries and to the manpower, economic and social environment of the locality, country or region as a whole. A major contribution of this division to the model is in the area of information collection and analysis. There is relatively little by way of direct, action-based interventions in the human resource domain in tourism.

Inputs to this division include:

- **B1   The national and/or local labour market environment**
  Information and analysis of current labour market trends and their implications for the tourism industry, including:

  - The national (or local) labour market structure by sector and region
  - Short, medium and long-term employment and unemployment situation
  - Description of employment and related trends, including moves to part-time, shared and other alternative work forms
  - Female/male, ethnic minority and immigrant participation in the workforce
  - Demographic trends and their relationship to the workforce
  - National skills audit and the identification of key areas of shortage and oversupply.

- **B2   Public   labour   market/employment/industrial   relations policies**
  Consideration of the above policies and interventions (or lack of them) and their impact on the operation of tourism businesses, including:

  - Minimum wage and related legislation
  - Controls over hours and conditions at work, for example components of the European Community's Social Chapter
  - Trade union legislation
  - Safety at work
  - Workplace hygiene legislation
  - The extent of government (local and national) intervention in employment protection/support
  - Employment creation initiatives and incentives

– Support for changes in the employment environment, for example incentives to invest in computerization/automation.

- **B3   Educational and training policies**
Consideration of public education and training policies and their implications for the tourism industry at a local and national level, including:

  – the relationship between 'academic' and 'vocational' strands within secondary and tertiary education
  – public funding of post-compulsory education
  – industrial training policies and the agencies with responsibility for this area
  – the role of private sector industry in training
  – public funding for training
  – the relationship, in terms of programme content and end qualifications, between education in school/college and training at work
  – The position and status of tourism education and training within national policies/provision
  – Public sector management responsibility for tourism education and training policies and implementation

- **B4   Quantitative and qualitative information about human resources in tourism**
Ensuring that human resource developments in tourism, at micro and macro levels, are implemented on the basis of valid, reliable and quality information, through:

  – Analysis and evaluation of macro-economic data on tourism employment
  – Undertaking of on-going and comprehensive direct surveys of the tourism industry in order to collect the range of necessary information (see Chapter 5)
  – Maintaining and up-dating data bases generated as a result of information collection processes
  – Evaluating and disseminating conclusions of surveys

- **B5   Other related considerations**

C   Tourism in the community

This division is concerned with the interaction of tourism, as an industry, with the society in which it is based. It is concerned with matters of social values, culture, the economy, conservation and the environment and how tourism, as an industry, impacts on these areas, to their benefit or detriment. It is also of great significance in that the human resources, upon which the tourism industry is totally dependent, are, generally, drawn from this community, whether national or local, and the interaction between tourism and its potential workforce is, therefore, crucial.

Inputs to this division include:

- **C1 National commitment to tourism**
  Information on the effects on the industry and its human resource environment of:
  - The attitude and policies of government (national and local) towards tourism as an industry
  - The policies enunciated and objectives set for tourism (foreign exchange earning, employment generation, international understanding) at national and local levels
  - The status and location of those allocated responsibility for tourism in government (full ministerial rank, part of a broader portfolio etc.)
  - Investment policies and levels in tourism at local and national levels (through promotion agencies/boards, tax allowances etc.)

- **C2 Public attitudes to/awareness of tourism as an industry**
  The impact of the perceptions and portrayal of tourism, at local, national and international levels, on human resource considerations, including:
  - Public attitudes to tourism and to tourists
  - Tourism development and local support/opposition at official and 'popular' levels
  - Attitudes resulting from cultural and environmental impact
  - Media portrayal of tourism as an industry

- **C3 Attitudes to and awareness of tourism as an employer**
  Information on how the tourism industry is perceived and portrayed as an employer, including:
  - Status of the industry, locally and nationally, relative to other areas of employment
  - Traditions of cultural and religious concern about employment in certain sectors of the tourism industry
  - Attitudes (cultural, religious, status) of parents, teachers and others to employment in tourism
  - Labour turnover/attrition rates for tourism relative to other employment areas
  - Actual comparative remuneration and conditions in tourism and other industries, locally, nationally and internationally

245

- School leaver and college graduate employment choices
- School leaver college course preferences
- The extent of industry's demonstrated commitment to ensuring a competitive and flexible employment environment (remuneration, conditions, benefits, job security etc.)
- Media portrayal of employment in tourism

- **C4 Tourism within education**
  The extent to which tourism, as an industry, is represented within educational curricula at all levels (see section D below) and the relationship of this to human resource concerns in tourism, including:

  - The study of tourism as an economic and social activity, in the school and college curricula, notably in association with geography, economics, social science etc.
  - Education through tourism: the use of field trips, visits etc. as part of the school and college curriculum

- **C5 Tourism and the media**
  Analysis of how tourism and tourists are portrayed by the local, national and international media (see C2 and C3 above), including:

  - Portrayal of domestic and international tourism options
  - Portrayal of visitors
  - Potrayal of the industry, from a business, environmental, cultural and employment perspective

- **C6 Careers awareness**
  The extent to which public sector, educational, manpower and tourism industry bodies take responsibility for the promotion of tourism careers to all target markets, including:

  - Careers information on tourism, available to school and college graduates
  - Careers information available to alternative, non-traditional sources of recruitment (older workers, women returners, ethnic minorities, immigrant communities at home and abroad)
  - Role of manpower/employment agencies in careers promotion
  - Special recruitment/careers awareness initiatives (media-based, special fairs etc.)
  - Initiatives aimed at teachers, careers advisers

- **C7 Other related considerations**

D Tourism and education

This division covers the role of the educational system at all appropriate levels, in developing the requisite skills and attitudes necessary for employment within tourism. Inputs, to this division, include:

- **D1 The administration and management of public sector tourism education**
  Allocation of responsibility for the administration and management of public sector tourism education, at local or national level to appropriate departments/agencies, including:

  - Identification of interested bodies in tourism, education and labour/manpower areas
  - Identification of component areas of tourism education and their existing administrative/management arrangements (covering schools, colleges and other higher education institutes, training centres, specialist external education and training for tour guides)
  - Establishment of coordinating mechanisms to cover all areas of tourism education, either under unitary policy and administrative management or through formalized and effective liaison systems
  - Development of links with private sector tourism education (schools, colleges, within industry) so as to ensure management of output, skills and qualifications equivalences
  - Ensuring comparability with other vocational sectors

- **D2 The funding of public sector tourism education**
  Identification of policies and provision of appropriate structures and resources for the funding of tourism education at all levels, including:

  - Allocation of resources from public taxation, local and national
  - Ensuring the support and the collection of appropriate resources from the private sector, through a levy or similar scheme
  - Ensuring equitable funding with other vocational education sectors
  - Ensuring that the funding allocated to tourism education is compatible with the priorities accorded the industry within national/local planning and development for tourism
  - Ensuring appropriate capital and recurrent allocations to meet the needs of practical education and training at all levels
  - Provision of funding sufficient to ensure the employment of quality, qualified and industrially experienced teachers and trainers

- **D3 Quality standards and qualifications equivalences in tourism education**
  Establishment of mechanisms and agencies to ensure the develop-

ment and maintenance of comparable quality standards and qualifications, where this is suitable, between all programmes, centres and levels, within tourism education, including:

- A national quality standards, qualifications and certification scheme to cover all tourism education and to ensure comparability with other vocational areas
- Linkage between this scheme and the outcomes of education and training within the private sector, both in schools/colleges and industry
- Ensuring broad comparability of all teaching and learning resources within institutions offering equivalent level programmes
- Establishment of mechanisms to conduct appropriate research in support of national/local curricula and quality standards guidelines (see B4 above)
- Agreement of national/local education, training and curricula development priorities and the translation of these into workable guidelines for implementation by providers
- Agreement of equivalences of learning outcomes and qualifications at all levels, so as to facilitate transfer and career development within tourism
- Linking, where possible, with equivalent schemes and systems in states and countries in close proximity (for example, within the European Community) so as to facilitate mobility.

- **D4 National assessment, examinations and awards**
  To provide the formal expression of the objectives within D3, by means of a specialist agency or by the coordination of the operations of other appropriate agencies, through
  - Coordination and execution, where appropriate, of national assessment of practical and course work within tourism education and training
  - Setting and marking of external examinations
  - Approval of internal examination standards
  - Awarding of appropriate certificates to graduates of programmes at all levels

- **D5 Education for tourism at secondary school level**
  To provide academic and vocational tourism education at secondary (or technical vocational) school level, including:

  - Tourism as a non-vocational subject of study, leading to examination and certification at appropriate levels up to final matriculation and comparable in status and standards to other academic disciplines

248

- Pre-employment and specific vocational education and training programmes, carrying recognized certification, and enabling graduates to:
  (a) take up positions at operative or semi-skilled levels in the tourism industry
  (b) join industry-based apprenticeship or training programmes, or
  (c) progress to programmes of further education and training within the education system
- Use of tourism case study material within general academic curricula (see C4 above)

- **D6 Vocational skills education for tourism at craft level**
Provision of craft education and training at post secondary school level and designed to meet identified needs for skilled employees within all sectors of the tourism industry (see B4). These should be courses:

- That are relevant to meet the needs of the local, national and international industry
- That are flexible in delivery, timing and location
- That combine and integrate practical and theoretical skills and knowledge
- That include supervised industrial experience and training
- That are offered in a wide range of disciplines, relevant to the needs of the local/national/international industry and which lead to the award of recognized certificates in areas that could include:

  o Food and beverage service, basic and advanced levels
  o Food preparation and production, basic, intermediate and advanced levels
  o Front office/reception operations, basic and advanced levels
  o Front office/portering operations, basic level
  o Front office/security operations, basic and advanced levels
  o Hotel housekeeping, basic and intermediate levels
  o Travel industry travel agency clerk, basic and advanced levels
  o Travel industry tour guides, advanced level
  o Tourism information operations, advanced level
  o Coach and taxi operations, basic level
  o Airline ticketing and check-in operations, basic and advanced levels
  o Retail industry sales operations, basic and advanced levels
  o General customer care operations

- Which may be located in either dedicated tourism education and training centres or within multi-faculty institutions of further/higher education

- That may be offered within either the public or private sector of education and training
- That may be offered through use of temporary or mobile training facilities, which can be instituted in, for example, seasonal hotels in order to meet local or specialist needs
- That are taught by quality, qualified and industry-experienced teachers and trainers
- That provide for progressive career development opportunities for skilled craft personnel in the tourism industry
- That allow recognized access to courses at more advanced, non-craft levels
- That provide training that develops flexible and transferable skills, for application within various sectors and jobs in the tourism industry
- That, above all, place particular emphasis on the development of generic skills and attitudes, especially in the customer service domain.

- **D7   Supervisory and management education for tourism**
  Provision of tourism education, at supervisory and management level, designed to meet the identified skills needs of all sectors of the industry, at local, national and international levels. These should be courses:

  - That are offered at a variety of levels (certificate, diploma, degree and postgraduate), appropriate both to the needs of the various sectors of the industry, locally and nationally, and to the aspirations of entrants
  - That are designed to be both sector-specific (where appropriate, e.g. hotel management; catering supervision; heritage management) and to include widely applicable business and management skills
  - That recognize the importance of small businesses and entrepreneurship within the tourism industries of many countries
  - That combine appropriate practical and applied theory components
  - That include real work industrial placement with supervisory/management responsibility
  - That are available on a flexible basis, through a variety of modes (full-time, part-time, block release, open learning) as appropriate
  - That are taught by teachers who combine academic expertise with relevant professional experience in the tourism industry
  - That provide for progressive career development opportunities to allow supervisory and junior management personnel to qualify for more senior positions

– That may be offered in the public or private sector of education

- **D8 Centres of excellence in tourism education**
To provide for specialist education, training and development needs to levels of excellence not normally achieved within mainstream education, through partnership between the tourism industry and education, and in areas such as

  – Culinary arts, in order to focus on excellence in local, regional and national cuisine and to contribute to the development of food as a marketable tourism product and to the training necessary to achieve this
  – Traditional performing and handicraft arts, to meet similar objectives to those of the culinary institute
  – Other areas of technical specialism such as airline pilot training and advanced tour guide education
  – Advanced postgraduate study and research, catering for the development of high level, academic skills in the tourism field

- **D9 National recruitment and selection of entrants to programmes of study in tourism**
Establishment of mechanisms to coordinate the local or national recruitment and selection of potential entrants to tourism education and training courses, especially in environments where there are identified skills or other personnel shortages, including:

  – Career awareness campaigns (see C6)
  – Institution of centralized applications procedures, either independent or in conjunction with other vocational areas
  – Operation of centrally coordinated but localized section testing and interviewing
  – Utilization of tourism industry expertise to support selection

- **D10 Teacher training for tourism**
Provision of a formalized system for the education and training of teachers to work within both the public and private sectors of tourism education and training, thus addressing one of the main weaknesses in many existing tourism education systems, to include:

  – Nationally recognized courses and centres for tourism teacher education
  – Requirement for all permanent teachers and trainers to receive appropriate training at time of recruitment
  – Recognition of professional and craft experience as appropriate for entry to courses

- **D11   Curriculum development centre for tourism**

  Provision of a local or national support centre, to work with institutions in the public and private sector as well as the industry itself and to assist in the development of quality and relevant education and training programmes, through:

  - Commissioning of specialist curriculum research in appropriate areas (see B4)
  - Interpretation and dissemination of curriculum and general manpower research findings, as they apply to education and training programmes
  - Development of local or national curricula, if required, for utilization within schools, colleges, training centres and industry
  - Development and publication of education and training support resources in print and other formats.

- **D12   Other related considerations**

E   *Human resource development in the tourism industry*

This division relates to the role of the tourism industry itself in the development of its human resources and the investment and provision which tourism businesses should make in order to ensure efficient and motivated staff of high quality. Inputs to this division include:

- **E1   Financing and investment in human resource development**

  Ensuring that the tourism industry, through its diverse businesses, meets, in full, its responsibilities for investment in human resource development through:

  - Operation of a national or local training level, remitted on acceptable evidence of training investment
  - Operation of tax and other fiscal incentives to invest in training and/or the development of specialist training facilities
  - Encouraging recognition of the business and competitive benefits, to individual companies, of investing in human resource development.

- **E2   In-company training policies and practices**

  Provision of training, for all levels of personnel within the industry, that is:

- Reflective of commitment to training from board room and chief executive level down
- Based on researched identified training needs within the company but also recognizing requirements at a local, national and international level
- Based upon clear and planned priorities within a given time frame
- Designed to meet the needs of all staff, from induction training through to senior management development
- Progressive and developmental, utilizing mechanisms such as career tracking and succession planning
- Proactive rather than reactive, designed to meet anticipated requirements rather than actual, emergency needs
- That maximizes the benefits of all sources of training, whether internal to the company or purchased from outside
- Carried out by skilled professionals, whether specialist trainers or operational supervisors/managers developed in the requisite skills.

- **E3 Recognition of industry-based training within local and national education and training provision**
  Provision of recognized links between the education and training which takes place in industry and that which is the responsibility of the external education and training system, through:

  - Institution of common and recognized awards for equivalent levels of education and training within both sectors
  - Facilitation of transfer mechanisms between the two systems and the institution of an Accreditation of Prior Learning (APL) scheme to cover both education and industry
  - Support for the development of specialist education and training centres, by the industry, which meet recognized national and international standards and criteria in terms of facilities, faculty, funding and curricula
  - Support for reciprocal mobility and cooperation (full-time and part-time) between training staff within the education system and those working in industry.

- **E4 Other related considerations**

Utilizing the conceptual framework

So far, we have identified some 28 inputs (as well as providing the scope for the addition of further concerns) into what is intended to be a comprehensive, integrated and cohesive human resource development framework for tourism. Each of these inputs, in turn, contains a number of specific components for its implementation. The inputs are diverse in terms of their objectives, their weight, and the resources that are required in order to implement them. Some inputs are of what might be styled an information collection, analysis and interpretation nature and are designed to contribute to the execution of the other category of inputs, those that relate to either policy formulation or the strategic implementation of human resource development initiatives.

Clearly, the individual inputs cannot be prescriptive, although those of an informational nature are highly recommended in that failure to access and consider these ranges of data must handicap policy formulation and strategy implementation. With reference to these latter inputs, a local or national response to the model will, inevitably, be influenced by a range of factors, historic, cultural, social, economic and political. However, this framework is intended to provide the structure upon which an integrated human resource development policy and strategy may be formulated. The framework may include most, if not all, the requisite components for this exercise as well as others that may be appropriate to add. All these components exist and operate within some of the world's tourism industries. The objective of this framework is to argue the case for their integrated implementation, so as to provide ultimate benefits to tourists, tourism industries and their employees.

References

Kurent, Heather (1991) Tourism in the 1990s: threats and opportunities. In *World Travel and Tourism Review*, vol. 1 (ed. Donald Hawkins and Brent Ritchie) CABI, Wallingford, Oxon.

Olsen, Michael, Crawford-Welch, Simon and Tse, Eliza (1991) The global hospitality industry of the 1990s. In *Strategic Hospitality Management: Theory and Practice for the 1990s* (ed Richard Teare and Andrew Boer), Cassell, London.

Index